4721800059067 2

Family Business:
A Memoir

In Memoriam, Prue Conradi, 1948-2013

Family Business: A Memoir

Peter J. Conradi

Seren is the book imprint of
Poetry Wales Press Ltd,
57 Nolton Street, Bridgend, Wales, CF31 3AE

www.serenbooks.com
facebook.com/SerenBooks
Twitter: @SerenBooks

ISBN
Hardback: 978-1-78172-501-6
Ebook: 978-1-78172-502-3
Kindle: 978-1-78172-503-0

A CIP record for this title is available from the British Library.

The publisher acknowledges the financial assistance of the Welsh Books Council.

Cover photograph: PC, Wales, c 1976.

Printed by TJ International, Cornwall.

Contents

Part Three: Iris Murdoch

Preface

The starting point for this book was the acquisition of various family pieces and papers. These came into my hands some years ago, leading to my desire to somehow document them and recover the life and times of my paternal grandmother, with whom I had a close relationship. It is her story with which the book begins and in writing it I realised that this would not only lead to the recreation of a larger family history, but would turn into an attempt to work out my own often troubled place in it. This led me to reflect on the sense and any purpose I have made of my own life, arising more immediately from the 'family drama' of my own (unhappy?) parents.

There are three distinct fields of enquiry which I found impossible to disentangle completely; hence the apparent digressive eccentricity of this book's construction: Early Years, Family History, and finally an account of my discipleship of Dame Iris Murdoch. It thus describes three trajectories in succession rather than a smooth chronology. Written topic-by-topic as a succession of stories, essays and pen-portraits, it combines social, family and personal history with a biographer's autobiography: a story made up of contrasting parts. Leading more than one life is what we all do; finding common threads can hopefully illuminate the whole.

In the 1980s I became deeply involved with the work and later – as her biographer – the life of Iris Murdoch. Her life and work seemed to me to reflect a set of psychological and philosophical issues that helped me understand not merely myself but also that larger history of my extended Jewish family against the background of European and American migration typical of the period. Iris Murdoch was first my admired friend and parent-surrogate, later my vulnerable subject. As I researched and drafted it dawned on me, that I had spent my first thirty-five years protecting my mother against my father; and my next thirty-five years protecting Iris Murdoch from the whole world. When, in chapter 22 of what follows, I protect a vulnerable Iris from a demonic Canetti, am I secretly re-living this old pattern? Both phases were at the time quixotic, neither fully conscious. Both entailed impracticality, idealism and hard work.

So a knight-errant's symmetry is implicit in what follows, that oddly medieval cultural marker, still alive in the modern world. This narrative starts by investigating the topic of solicitude, the quality knight-errants are hardwired to display. Murdoch's fiction and philosophy might be said to be concerned with the possibility of the idealism and solicitude involved in 'knight-errantry'. What may bring the different parts of the book together is its exploration of this recurring pattern of anxious solicitude for others, first in my own make-up, then also in wider fields of speculation. Part One explores solicitude for my younger self; Part Two solicitude for my ancestry; Part Three for Iris Murdoch.

Prologue: Solicitude

I occasionally sleep in my American grandmother's very comfortable bed, a useful (and unusual) width of four foot across. It was just large enough to accommodate her plump body together with the last of a succession of the poodles she adored, a miniature called Spice, in a series starting with Penny, her first big dog.

Florence Conradi and Penny, 1950s

I also possess – among much else that was hers – the low wicker nursing-chair on which she breast-fed my father in Coleherne Court a century ago in 1916, her sketching stool – still serviceable for weeding in the garden – her fire-screen, foot-stool and cushions all embroidered in her *petit point*, a magnificent blue Isfahan rug, and the elegant, round copper tray she used for her letters to sit upon.

Things often outlive their owners. She died aged ninety-one, in 1983, but all her diaries of annual trips to Europe before World War I survive, stuffed with picture post-cards of sights and cities visited, together with many home-made Alice-in-Wonderland cards from a surprise birthday party around 1898 that gave her joy to remember.

Granma also kept a fat scrapbook from the winter of 1909-10, when her elder sister Beatrice – of whom she was all her life passionately jealous – married a clothier called Leo Sulzberger, whose family co-owned the *New York Times*. Jealousy was probably one spur to her first idly but compulsively collecting, and then later conserving, mementoes. The cut-and-glued frippery that fills this packed-to-overflowing scrap-book includes humorous cartoons of beautiful and supercilious swan-necked Gibson Girls and dried flowers. From this collection I learn that in one short season, among many other engagements (including much Vaudeville), she watched Princeton beat Yale at ice-hockey in the St Nicholas rink in New York City on 26 January 1910, saw Lionel Monckton's musical comedy *The Arcadians* and Conan Doyle's new play *The Fires of Fate*, heard Sergei Rachmaninoff perform, partook of a ten-course banquet in Atlantic City on 5 January, sent and received Valentine cards, went to the races on 23 March in New Haven, Connecticut and saved the race-cards, watched *Coppelia* with Pavlova as lead-dancer, Massenet's opera *Thais* at the Met, and at the Manhattan Opera House Debussy's *Pelleas et Melisande* and Offenbach's *Tales of Hoffmann* on 19 March. Then there was Barnum and Bailey's circus – 'Greatest Show on Earth' – in Madison Square Garden. A busy winter.

Mementos of her elder sister's New York wedding reception at the new St Regis Hotel that she taped into this scrap-book include a maraschino liqueur chocolate that – over a period of over a century – has dissolved, leaving a brown stain that soaks through many pages, sticking them together. Her dried flowers have long since faded, their perfume lost and – brittle now – their petals rapidly turned to powder. The clear scent of young Florence's personality nonetheless lingers: a seventeen year-old American girl on the brink of grown-up adventures, a budding aesthete hungry for culture, eager for travel and for attention, spoiled, charming, headstrong and missish. She was to be, while I was growing up, my closest friend.

Dying relatives often bequeath me trunk-loads of papers which I treat with superstitious reverence and have no idea what to do with and so stuff into cupboards, lacking the courage or resolution to burn or discard. Pride of ownership is also hard to surrender. Living relatives off-load papers and objects too.

I've inherited Florence's mother's sizeable library, which includes her

Studio portrait of Florence, c 1909

Warne's Model Cookery (1900) and her various 'guides to modern opera' from 1909. A Hebrew Bar-Mitzvah prayer book published in Sulzbach in Germany and dated 1833, and a pen-and-ink drawing and also a framed daguerreotype of my great-great grandmother from the same period. Father's wooden darning mushroom and needle from Normandy in 1940 and his solar topee from Nigeria in 1945; the violin of my Uncle John, shot down with the RAF and killed, aged 19, in 1941; and the essays he wrote at Clifton College, calf-bound by his grief-stricken mother, my other Granny. My mother's egg-preserving pail from World War Two, in which she dunked eggs in isinglass extracted from the air-bladders of fish. (Where did you buy fish air-bladders to get isinglass? It was evidently both universally available and presumably cheap. The chemist maybe.) The deed-box of my great-great-grandfather George Cohen, who founded in 1834 what became the biggest scrap metal merchant in the UK, George Cohen & Sons, which demolished the Crystal Palace in 1936. He died in 1890, having started a dynasty as well as a big firm. My Franco-German great-grandparents' papers survive from 1870, when they escaped from Paris and its attacking Prussians. There are also some fine pictures and good furniture.

No doubt because the dead no longer exist, their bygones come charged with an extra freight of responsibility and piety, suggesting other customs, other times – 'Alas, poor ghost(s)'. We seem partly made up out of stories concerning dead people we never chose to be kin to and scarcely know. And if the oft-repeated truism that we suffer two deaths is accurate, the first when our hearts stop, the second at the point when nobody is left alive on earth who remembers us, then the act of burning old boxes of papers foreshadows final extinction or – more fancifully – slaughter.

Is it feeble-minded to feel sorry for and to want to stay loyal to the past? To worry and want to look after it? God has gone – together with his careful databases chronicling each human existence. Biographers alone now measure the *weight* of an individual life, and may feel that every human soul has a story worth safeguarding. Since I was a child I've felt an abstract pity for the lost and speechless generations fading silently into nothingness with no one to mourn or celebrate them.

A tipping point in later life comes when your address book contains more dead than living and many of the friends you talk to in your head cannot reply. We commune with spirits. 'As for man, his days are as grass: as a flower of the field, so he flourisheth./ For the wind passeth over it, and it is gone; and the place thereof shall know it no more', as Psalm 103 thrillingly has it. I feel sorry for the past, for the detritus of trivia its successive waves leave beached behind.

The task of looking after the possessions of the dead is a familiar one, for I was born to time-consuming, heavy responsibilities, my role as knight-errant defined early. Schooled to protect, from age six, my warring and unhappy parents from each other, and myself from them, I eventually graduated to rescuing wives-in-general from their husbands, regardless of their own wishes. This quixotic training had other long-term consequences. I volunteered during the Six Day War in 1967 to go to Israel to protect the Jews there for a lengthy thirteen months of kibbutz life, helped pioneer the UK's first gay-lib magazine around 1972 and moved to Poland after the Berlin Wall fell to help save the Poles from their history. That took two years.

PC, Kibbutz Alonim, 1967

Then, in 1996-99 I and my partner spent an aggregate of eight months caring for the ailing Dame Iris Murdoch in our house in Wales, at the same time that I was starting to try to write her biography. I recently found in Wales a random cache of stones she had collected and taken into her own protective care. The history of my solicitude for her – which has dominated the last three decades – forms the substance of the last, very different, third of this narrative.

***

But it seems to me that my final solicitude, which might also have been my first, might be towards myself. *Who was I*? is a real question, albeit a teasing one, with no correct answer, and in my case a question comically complicated by my having a name-sake who is a writer on the *Sunday Times*. We two Peter Conradis have never met but share an optician who once offered me his new spectacles instead of my own, so the world was out-of-focus. In 2004 during the same week we both gave talks at the Savile Club and at the end of my evening an elderly man rose to his feet to say he had driven all the way from Doncaster (an ominous beginning) to hear me talk about being Hitler's piano player and I had to tell him that that particular Peter Conradi's talk had happened four days earlier. In 1987 his mother rang me out of the blue to suggest that as everyone confused us, and as her son was the better-known, it would behove me to change my name. 'What name do you think might suit me?' I should have asked. Her Conradis were Dutch Protestants, I learnt, while mine were German Jews, on which topic more, later.

How do you recapture your childhood self? When I try, it feels like introjecting my present self into a faraway scene, rather like Scrooge guided by the Ghost of Christmas Past, or the ancient Professor Borg in Ingmar Bergman's *Wild Strawberries*, who similarly haunts scenes from his own childhood as a silent and sometimes invisible interloper. (Surely Bergman's film feeds off *A Christmas Carol*, both concerned with how apprehending the past might trigger a change-of-heart? Both configure remembering as an act of renewal, of redeeming lost time.)

This act of remembering, which sounds so simple, seems less so when subjected to analysis. My old PhD supervisor A.S. Byatt, together with my boss for two years at the British Council Harriet Harvey Wood, made an admirable anthology entitled *Memory*. The closer you get, the odder the act of recall appears. Not merely can we vividly remember events that never occurred, and forget those that did... but even the attempt to recapture the past alters it too. Moreover writing about it, which looks like a way of owning it, turns out also to be a way of making peace with it, and letting it go.

Part One: Early Years

1. Florence Alice Conradi, 1892-1983

When we went into Notre Dame Cathedral together my grandmother Florence Conradi wept. This was January 1967. She had thought she would never see Paris again. She recounted to me her first visit sixty years before, occasioned by her parents' attempt to prevent her elder sister from marrying Leo Sulzberger. He managed the family cotton-goods business (N. Erlanger, Blumgarten & Co) on Fourth Avenue in Manhattan's SoHo district and was brother of the future *New York Times* owner Arthur Hays Sulzberger. Probably they thought Beatrice – at 18 – too young to marry. As a *voyage d'oubli* or plan for diverting her energies, the scheme failed: the marriage took place the following year on 17 November 1909. Indeed Florence and I were now in Paris for the wedding of Beatrice's granddaughter – our cousin Marina Sulzberger – who married Adrian Berry (later 4th Viscount Camrose) in a Greek Orthodox ceremony on the rue Georges Bizet followed by a reception a mile away at the Ritz in the Place Vendôme. Adrian's mother was Lady Pamela Hartwell, daughter of F.E. Smith, society hostess, friend to Evelyn Waugh and wife of the then owner of the *Daily* and *Sunday Telegraph*. This was in a sense an alliance of two newspaper dynasties, the *New York Times* and *Telegraph*.

I was wearing desert boots with a mixture of defiance and shame: partly because they felt so comfortable but also because I relished feeling an imposter and out-of-place. Cousin David Sulzberger was handsome and charming; and kindly East Coasters, many of whom seemed to have flown in for the weekend from JFK, also tried – with limited success – to put me at my ease. To lack the knack of feeling at home seemed a token of authenticity.

Henry James wrote on the death of an old woman friend that 'A window on the past has closed for good: henceforth there will be – for those of us who remain – that much less light and so much less air'. Granma – who remembered what she was doing on the day that President McKinley was shot by an anarchist in 1901 (she was attending the co-educational Horace Mann school, so progressive that boys were taught to sew while girls tended the garden; Jack Kerouac attended the school later) – was my window onto vanishing worlds.

Firstly a window onto the pleasurable cavalcade – pleasurable so long as you were well-to-do – of Europe before World War I, of ragtime and Baedeker Guides (many of hers survive, well-thumbed) and of easy travel in a world still innocent of passports. In the Grünewald outside Berlin there were brightly uniformed Guards officers, with one of whom she had a dalliance; while in London straw was still put down outside the houses of the prosperous sick to dull the sounds of the carriage wheels that might disturb them. In London too, they watched Isadora Duncan dance at the Alhambra in Leicester Square. Here they learnt a new and expressive dance themselves – the Maxixe (pronounced Mashish) or Brazilian Tango. Girls in that far-off epoch carried dance-cards and fans and wore aigrettes in hair that was 'dressed', not cut: after she died in 1983 we would find a dozen of these feather-sprays, of all colours, in her flat. Georges Clemenceau, she told me, watching the London young dance the Bunny-hug in the Connaught rooms, mused to Lloyd George that the English – despite their '*visages tristes*' – sported when they danced '*des derrières gaies*'. It vexed her that being invited to dance made her blush.

Books helped me to understand our like-mindedness.... When I read Truman Capote's 'A Christmas Memory' I recognised the boy child's affinity with the old lady, and the easier understanding that can exist between distant generations. We conspired together to visit (one day, we hoped) New England to see the trees in their autumn colours, St Petersburg's Winter Palace – we checked its accessibility to wheelchairs – and (improbably) Albania by coach. We liked and enjoyed each others's minds. I was pleased to find sociologists describe this 'reciprocity of alternate generations' as a nearly universal phenomenon. So on reading Proust I was moved when the narrator's grandmother Bathilde Amédée averts her face in the Gardens by the public lavatory. Having suffered a stroke she wishes to protect her grandson from seeing that she is dying. Granma and I, I thought, resembled this narrator and his grandmother, secret allies.

At any rate I loved her tales, her taste, her aestheticism and shared her love of dogs. She kept up with books, from *Elizabeth and her German Garden* as a small child in 1898, buying and devouring Hemingway's *A Moveable Feast* as soon as it was published in 1964 and Doris Lessing's *Memoirs of a Survivor* in 1974. That made another link. We were in league together to worship beauty and this pact made us superior to everyone else, especially my father. Father belonged to the merely humdrum activity of making the money that clothed and fed us: all his hard work over the years meant we could safely afford to look down on him. Meanwhile we sighed in sympathy over each other's sorrows. Granma had problems with her beloved younger son's hostile second wife, who kept her at a distance while Eric was dying, aged 52, of Hodgkins's lymphoma; while we both boasted that my father didn't much like either of us.

If money-making was tasteless and if work of the kind Father did was philistine and bourgeois, Granma's world by contrast was rich and rare. Her sister Beatrice's remarkable first marriage gave her access to the *New York Times*, and after Leo's early death from pneumonia (1926) her second marriage was to the 'socially acceptable' architect Eli Jacques Kahn who designed art deco masterpieces like New York's Squibb Building, 261 Fifth Avenue, 120 Wall Street and the glamorous Film Center building on Ninth Avenue. Granma referred to him – perhaps confusing him with Louis Kahn (no relation) – as Frank Lloyd Wright's premier pupil.

When Uncle Eli visited London, he bought gifts of the good water-colours he liked to paint. He entranced me by comparing this medium 'to morality itself', adding that both were a matter of '*premier coup*'. He meant that working in oils you could always over-paint and conceal your mistakes: while with water-colours your first attempt was also your last, and exposed your frailties for ever. In Manhattan close to Central Park he had a collection of phosphorescent glass phials and bottles that I was awed to learn were Phoenician and destined for the Metropolitan Museum.

From Granma I thought as a child that all Americans were patricians who spoke three languages and came out of worlds we recognised because Henry James and Edith Wharton had mapped them for us. Albeit a Jewish version.

***

Florence Josephi was brought up in a flat on the Upper West side of New York City between 100th and 101st St and at 853, West End Avenue. It

Florence, Nettie, Beatrice

was furnished in what Americans called 'Mission Style': Arts-and-Crafts. It cost a cent to walk across the pedestrian promenade on Brooklyn Bridge, two cents for a hog or a sheep, five for a cow or a horse. There was still a farm on 121st Street. Her parents took her out of school to travel. She was glad to get away from the elderly Miss Cornelia Frances Baird, who wore bombazine and ran an Academy two hours out of Manhattan by train, in Norwalk, Conn. They sailed first-class to Cherbourg on the Hamburg-America line (the *SS President Lincoln*), arrived on 15 June 1908 and stayed till October, making travel arrangements by 'Marconigram', as cables were then known. Meanwhile they went sight-seeing in city after city, seeing opera and operetta, visiting museums, cathedrals, inns, great houses: her diaries are exhausting to read.

In Karlsbad on 27 August she and her Papa spotted King Edward VII riding by in a carriage with black horses looking 'very pleasant but not at

Sight-seeing. Florence's album

all imposing' with three adjutants and liveried coachmen, 'everyone wearing black like undertakers'. She wrote to friends back home that he 'walks around and takes his cure like everyone else, talks and smiles at all and sundry, and anyone who wishes may speak to him'. Flo's Papa, a prosperous clothier, had been prescribed a one month's cure too. This is the first instance of her interest in the British royal family: her identification with Edward's daughter-in-law Queen Mary belongs a little later in this narrative.

She was only sixteen. From her bossy letters it is clear that she looked older and flirted with Ivy League sophomores and handsome German students scar-faced from duelling.... The girls were brought up with some freedom. Flo comments on her own hypocrisy (this was July 1912, so she was 19) in asking an over-attentive suitor to request her mother's permission for them to meet the following day: 'That I, an American girl, should use this ploy!' She could 'get along nicely with French' and could follow a poor play in her 'indifferent German', their Swiss governess Antoinette Sellner having taught them both languages. Europe thrilled her. Of 'old' Heidelberg, she wrote that 'no artist can paint or orator describe [it] ... the castle is known to be the largest in the world' while Wiesbaden's recently built Kurhaus (1907) was '... the finest in the world'. Her propensity for boastful hyperbole was life-long.

Florence with her parents

Henceforth a family trip to Europe happened most years. In May 1910 the Josephi family who had travelled elsewhere in Europe made their first trip together to London, on the *RMS Mauretania*, then the world's largest ship. Actor-manager Forbes Robertson had the stateroom directly next to the Josephis; they docked at Fishguard, taking a Cunard 'special' train to London, where they stayed at the old Carlton Hotel (1899-1940) on Haymarket where it met Pall Mall. Their arrival coincided with Edward VII's death and two women in their large party, despite being American, changed to wear 'full' mourning dress, which gives some idea of the astonishing quantity of luggage with which they must have travelled.

They visited Selfridges, which had opened in 1909, termed by Flo 'the new American-plan' store, where they ordered ice-cream sodas. That only one American was available to make these drinks they thought probably accounted for their poor quality. However 'all the sales people were most polite and courteous – quite a contrast to NYC'. At Marlborough House they had 'dandy' views of the state funeral and of the new King George V and Mary looking 'very sad' as they drove by. One old soldier came out crying; Flo cried in sympathy.

At eight her hero had been the pioneering French woman painter Rosa Bonheur and by 1910 she knew she wanted to be an artist herself: she spent weeks in the Tyrol studying how to create dramatic landscape wood engravings with mad King Ludwig II's wood-worker Herr von Untertusch; then crossed the Dolomites in an open Victoria. Around December

Florence at her easel

1912 she met Emil Conradi, an Englishman, in St Moritz. Flo was coming down the hotel stairway wearing a whimsical muff in the shape of a pig (a life-long fetish: a colony of small pigs lived on her sill and the gift of a new wooden or glass pig was always a welcome addition).... He invited her to dance: she accepted. Discouraged from matrimony while hostilities lasted, they none the less married on 24 March 1915. Leo Sulzberger witnessed. The reception was at Manhattan's Hotel St Regis: 'Dancing at ten o'clock'. Emil called her 'F' by her initial letter; while he was 'E'.

She had married an Englishman and would live in London for the next sixty-eight years. The American writer Alice Duer Miller's best-selling poem sequence *White Cliffs of Dover*, a copy of which Granma cherished from its publication in 1941, ends with its American heroine, who had married an Englishman before World War I, reflecting:

> ...I am American bred
> I have seen much to hate here – much to forgive,
> But in a world in which England is finished and dead,
> I do not wish to live.

Perhaps this dramatised some of her own mixed feelings about her adoptive land.

The newly-weds cancelled their crossing on 1 May on the *Lusitania*, on which they had first booked, and which was sunk by U-boats eight miles off the coast of Ireland with huge loss of life. They came instead, a month earlier, on the *New York* on 3 April, on the American Line, docking at Liverpool. She kept up the habit of sailing the Atlantic for sixty-five years, into the age of jet travel. Over eighty in the early 1970s and dining at the captain's table, she was still cultivating new and useful acquaintances.

***

She sometimes claimed her family had owned the site on which the Bank of England was built in 1694. Noticing that her picturesque tales were embellished differently to suit each new occasion, we understood and sympathised with her need to impress. Much contributed to her sense of insecurity. She had lost one entire year of schooling after contracting typhus and spinal meningitis, during which her hair was shaved off to 'save her brain from over-heating'. She was incontinent for a while afterwards, and always very jealous of her sister Beatrice's healthy smartness and beauty and 'great blue eyes'. Flo and Beatrice fought like cats and dogs. We thought her a fantasist or romancer, who liked to 'talk the family *up*'.

Jack Worthing, at the end of *The Importance of Being Earnest*, quips that it is a terrible thing for a man to find out suddenly that all his life he has been speaking nothing but the truth. Florence's unexpected truth-telling propensity became clear only after her death in 1983. A sober-headed English cousin researching the family showed that her tales often carried credence. There was the odd exception such as her probably silly assertion to Emil that 'the Josephis were once of noble blood'. Other tales turned out to be based on fact: that the Josephis became court jewellers and so-called Schütz-Juden to the Russian Czar in the eighteenth century, following their skilfully engraving the flaw within a gem-stone into a rose; that they fled Riga once a Grand-Duke threatened to adopt one of their sons; that her grandfather paid for his voyage to Chicago by purchasing in Paris a cheap stone that turned out to be a fine jewel.

I loved this latter tale with its happy ending. Nearing the end of his apprenticeship in Paris around 1850 and living in a slum room on the Left bank, her grandfather was starving himself so he could afford to visit all the museums. On his last day he bought for almost nothing what turned out to be a fine emerald. He was playing with it, tossing it up in the air when his boss identified it: the said boss then sold the gem to an Indian Rajah (of course) enabling her grandfather to leave for Chicago, where he opened a successful jewellery business, and to send for Celia Cohen, whom he loved and who sailed to join him.

The Bank of England story – it turned out – was widely circulated and believed. I have copies of Josephi letters seeking to recover this lost inheritance – a sum they believed to be held in Chancery – in Hebrew from Riga in 1813 and 1829, in German from Petersburg in 1833 and in English from New York in 1909, all concerning the contested estate of 'an immensely rich Jew broker' Benjamin Levy, an East India Company founder who conducted financial dealings on a grand scale in London from 1669.

***

When I read *The Portrait of a Lady* I recognised her compatriot Mme Merle's pragmatic attire: stout boots, umbrella, waterproof overcoat. Granma went out, an American matron and redoubtable pilgrim, equipped with sensible shoes, plastic mac, a pleated plastic hood that concertinaed down into a convenient strip, and a bottle of Milton's disinfectant to keep Old World germs at bay. She was my exotic grandmother, strange because of her American-ness. Her speech fascinated me. 'Good' when she was a girl had still been 'dandy'. She was never thwarted but sometimes 'stymied' instead; when things went wrong they 'gave her gyp'. And of discipline at my prep school, she remarked 'I guess they whack you some'. Rich people were 'swells'. Even her kitchen was different, from which she conjured corn-on-the-cob held at each end with tiny finger-sized forks to stop your hands getting buttered, long thin spoons to scoop marrow from bones, a waffle iron, a broiling pan, Hellmann's mayonnaise before it became commonplace and a special almost black American chocolate cake with white icing. Her good American silver, exotically hall-marked by the maker and belonging to her mother c. 1880, somehow (to me) conveyed the easy optimism of that period.

She cost my father both money and peace of mind. In the 1920s she started her own company, called Durée, off Hanover Square, selling expensive buckram and parchment lamp-shades hand-painted with Chinoiserie figures by herself and three girl apprentices. She met Somerset Maugham's wife Syrie, a legendary interior designer, and visited her house at 213 King's Road. But her greatest coup lay elsewhere: in a memorable fog on Albemarle Street she once spotted a great car that had broken down, stopped and offered Queen Mary in the back a lift. She graciously accepted. Or so one unlikely story went. Florence unquestionably attracted her attention, winning a commission to design and make lamp-shades for Sandringham. (Only one of these lamp-shades, the figure-painting sadly faded and a ghost of its former self, survives.)

Queen Mary – aka the Dragon – henceforth became an object of fantasy-projection, together with her toques, eagle-headed umbrellas and covetings of others' furniture. In Granma's fanciful account, their paths kept crossing. In the 1920s when chromium furniture became fashionable Queen Mary tried a chair in Fortnums ('It *looks* very nice, but is it comfortable?'), got stuck and had to be pulled out. Laughter ensued: hers too. Granma saw her stomping around the Rose Garden in Regent's Park once it was opened in the early 1930s, in a cut-away jacket, long-skirted, heavy-shoed, be-toqued, one lady-in-waiting with her, two following discreetly at a distance. Granma visited Spinks auction house on Southampton Row on the day the future Edward VIII and the Princess Royal were there and treasured the story that he left the ash-trays full, exhorting his sister, 'Do hurry up May or we shall have George and the Dragon after us'. Aside from the snobbish and banal interest in royalty it was apparent that this dragon-persona fascinated her. Here was one role model for a woman exercising power.

She got permission from the Lord Chamberlain to take her boys round Buckingham Palace and sat them both experimentally on the thrones in the throne-room. (Angus Wilson collected these stories from me during the 1970s and from them wove the figure of Lady Mosson, an American grandee in a Baroque mansion competing with the royal family, in his final novel *Setting the World on Fire*. He admitted as much to me, and he catches her voice uncannily, considering he never met her.) When she tried again to secure the same permission for me and my brothers in the 1950s, she failed.

Durée lost large sums of money for each of its eight years, after which further difficulties followed when my grandparents could not sell the lease-hold during the Depression: their premature removal of my father from school before he matriculated – on financial grounds – was one direct consequence.

It took me years to understand that the whole rich panoply of her existence was entirely dependent upon my father and so a source of contention. Once he took over the family firm, after Emil's death in 1947, he did the hard work, while his mother reaped considerable financial rewards and moreover as Chairman attended Board meetings to which she contributed with infuriating inconsequentiality. She arrived one day at the Institute of Directors, 5 Belgrave Square and claimed then and there to have registered as the first woman member. For my father she must have combined the roles of tyrant and parasite. In her turn she resented him because she had always preferred – indeed adored – his younger brother.

Her luxurious Kensington flat for which her son worked so hard was painted a pale green she termed *eau-de-nil*. There were stunning blue Isfahan rugs and Whistler etchings that included his 1858 *La Marchande du Moutarde* with its Vermeer-like sense of inviting you into a mysterious interior. There were also two gorgeous miniatures by her beloved uncle

Ike Josephi, founder and first President of the American Society of Miniature Painters: a portrait on ivory of a Gilded Age lady ('Ike's lady-friend', who resembles a Gibson Girl) wearing peacock colours, and a landscape she claimed – after she had admired the full-size original – that he miniaturised in a week for her in 1899. Entrancing bibelots apart, she had curtains of Thai silk, sheets of Egyptian cotton and blankets spun from camel-hair, while the goose-down cushions on her pink settee sighed as you sat on them, taking their time to work out how best to support your behind. She displayed her mother's stately library, which boasted bound editions of Guizot's *History of France*, Hugo's five volume *Les Miserables*, Ruskin's *Stones of Venice*, together with the collected works of Maupassant, Flaubert, Kipling, Robert Louis Stevenson and Goethe. A library conventionally Europhile and aesthetic.

She summoned her housekeeper with a Swiss cow-bell, kept a chauffeur and entertained liberally, from American friends staying at Brown's Hotel to Lady Baden-Powell visiting from her grace-and-favour flat in Hampton Court. Little Miss Margaret Popham, ex-head-mistress of Cheltenham Ladies College, came down from the flat above every week for supper. 'Why do you bother to go to Brighton?' asked Miss Popham idly one evening: 'It's nothing but Jews and jelly-fish.' Granma took a few careful moments to savour and then explain this discourtesy. Friendship survived.

She knew and loved London as only an American can, always hungering to know it better and conveying to me a potent sense of its romance. She taught me not just Rotten Row and Richmond (where in the Park she and her closest friend Polly Gordon-Roberts – a Brigadier's widow from Idaho – always known to one another as 'Comrade', liked to roll sideways down a slope together after picnics) but the Chiltern villages, and the Epstein mother-and-child on the Cavendish Square convent. She also knew a terrace in Campden Hill created by a speculative builder who – if Napoleon had successfully invaded the UK – wished to profiteer from French officers' need for housing. In *A Handful of Dust* (1934) Evelyn Waugh created an interior decorator called Mrs Beaver, full of comical energy and networking ability, who is also the secret agent of a destructive modernity. Florence seemed to me an essentially *benign* Mrs Beaver who knew how to find the best joiners in Stepney or Peckham – i.e. hidden London – and where to go to buy not just chandeliers but Venetian rowlocks and then how to adapt these as andirons or fire-dogs.

***

When I read Thomas Mann's magnificent artist-tales – especially *Buddenbrooks* and *Tonio Kroeger* – I recognised his depiction of business families throwing up writer-aesthetes as a kind of final and unhealthy biological 'sport'. I identified with Tonio Kroeger's attraction to those who were happy in their skins and un-fussed by the world, like his beloved Hans Hansen and Inge. Mann was evoking himself in these characters; he was also describing me. I knew what he meant when Tonio is described as 'rasped by the banal', irritated by any conventional expression and so tiresomely supercilious. 'The thing about intellectuals,' a cousin once told me, 'is, you think you're getting on perfectly well with them, plain sailing and so forth; and then suddenly, completely out-of-the-blue, *they say something sour.* Now why do they do that?'. I had plenty of sour things to say. Sourness and articulacy were ways of surviving parental battles, and of holding my own.

Worrying about being gay and aged 20 or so, I decided to sound Granma out as to what she felt about homosexuals. The comical inadvertence of her reply – no doubt fuelled by encounters with inter-war interior designers – delighted me. 'What they *do* is quite disgusting,' she pronounced with solemnity. 'But they all have perfect manners.'

I was aware very young of needing to flirt with old ladies, and the efficacy of politeness in doing so. Recruiting my father's mother in this way as my intimate ally – together with my mother as the person I had to rescue – meant that my father was now perfectly encircled. The two most important women in his life had joined my side in the family war and the scene set for battle.

2. Parents-at-War, 1945-72

I was born on VE day, 8 May 1945, and lucky not to be called Victor: perhaps I did not want to be a war-baby and in any case waited three weeks after full 'term' for peace to arrive. A plump baby – which I was – was particularly admired during that time of austerity and rationing. But my father, stationed at army barracks in Catterick in the Yorkshire dales, did not learn of my arrival for some days: telephone operators went AWOL during the celebrations and telegrams were delayed. He was soon stationed in Nigeria for six months and I bonded with my mother, not him.

***

PC, Mother, Richard, 1945

The lost little boy I once was survives only as a ghost, and ghosts are sad when they need our help. If I invoke the spirit of this child he politely shows up again without expecting that anyone can do much for him. Embattled in his time by the grown-ups, sharp-wittedness and fluency were his chief ways of negotiating trouble.... Language and wit were his firepower. I loved learning new words. I learnt the word 'disturbed' when I was very small indeed.

When, aged six, I asked Mother 'why my father hated me', he had probably shown reasonable impatience at some now forgotten misdemeanour on my part. But her reply after a pause was unexpected: 'You have to understand, Darling, that he is psychologically disturbed'.

She was busy drying me with a large fluffy white towel after a bath. What did 'disturbed' mean? I gazed at my parents with new eyes and thrilled with pity and importance: my beautiful mother had to cope with a man suffering from the condition of *disturbance*. Here was a brand new word to savour, treasure and try out. I could guess from her demeanour that being disturbed was worse than chilblains, tonsillitis, or whooping cough. Being disturbed was clearly sad, dangerous and offensive. But by happy chance there I was, willing and able to help, living in a permanent state of Boy Scout-like preparedness, on red alert.

Sixty years later I see that 'disturbed' probably referred to his dalliances with other women; that he never wished to hate me, and that my alliance with my mother, cemented now by this single terrible phrase, excluded and disempowered him cruelly, rendering him understandably jealous.

No doubt it was because of his being disturbed that my parents had such weirdly violent arguments. Over high tea with buttered toast and jam, she once spat at him, 'How DARE you?! You are an absolute menace!' He came back at once and unexpectedly with 'And you're as bad as the Japanese'. Evidently the Japanese were disturbed too. 'Pah!' my mother retorted, winning this round with suspicious ease: 'You are *even WORSE* than the Japanese, you're the giddy limit'. She favoured conversation-by-flat-contradiction and frequently came out with strange comments that baffled. The chief problem with the Soviet Union, she once observed confidently if to general puzzlement, was that everyone there was believed to be harbouring an ulterior motive.

Understanding adults was a challenge. Mr Cooper, headmaster of the local kindergarten (where I much later discovered the writer Roger Deakin was at the same time), called the school together as the King

(George VI) had died, school was dismissed, and, as he explained, 'All the shops in the country were to close in sympathy'. By strange chance he had a big dog he loved whose name was 'King', and I at once understood that he was, reasonably enough, announcing the death of this Alsatian. I walked home and saw that all the shops were indeed closing; I remarked to my mother, deeply impressed, 'Boy!... *What a dog*!'

Nor did I understand why the Monarch had such a voracious appetite for plums that the country at large sang 'Send her Victorias'. Adults often mis-communicated, I saw. Perhaps the entire adult world needed my childish help, prone as it clearly was to ambiguity and disturbance? My life task might be rescuing and protecting adults. They were given to ailments with mystery-names like 'lumbago' and 'sciatica'. Meanwhile I could practise defending my mother from my father.

My parents had been happy at first. Early photos give out warmth and mutual affection and there were still long peaceable interludes. They were in themselves entirely admirable people – kindly, well-intentioned, public-spirited – yet increasingly unhappy together. Mother came home unexpectedly one day and found him in the arms of a woman she termed a prostitute. Twice when Father was found out in this manner he bought and thus tried to seal the peace with the gift of an oil painting.

When a marriage decays, the bedroom is implicated sooner or later. Maybe Mother could not, in great-aunt Betty's old-fashioned and graphic phrase, 'take the blanket off the bed': perhaps she became frigid. In any case Father had a dominant sexual drive and, when he was caught straying, mistrust grew. Visitors stayed away, complaining of the black atmosphere, and we children experienced at home a Pooter-ish Dance of Death, our version of the Strindberg play about a marriage locked in hate-filled warfare, staged with all possible suburban bathos.

If Mother felt she were losing a round, cornered or found out, tears, then tiredness were weapons of last resort. She would announce, 'I'm afraid I'm feeling very tired', a deadly ruse that drove us all into guilty silence, so energetic and capable was she really. Her tiredness must be our fault and we dreaded its onset: our frailties and imperfections had exhausted her.

If Father felt he were losing he was by contrast capable of violence. He once threw our part-corgi mongrel dog, whom we loved despite his habits of ring-barking trees and biting our friends, down the staircase by its tail. Later this dog was destroyed without our foreknowledge, and we children huddled together in whispered conspiracy while the adult emotional storms blew downstairs in the living-room. The following morning, as compensation for the disappearance of the dog, a blue budgerigar arrived.

***

In September 2008, I rang my mother, then dying of double pneumonia, to commiserate. 'How are you?' I asked. Wheezing, very frail, about to enter a coma, she retorted with faint but still brisk vigour, 'It could be A LOT WORSE'. The phrase 'Blitz spirit' was meant for her. She told frequently of carrying my baby elder brother in pitch darkness through their West Hampstead flat strewn with the broken window-glass caused by bomb-blast in the quarter-mile radius around each dropped bomb: war-time provided a bonanza for glaziers. I could not save my mother from the glass or the Blitz, being as yet un-born. But, accident-prone, she imported Blitz spirit into post-war life.

She was a bad driver. In her very first car, a black two-doored Austin A30, sometime in the early 1950s she took a bend so fast that the car rolled onto its side. Her passenger Great-uncle J. (aka Jules), born in Paris in 1870 and now eighty years old, fell out of the unlocked door just before the car overturned. He had lost his right leg during the 1916 Zeppelin raid on Hull and his ill-fitting wooden prosthesis came unclipped and was discovered some distance away. Everyone was shaken, nobody hurt. On a separate occasion with another driver she leant against the old-fashioned door-handle and fell out herself. Some doubted whether Mother had a sense of humour: when she laughed she sounded in pain. None the less both episodes were considered excellent jokes.

In a similar spirit of accident-prone-ness, when she visited a local school on sports day she fell through a rotten patch on the cricket pavilion floor and came home sedately with one leg badly grazed and bloodied. When she flopped into her favourite armchair, a malicious knitting needle penetrated her buttock. She coped heroically. Working her Singer sewing machine – electric but with a treadle – the needle once shockingly pierced both her finger and finger-nail. She made little fuss. If she picked an apple, there would be a wasp or bee crawling over its under-side to be stung by.

Comedy did not always belong within this picture. Shopping with me once during a rain-storm, she froze for long minutes in a rictus of pain, breathing carefully and bravely telling me to go home without her, suffering a prolapsed uterus. Later her bladder prolapsed. She also suffered, among other internal disorders, anaemia and diverticulitis, conditions requiring regular ingestion of pills or a granular green powder. In later life she developed a duck-egg sized brain tumour that, though benign, required surgery and left her permanently unbalanced, given to knocking over waiters and wildly dangerous during Scottish reels. There were many falls and broken bones: two broken arms and four hip-operations.

She was always cheerful and gallant in hospital, garnering fascinating details about the private lives of her nurses and doctors. Perhaps the mugs of tea and camaraderie amongst the wounded recalled war-time? But she seemed always to be threatened by tempests and perils, which my evidently imperfect love could not prevent. For I was her squire, chaperoning her against harm, her Special Ally, St George against the dragons of adversity. I loved her beauty, her air of certainty, her scent and clothes: the sequined dress she had married in in 1940 that still hung in her wardrobe; the way she shopped wearing gloves and a hat and (once) a demi-voile that flattered her wonderfully blue eyes. I identified with the child in A.A. Milne's 'Disobedience': 'James James/Morrison Morrison/Weatherby George Dupree/Took great/ Care of his Mother/Though he was only three./ James James Said to his Mother,/ "Mother," he said, said he;/ "You must never go down/ to the end of the town, /if you don't go down with me." '

But my mother was more headstrong than Milne's, and also suffered from one peculiar and unique threat to her health and well-being: Father. Most of her ills and accidents I could do nothing to help. My father by contrast represented a jeopardy carrying with it the greatest charge of fear but I could happily resist and attack him on her behalf.

Home life muddled and dirtied all four children; it also taught us to walk on egg-shells. Where would the next hidden mine explode? We felt doomed to tension and thrilled with guilt; in my case I acquired a lifelong tendency to hyper-vigilance, looking for danger. Henry James wrote in 1895, 'I have the imagination of disaster, and see life as ferocious and sinister': yes. We all suffered an exaggerated, perhaps Kafka-esque sense of responsibility. Supervising my doctorate A.S. Byatt once cheerfully proposed that I write up the slogan 'The world is not my fault' as a frieze around my study: good advice for my siblings too. I notice in myself a desire to mediate and reconcile where this is not my business; it has the same cause.

Tension at home was not eased after 1958 when she became an early Marriage Guidance Counsellor and then a psychotherapist. When the first cheque arrived, she framed it on the mantelpiece rather than banking it, so proud was she of having earned money herself. She could now try out her 'marriage counselling' skills on Father, maintaining that the 'blame' for her failing marriage always lay outside herself. That she had independent means could not always have been comfortable for him either.

***

Another vignette from early childhood. I'm holding pale blue wool for Mother between my two upright hands, which she patiently spools off

Peter, Prue, Richard, 1952

into a ball. When my mother puts down the wool and unexpectedly hugs me, I ask what I did to deserve this favour? It stands out in my memory as having neither pre-amble nor sequel. She explained that the hug was not a reward for good behaviour but that she had just read in Dr Benjamin Spock's *Baby and Child Care* that a limited amount of physical affection can be a jolly good thing for everybody concerned. She fully intended, she added, to give both my brothers and my sister a hug too. As a child she was shown off to her parents for an hour only before bed-time and any warmth she received had been from her Nanny Fraser, who lived to be one hundred on the south coast, where it seemed to me that all Nannies went into retirement: our Nanny Pett retired to Emsworth. So physical affection happened rarely. (No accident surely that my sister Prue and I both liked mountains of blankets on our beds at night for comfort and made a cult of open fires.)

Mother would say that whereas her sister in South Africa had always liked dogs, she herself preferred children. But if that implied that we had a better deal than her sister's child, a dream she confided late in life suggests another reading: she dreamt that she re-inserted each of us, one by one, back into her womb in reverse order. Perhaps she never saw us as entirely separate from herself.

***

At prep school the burly and kindly head-master Mr Meikle was a wonderful story-teller. Wearing his red polka-dot bow-tie he spent an hour each Sunday telling the tale of one chapter from Homer's *Odyssey* after another, perhaps as a corrective to Anglicanism. He did this from memory, without any text in sight. We sat at his feet or lay on the floor and drank it all in. When he described Odysseus's escape from the Cyclops's cave, I thought he had blinded Polyphemus himself by plunging that stake into his eye and then clung bravely to the under-belly of the giant sheep to escape. He also loved Conan Doyle's Étienne Gerard stories. He took good care of his charges, which included our indisposi-tions.

Early on I sat at the front of his French class while he gently asked whether I needed to be excused? I denied this while a hot and steaming puddle gathered around my shoes, as I pissed myself in public, drawing attention to my predicament through being too shy to make a request. When I wet my bed, I sometimes got a beating from my father.

I also suffered from bronchial asthma, for which Vick was rubbed into the chest, or a steam inhalation taken; and flat feet about which nothing was to be done. Then there was a weird involuntary form of spasm or panic during which the glands in my neck swelled up visibly, like a bullfrog, till they became rock-hard and condemned me to swallowing saliva hard non-stop for five or ten minutes during which I had perforce to be silent. I grew used to forewarning people that I was about to go incommunicado and that they were to continue chatting informally among themselves without giving me further thought.

On one afternoon out from Winchester House prep school we all three visited Blenheim Palace, whose majestic gardens included facing groups of trees representing the embattled armies confronting one another during the wars of the Spanish Succession. I was eight years old and carefully explained to my parents the Auld Alliance between Scots and French in a manner that deliberately, provocatively alluded to my and my mother's complicity. Small wonder, perhaps, that in 1970, when my father attempted for the first time, and as yet unsuccessfully, to leave my mother, his parting words were 'You have to choose between Peter and me'.

***

From the early twentieth century Pears soap was famous for its annual 'Miss Pears' competition, in which parents entered their children into the high-profile hunt for a young brand ambassador to be used on packaging and in consumer promotions. Many Miss Pearses subsequently entered acting or modelling. When she was three and I was five, my sister Prue and I auditioned as Pears Babies and indeed for a season her photograph, wide-eyed, adorable, flirting outrageously from under the bed-clothes and hugging her favourite black-faced doll, was to be seen on hoardings everywhere across the country.

Prue and I – of the four of us – were always allies, and in 2001 she wrote to me about our joint childhoods. Our elder brother suffered greatly for around twenty years from working in the family firm with Father; our youngest seemed to us too young to understand much. Prue's response to the powerlessness our family troubles induced in her was to become a psychotherapist, and she wrote from this perspective. Perhaps this point of view helped save her from the various panic attacks that all three of us boys suffered for many decades. My elder brother, who suffered for years forms of heart arrhythmia, believes these attacks probably related to the domestic warfare we witnessed for so long. The warfare is long past; the panic attacks are hardier and outlive the strife.

Prue, c 1970

Prue described our parents as two very willful people locked in battle and their marriage as 'hugely conflicted'. She saw our mother as original but trapped in conventionality, tough and stubborn. She believed that she and I had 'carried the consciousness' of the family psyche or trauma and that this always constituted a deep bond between us. Did 'carrying consciousness' mean that we were the ones who tried to 'understand' and mediate? Perhaps. She added 'I sense … that the family drama was played out with you very much in the centre of it. I saw Father as quite unable to relate to you as a highly gifted and sensitive child. Instead he was deeply antagonistic, whereas Mother … "doted" upon you.' After she died I found that she had over the years indeed cached letters of no special interest from me.

Here was a typical Oedipal configuration. Prue argued that Father's jealous childhood trauma of being excluded by his mother in favour of his younger brother was replicated by my birth. 'The deep bond that the mother makes with her baby, and her adoration of the baby potentially can feel excluding to the father or cause his extreme jealousy…. If you really think of Father's unconscious patterning with respect to Grandma, then this moment of his wife turning her attention to the baby, first Richard, then you, then me, this situation would have caused ripe conditions for a re-constellation of Father's own childhood trauma, where it seems it was his mother who primarily in his eyes did all the damage. Perhaps the rift in the marriage was already there after Richard's birth. But it was also due to the second born son in his childhood, and you as the second born son may have unconsciously replicated this for him. Such a trauma is bound to be replayed if it is not made conscious. (The sins of the fathers, etc)'.

Prue's reflections were written half a century later. At the time we were all aware of a mechanism which trapped us, but which made little sense either to outsiders or to ourselves. And that baffled state is itself hard to recover. I don't recognise the slightly sissy pretty-boy of family snaps: I felt gangly, un-athletic, uncoordinated and unworthy, at best *beau laid*. Feeling that you are different is common to most children. In my own case I made sure that cleverness and love of art set me apart.

PC c 1960

***

My family might be reconciled to the 'long littleness of life': I was not, and hungered for more, and for elsewhere. I wished to rescue my philistine family for 'culture', for the life of the mind and for an emotional worship of beauty, as – if possible – of tragedy too. This ideally meant *Swan Lake* at Covent Garden, for the family Christmas outing. My mother pleaded my cause. She and I once inflicted all four movements of a Tchaikovsky symphony on my father and patient and good-humoured siblings. If I lost this battle over the Christmas entertainment what we got instead was often the Crazy Gang's slapstick at the Victoria Palace, Cinderella-on-Ice in Golders Green, or an extended family dinner at the Trocadero, for which grandfather had provided the lighting, or the Criterion; followed by my dutifully foxtrotting around on the dance-floor with my mother, impersonating a grown-up. Cousin Martin remembers how elegantly my parents danced together.

There was an element of pose in these culture wars: I had played Helena in *A Midsummer Night's Dream*, aged 12, and Portia in *The Merchant of Venice* at 15, but secretly thought *South Pacific*, most of which I could play by ear on the piano, roughly as good.

The coldness of a child, Iris Murdoch once observed, can hurt just as much as an adult's. I would goad and taunt my father by speaking of the need for provisional parenting licences on the model of provisional driving licences. You could, I hinted priggishly, be biologically capable of fathering a child but should still have to prove that you were stable or mature enough.

One notable crisis happened when I was sixteen and we were holidaying with Dutch friends at Petten on the north Holland coast. Mealtimes were tense with miscommunication, blame and drama; and my mother, always an uncertain cook, had made a highly experimental carrot soup that we were eating outside in the garden when a dispute about this meal triggered a row. It started at a slow tempo but rapidly grew first wild and then quickly out of control. Details are now hazy but my father and I exchanged hate-stares till I managed to provoke him into threatening 'to beat me until the blood ran'. 'Against international law', I sanctimoniously goaded. At this point he jumped up, red-faced and furious, manhandled me into an awkward half-nelson, trying to force-march me into the house for punishment.

Everyone was by now shouting at the tops of their voices. My four-year old brother Stephen wept, my sister jumped up and down and yelled while my mother beat his shoulders vehemently with an egg whisk and told him to let me go. The violence also attracted the interest and concern of our Dutch neighbours and friends. All this brouhaha distracted him during the crucial second it took me to escape, panting and trembling, through a ground-floor window, grab a bicycle and ride off into the evening with my sister. In Holland, two are allowed onto one bike together and we rode away – allies in misery always – condoling with each other as we often did about the stupidity and cruelty of adults. An early satellite was orbiting the heavens that night as if catapulted there with such force, I remember, that it suggested the loopings of a crazed planet.

The following morning saw a painful coda. My father, I learnt, had gone on a long, long walk into the small hours to work off his feelings and regain balance. 'That is what he does', my mother explained. She next told me that I must now go up to his room to apologise. But, I piteously objected, he was forty-five while I was only just sixteen and the fracas had been his fault, not mine. That made no difference, she replied. *Someone* had to act the grown-up, express regret and start a reconciliation, she explained, and he would be able to do neither.

Hating my mother's logic, I saw no way of avoiding its forlorn conclusion. So dragging my feet, swallowing my pride, I went upstairs, knocked on his door, and apologised. He duly forgave me and we sheepishly shook hands. Her making me initiate this act of contrition was partly because this was a way in which we could all move forward, but perhaps partly also a device for humbling him further.

It had another significance too, which I now begin to understand and formulate. I longed for an older man to hold me, be proud of me and show me how to grow into a man. I longed for signs of his love and approval. But our unhappy family dynamic ruled this out. I was coming to the sad conclusion that, matters standing as they did, I would probably have to learn to be my own father.

I soon got permission to hitch-hike from Holland to stay with my elder brother, who was working for four months in Marseille. Hitch-hiking there took two days. I secretly yearned to be picked up by an attractive man, yet when a handsome, dark and kindly Frenchman of twenty-four offered to share his hotel room with me for the night near Valence, I was too inhibited to accept. I fled onwards to reach 107, avenue de St Julien, Marseille, 12e – where Richard was staying – around 5 am and sat out in the courtyard garden with its bougainvillea. Relaxing a little, I drank my first café-au-lait from a deep cup, ate a croissant, gloried in the pantiled roofs and scented air, and the hot bright clear southern light.

This was the first of many hikes. During the following three years I hitched to Israel, to Algeria just after the war of independence, to Berlin to see the Wall open up for the first time for Christmas 1962 – a very moving and distressing scene of reunions and farewells – to Paris to stay in the famous book-shop, Shakespeare & Co, and then twice to Greece, and once to Nordkap in the Arctic wastes of north Norway. I had time to do all this because I left school in December 1962, after creating a minor scandal by refusing to accept another beating. That my parents allowed me at sixteen to nineteen so to travel was brave on their part – albeit the world seemed safer then. My restlessness is not hard to deconstruct: as well as exploring new scenes I was longing for escape. Thom Gunn's poem 'On the Move' resonated with me: 'At worst, one is in motion; and at best, /Reaching no absolute, in which to rest, / One is always nearer by not keeping still.' No doubt my father was glad to see the back of me, too.

3. Being German

A comical tale is told of a visit made around 1925 to my grandfather Emil Conradi, who had established his own successful electrical wholesaling company in 1908 on Rosebery Avenue near Finsbury Town Hall. He received a call from a Scottish engineer in his thirties seeking a substantial investment to develop a new idea.

When Emil asked what this novel invention might achieve, he was assured that it was 'a seeing wireless' that – with a camera installed in a kitchen – could be watched on a flickering screen from the living-room. Emil puffed at his pipe before pronouncing 'A bad idea with no possible future'. So – none the better for his visit – James Logie Baird departed into the afternoon with his pioneer television set undemonstrated. And my grandfather might be indicted for being both *Besser-Wisser* and *verbissen*, two German words without English equivalents. His family had after all decamped from Dresden (via Paris) to London only in 1870.

Being a *Besser-Wisser* is a charge often levelled against Saxons – as Emil was by descent – and signifies a Know-All who can therefore learn nothing new; while *verbissen* means 'dogged', 'tenacious' or 'determined' and implies an unwavering one-track-mind. Emil sometimes found it hard to think 'laterally'. As for Baird, we now know that by 1937 the BBC adopted Marconi-EMI's method of televising in preference to his; and Baird's widow when she died in 1996 is said to have been penniless. So perhaps Emil's *Verbissenheit* was not entirely stupid.

The Conradis struck my cousin Freda Morris as rather German. She once commented on what she perceived as tribal differences between her father's family, the Russian Pale-descended Abelsons, and her mother's Dresden-descended Conradis. She believed Abelsons to be artistic and to have what she called 'dash' or flair, while Conradis by contrast – even when charming or good-looking – tended to be 'rigid and neurotic perfectionists'. She had experienced her grandfather Heinrich (later, Henry) Conradi as strict, officious and difficult. He was not averse to the use of a strap for punishing his children. Heinrich was Emil's father and, like him, an electrical engineer.

There were two Conradi-Abelson marriages in the 1890s, one between beautiful, spirited, good-humoured Adele Conradi, born in 1880, and the worldly, attractive businessman and *coureur de jupons* Seymour Abelson, whom she met when a very young assistant teacher and married at nineteen; the second between Adele's half-brother Leon, who three years before married Seymour's gloomy sister Alma. Such complex intermarriages were common until recently among so-called Anglo-Jews.

Freda's had been a difficult birth; and Adele, horrified in 1910 at getting pregnant again for the sixth time, consulted a close friend who came up with the idea of employing a knitting needle – unsterilised – to induce a miscarriage. She died of scepticaemia after a few days. She was thirty. Freda was less than one year old and had no memories of her mother. After this half-orphaning, her German grandfather Heinrich loomed large in her young life. He came from that mysterious and off-putting land where Rupert Brooke had warned that even 'tulips bloom as they are told' – a disciplinarian whose concern for correct behaviour thoroughly alarmed his grandchildren.

Freda grew up to be an amateur painter and married a successful property developer: they bought an elegant Georgian house in Edwardes Square, Kensington and put down their sons for Eton. Later she would choose Bohemian St Ives, Cornwall to over-winter, where to her satisfaction unconventional painters abounded. Her reflections on the Conradis have led me to think about being German and – a recovering perfectionist myself – about how my family found their lucky way to London from their ancient base in Dresden in Saxony. Conradi men in England even today occasionally appear to me 'somewhat German' – arrogant, officious, or blinkered – and I ponder the meaning of being German-descended. When my father first worked in the family electrical wholesaling business in the 1940s he had the temerity to install fluorescent lighting during one of his father's absences; he feared his father's fury and suffered greatly, even wondering whether his father might sack him. An addiction to micro-management runs in our family DNA. How much of Henry's and Emil's characters was due to nationality and how much to their genes? And how much to the long-term effects of Henry's forcible exile in 1870? And how much of all this do I inherit?

***

One Dresden Conradi invented the Leibniz biscuit while his brother published *Der Zauberspiegel* – The Magic Mirror – and created a set of magic tricks still known today as 'Conradi Magic Acts'. I should like to be descended from the biscuit-maker and the conjuror but cannot prove this provenance. Henry's branch of the Conradis believed – according to one source – that they descended from Subiza Jews from Spain, plus France and Holland.

Although post-Holocaust it is Protestant Conradis only who survive in Germany, Conradi is still a common surname there. The Dresden community of over 3000 Jews in 1904 was decimated to around sixty by 1945, and six of Henry's nieces and nephews, many of them by now in their eighties, together with their spouses, children and grandchildren, were among the millions gassed. Henry himself had died, in safety and in London, in 1920.

That sixty survived at all constitutes a perverse miracle: the diarist Victor Klemperer believed that the chances of survival of the few dozen Dresden Jews still alive in the last months of the war were greatly helped by the terrible fire-bombing of February 1945: any survivors after that date with a Dresden accent were excused from having to carry the obligatory racial papers demonstrating that they were Aryan, since so much paper-work had been consumed in the flames. Those indemnified in this way did not include a new Dresden friend of Klemperer's, a Professor Conradi arrested in 1943 for buying radishes – for vegetables were then forbidden to Jews – and sent to Auschwitz.

It is well-known that Jews from the diverse European countries often disliked each other and differed radically. Their distinguishing features cannot simply be put down to protective camouflage: the differences are more than skin-deep. German Jews were famously *plus royaliste que le roi* or, as we might say in this connection, more German than the Germans. Henry had an elder brother named at birth in 1826 Sigismund, a variant of Siegmund, name both of a Holy Roman Emperor and in Germanic myth of Wotan's son, twin brother-and-lover of Sieglinde, and father of Siegfried. Sigmund was of course also the name given in Moravia in 1856 to Freud. Such proud post-Enlightenment identification with Germanic culture was passionate and deep; so that the rejection of German Jews by their beloved host culture was, as well as murderous, heart-stoppingly cruel.

Being a Francophile and a reluctant Germanophobe I would much prefer to dwell on my Paris-born great-grandmother. Yet I don't think my awareness of something German in the male line of my family – and within myself – fantastical or forced. When I lived on an Israeli kibbutz for more than one year in 1967-68, any Jew who came from Germany was unkindly known as a 'Yekke' from the Hebrew 'Meduyak' meaning *precise* and also *punctual*. *Yekkim* were disliked for exactly these reasons, among the other more Levantine – and therefore more relaxed and unpunctual – Israelis.

The whole idea of 'German-ness' was of course in a sense Bismarck's flimsy 1871 invention; and can be a convenient portmanteau or scapegoat for a variety of unrelated traits. When my ancient great-aunt Poulot went yellow from over-dosing on dandelion leaves, we thought that here was one last instance of the German sense of duty that had always marked her. She had watched her first-born die of ptomaine poisoning from a bad fish; done years of voluntary work in the Jewish East End; then, widowed young, she dutifully brought up her beloved grandson Peter – fruit of her reprobate son's indiscretion with a *demi-mondaine* – only for him to be killed when a following Lancaster bomber crashed into his, on take-off for a raid. We attributed Poulot's faddish regimen and yellow complexion to the Germanic duty to eat herbs: and it suited our narrative that the equally yellow companion who encouraged this zany diet came from Potsdam.

Our father could pursue a single wasp with a rolled-up newspaper for up to an hour, cursing with the purest *Verbissenheit* 'This bloody animal', enraged by its wicked zigzag flight and its perverse refusal to die. Other explanations were also possible for our father returning his children's letters with each mistake officiously under-lined and corrected in red ink in the margin. General knowledge quizzes were administered at meal-times – 'What is the capital of Guatemala?' – that terrified Prue. His letters were usually round robin affairs, typed out by his secretary, with each of us receiving successively fainter and fainter carbon copies signed 'Your affectionate father'. They nonetheless employed underlinings reminiscent of Queen Victoria's, uses of Upper Case, and italicisings that all betrayed the fear of not being listened to, as well as an addiction to getting one's way. There would often be news of some new domestic acquisition which he would inform us had 'revolutionised our lives'. I relished the phrase 'revolutionise our lives', which could refer to the effect of an electrically vibrating carving-knife that accelerated the carving of the Sunday roast, and/or a cork-screw whose needle pumped air through the cork either causing it to rise or the bottle to explode. This helped with Piesporter Michelsberg though less with Mateus Rosé, which was semi-sparkling.

Life itself often exasperated Father. The racking coughs of heavy smokers – especially if they were women – offended him. Heavy drinking annoyed him. My gawkiness at fifteen and the uglinesss of one woman friend of mine were cause for satirical comment for days. He policed and micro-managed our table manners, was accordingly censorious about chain-smoking and drinking amongst much else. He led – at least on the surface – a hyper-orderly life, attested by his hundreds of tool-shed drawers, each accurately labelled e.g. 'screws, ¼ inch, ½ inch, ⅛ inch' and by his valuable stamp-collection, including many Penny Reds and Blacks, and even some Tuppenny Blues. After a dinner with guests he circulated a typed alphabetical list of liqueurs, starting methodically with 'advocaat' and ending with 'schnapps'. As my mother's father George had been a twin, and George's sister one of another set of twins, Father took out insurance against siring twins himself.

He would sit at weekends at the centre of the silent sphere of light shed by his angle-poise lamp, hinging and docketing and indexing, page after page and book after book of stamps, reaching out from time to time from his abstraction to take a jelly-baby from a large tin, a childlike comfort we imagined compensating him a little for his loveless childhood and sweetening his unhappy marriage. Perhaps he would be playing a song by his favourite French singer 'Patachou', or Offenbach's *Barcarolle*, on the gramophone.

He had his own way of being *Besser-Wisser*: an impatience with difference, flagged with sentences that started 'I simply cannot believe how he behaves like that…' or 'I fail to understand why she thinks that…'. Failure to understand and inability to believe were presented as badges of authenticity or tokens of good faith: it was the world's fault rarely to render itself comprehensible, never our responsibility to widen our grasp of the possible.

Five generations of Conradis have been engineers, starting with Henry's father Samuel, born in Dresden in 1790, and continuing for over two centuries to my electrical engineer father and both my brothers.

Some necessary connection exists – at least in my head – between this profession of engineering, for which precision and accuracy are prerequisite, and 'German' perfectionism. Conradis have also been inventors: Henry invented an arrow-head shaped scoop to push fallen pedestrians out of the way of the first Paris trams and thus prevent their being crushed to death. His son, my grandfather Emil, made his name in 1930 with the gripper hand-lamp for use in workshops and garages and was responsible for ten patents during the second war alone.

I feared that the German-ness I inherit is not the German-ness I most love and admire, i.e. an intellectual and cultured German-ness; and a further digression belongs here. In the London flat of Poulot's daughter in the 1960s hung a beautiful small framed portrait in oils dating from around 1840. On enquiring, I was told 'Just some German poet, some ancestor of Poulot's Edelsten in-laws'. Then, when I pressed my enquiry, I heard 'Just someone called Heinrich Heine'.

This cousin was a concert pianist with good reason to know that Heine's lyrics were set to music by every great composer from Schubert and Schumann to Wolf, Brahms, Mendelssohn, Wagner, and Richard Strauss. Heine was one of the most influential German Jews, the greatest German writer after Goethe, and arguably Europe's second most important poet after Byron. The momentousness and casualness of Fifi's reply equally took my breath away: as if a cousin had down-played the discovery that you shared a kinship with Shakespeare.

I reluctantly drew my own conclusion: that I came from a family of Philistines, people who in Russia would have been dismissed as *nie-kulturny*. But this snobbish and aesthetic fear – once I started to explore my own ancestry from around the year 1870 – proved somewhat misplaced.

4. Being English

My maternal forebears came to England in the eighteenth century from central Europe. I never met anyone who knew precisely where – or who worried about it. There was a persistent rumour that they were at least in part Sephardi, which might conceivably be true: one cousin maintained that the family had changed its names from Leon to Levy after a father-son quarrel in the late eighteenth century. 'Cohen', 'Levy' and 'Isaacs', despite sounding Ashkenazi, are occasionally Sephardic surnames too; and Judge Neville Laski (1890-1969), elder brother of Harold Laski of the LSE, who worshipped at the Spanish synagogue on Lauderdale Road, was a family friend. But they felt themselves to be English and did not investigate further.

When my parents dined with my great-aunt Katie van Zwanenburg in March 1970, the phone rang and Katie heard that her favourite grand-child Anna, who was thirty-four, had been killed in a car-crash. Anna's marriage was in difficulties and she was at this time peculiarly reliant on her grandmother. Katie stood up, told my parents she would retire to her room, and left them for twenty minutes. After this, dinner resumed. Katie was shaken but composed.

I often ponder this uncanny composure. My mother's family, especially the womenfolk, had about them an Edwardian sense of certainty, of belonging on the planet, and a tough way of knowing – or not minding – who they were. They did not indulge in the self-questioning that weakened my own post-war generation. But other elements were at work here too: a sense of what 'acting English' required in a century that had seen the English beleaguered during two world wars, and a related sense that to act less than stoically might risk appearing dangerously foreign. They accordingly looked as English as a Mark Boxer cartoon. There were cousins whose grand-parents came from *Mittel-Europa*, who sometimes seemed to be impersonating Pierre Daninos's comically stereotypical Major Thompson.

So-called Anglo-Jews feature in many post-war novels. Anthony Powell describes Rosie Manasch in *A Buyer's Market* (1952) as 'at once coarser in texture and at the same time more subtle' than the gentile girls in her debutante 'set'; I suspect Powell sees subtlety as a secret mask for coarseness, and sees both as related to the fear of exclusion.

Excess of scruple is something I recognise in myself, manifesting in a Byzantine tendency towards worrying about many possible scenarios at once, especially random punishment and losing favour. Iris Murdoch in *The Philosopher's Pupil* (1983) writes of the Jewishness of Stella McCaffrey (née Henriques) as 'an alienation from English society … a kind of empty secret freedom, as if she were less densely made than other people'; while in *Nuns and Soldiers* (1980) she accurately captures the tribal clannishness of the Anglo-Jewish Openshaws, who operate in relation to the central characters as a comical chorus known as '*les cousins et les tantes*'. I recognise that, too.

***

When I was seventeen Katie's sister Ruby – my maternal grandmother – took an overdose and died. There is still family debate about how befuddled whisky had made her when she kept swallowing those sleeping pills, and how desperate she was. I, from the age of ten, used at her request to sneak to the whisky decanter to freshen her glass: she was undergoing a pointless and cruel form of aversion therapy for her alcoholism. What she needed was to be listened to. But acknowledging what you are feeling was not then – as she knew to her cost – considered English. In her generation emotions 'did not do'; and this was a harsh lesson in which she had been cruelly coached.

Her despair began twenty years before when her favourite child, blond, blue-eyed and weeks shy of his twentieth birthday, was shot down and killed on his final trainee navigator's flight, on 15 November 1941. My mother recalled the extensive cousinry assembling at Frognal Lane to urge a stiff upper lip. Such repression of public displays of grief was common during that war. It probably helped kill her later. By an astonishing chance her grave-digger turned out not merely to have dug her son's twenty years before, but had worked out for himself the association between them. I remember his startling us by asking – vividly recalling her pain – whether she had ever 'got over it?' In some sense she had not.

John Cohen, 1941

On the day in question her expected bridge partners had failed to arrive. She was sixty-nine, lonely and sorry for herself. She had worn her son's 'wings', made up as a marcasite brooch, for her last twenty years of good works, tippling and bridge. His violin and his calf-bound Clifton College essays, all of which I have – unremarkable apart from one extra-mural one on Jewishness – became sacred relics. I was named after this dead uncle. So were two second cousins.

Katie had been born in 1885 and Ruby in 1892, into what had once been a doctor's residence, on what we always called the 'open Bow Road'. There was a pub opposite whose weekend drunks tumbling out onto the street they loved to watch. Did the word 'Open' distinguish the residences of city gentlemen in East Bow from slum tenements elsewhere? They were a family of nine children, including three girls, all of whom married well. Born Isaacs, they changed their name to the more English-sounding 'Phillips' – though one dim-witted brother opted instead for the double-barrelled 'Isaacs-Phillips', rather missing the point. *Sotto voce*, they used the coinage '*un de nous*', i.e 'one of us', when identifying whether a passing stranger or new friend was a co-religionist. Sounding – and also seeming – less Jewish mattered. Katie paid for one niece to have an operation on her nose. But they stayed within the faith, worshipping at Dennington Park Road synagogue. After their father did well importing coconuts, they moved to a bigger house in Highbury New Park with four live-in servants.

Katie married Anglo-Dutch Fritz van Zwanenburg, hard-working and a practical joker; while her youngest brother Manny married a Vandenburg (aka van den Burgh in Holland), from another branch of the same family, both from Oss in Brabant, names associated with the meat-trade and the discovery of margarine and, after 1929, with Unilever. These two great-aunts' memories went back before the Great War and both described to me on different occasions 'Jack' (John Benjamin) Sainsbury – whose father founded the Sainsbury dynasty and empire – in his earliest incarnation pretending to be a countryman in Hampstead, and fancifully sporting a Norfolk jacket and gaiters. He inaugurated the Sainsbury tradition of marrying a Jewish Vandenberg girl (more recently Robert Sainsbury married Lisa Van den Bergh), while 'we' loaned him £100 to pay for some early shops. The legend in our family was that in return he agreed to be circumcised, a horrible and painful procedure for an adult and accordingly thought hilarious. This story is contradicted by Sainsbury sources which – curiously – award him a Christian wedding.

The family business plan was that there should be branches both in Holland and England in order to exploit two markets. Happily Dutch and English cousins liked one another too. My mother before the war often visited two Vandenburg cousins in 'Cape Farewell', their big house at Wargrave-on-Thames, where the music-hall pair and house-guests Mr Flotsam and Mr Jetsam entertained the company after supper singing 'Little Betty Bouncer/Loves an announcer/ Down at the BBC....' Another Dutch cousin called Sydney van den Bergh escaped across the North Sea to Frinton in 1940. He had been deputed to parley with the Germans before they invaded and chose a railway carriage made in Uruguay which he hoped was neutral territory for the meeting – unsuccessfully, as we know. Rotterdam was soon and quickly bombed to pieces and the cousin arrived on his own yacht in Frinton dressed in his tennis whites, ready for a game. After the war he was Dutch Minister of Defence.

When one of Katie's granddaughters married in 1960 my sister Prue and cousin Jenny Hartley were bridesmaids of choice since related not just to one another (on both sides) but also to both bride and groom (who had themselves many further degrees of kinship in common). Jewish families established before the Great War – the so-called 'ten thousand' – until recently tended to inter-marry, and my mother carried in her head and could recite at will a vast and complex genealogy of some hundred or so cousins all of whom she could precisely 'place'. They tended to 'nest' together, mainly in and around Hampstead: Katie and her daughter Nancy both had flats above Granny's in Bickenhall Mansions W.1, and for summers and weekends both also owned houses neighbouring hers at Frinton-on-Sea. Frank Longford, who with others including my great-aunt Betty Philips helped form a prison visiting group (New Bridge), once told me that aristocrats resemble Jews: both belong to a strange and inbred ancient minority whom nobody much likes or understands, but whom a stubborn sense of pride fortifies none the less.

It is said that when the 1905 Aliens Act was passed – limiting for the first time the number of immigrants from the Russian pogroms allowed into the UK – that powerful Jewish families supported this restriction, ring-fencing their hard-won privileges. Hitler – had he invaded – would of course have made no distinction whatsoever between assimilated Jews and newcomers: and of this they must later have become uncomfortably aware. Yet that distinction was none the less there.

Katie and Ruby's grandmother Hannah Levy bought and fried each Friday sole, dabs and haddock, which the children then delivered to poor East End Jewish refugee families whose superstitious customs they found outlandish or comical but whose destitution they pitied. This double way of thinking about the Ost-Juden survived into the 1930s during which my mother – then working in her spare time with an organisation dispensing soup and warm clothing to Jewish refugees on Upper Berkeley Street – commented pointedly, 'We opened our homes: but not our hearts'. The family pulled its weight. Great-aunt Betty Phillips (born a Sternberg in Berlin, c. 1900) regularly took her passport down to the Jewish Agency, which shipped it into Germany for Jewish girls, pretending to her identity, to use to get to safety in England.

Katie's self-assurance helped her around 1920 when she travelled to

Derbyshire to interview the then head-master Geoffrey Fisher – not yet Archbishop of Canterbury – about whether Repton was a suitable school for her boys and – in particular – whether they could expect to meet anti-semitism. Fisher – an early champion of inter-faith dialogue – admitted that he allowed in only a small number of Jews 'to stop their becoming too cliquey' and satisfied Katie that her sons could be happy there.

Katie was in the 1920s lady captain of the Frinton golf club, no mean feat in that snobbish and parochial town, saying much for her sociability and strength of character as well as for her golf. When the committee refused to admit a new member solely because he was Jewish – albeit a man Katie termed a 'decent-class Jew' – Katie organised the campaign of protest until a letter of apology was after much drama extracted.

Katie's inner strength of character made her *de facto* the Materfamilias. This was on show in the last decades of her life in her decision to avoid the twin plagues of family Christmases and cold weather by sailing the South China Sea in a small merchant steamer for the winter months. A halt was put to this when regulations required each such passenger-carrying ship to have a doctor on board; most ships were too small and poor to do so.

5. Frinton-on-Sea

Frinton was made fashionable by actress Gladys Cooper and the then Prince of Wales. It was where I happily spent my first eight summers and many weekends, a sort of Music Hall joke of a place: by-laws were rumoured to prevent the opening of pubs or the parking of cars on the street, as if every Frintonian possessed her own carriage drive, and the theatre to this day plays the National Anthem at performances, as if it were still 1950. As a small child I appreciated the sense of security it afforded more than I resented – or was aware of – its smug exclusiveness. Randolph Churchill sometimes lodged his daughter in a nearby house where a flotilla of nannies and Norland nurses with their charges seemed to be in semi-permanent residence.

Once you drove through the raised level crossing gates – an exciting, long-anticipated moment – Frinton in the 1950s had a quiet air of being pocketed outside time. This was its point. A framed pre-war photograph froze a line of smiling young Frinton friends carrying tennis rackets and walking happily together arm-in-arm into the future, eternally unaware of the terrors of adult life or the coming conflict. This snap was of my mother, her siblings and the handsome Romain brothers – who believed their Sephardi ancestor sailed here from Gibraltar on HMS *Victory* after the battle of Cape St Vincent in 1797. 'Anidjar', which I took to be Spanish, was their middle name. Post-war, the tennis club fancy-dress party still provided Frinton's social highlight, while a rep company put on performances of *Rebecca*, or you could watch Jessie Matthews in a wooden Agatha Christie play.

My grandmother's summer house, Chesterford, near the Grand Hotel, boasted bedrooms full of sea-light and views over the North Sea. It fronted the esplanade with its single wind-tormented tree and (often) an errant child's kite lodged high in its branches. At low tide you could wander for a mile on the vast beach towards the horizon under the big sky a Dutch landscapist might have loved to paint.... Beyond the concrete and wooden break-waters, the warm sands displayed those satisfying and echoing undulating parallel lines David Hockney later taught the world to recognise, and shrimp wriggled and tickled your toes.

The Frinton house-keeper Florence Reynolds sounded the gong for meal-times. I loved her tact and gentleness and would sit shelling peas with her in her kitchen, listening to her tremulous south Lancashire brogue. We laughed when we imitated the BBC weather forecast together for neither of us could pronounce the word 'visibility', she because it was unfamiliar and posh and me because I was five years old. Weather mattered. The grown-ups tapped the barometer in the hall while an oracular doll's house contained a tiny blue man with an umbrella who came out to announce advancing rain, while a pink lady with a parasol declared sunshine. The primitive weather-vane in Granny's hut on the sea-front where we changed for swimming was bladder-wrack. We boiled water to make tea there on a primus stove and at Granny's request collected buckets of sea-water that she applied to her neck and face because – she explained – sea-water contained much health-giving ozone. Jam-jars were rigged to entrap and drown wasps in their dozens while Reckitts Blue bag mitigated the pain of stings when the jars failed.

Florence, from a mill-town where clogs were still worn, had started out aged fourteen as in-between maid in a big house, on half a crown a week. She fell in love with Pykle, a merchant seaman whose name was Essex dialect for apple-thief, and Granny encouraged them to marry. As nothing had been heard of Pykle's first wife for over seven years, a second marriage, she explained, could not in law be deemed bigamous. Pykle duly tended the garden and its hens, and scared me by showing off how to kill a rabbit, holding it by the ears while delivering an oblique blow to its neck. Chickens and rabbits had helped mitigate war-time food shortages. Florence told me how Pykle had once nearly died of food poisoning from badly prepared mussels, and – improbably – how over-dosing on salt or possibly mustard, made him sick and saved his life. She favoured buttering a cat's paws to stop it straying; and commended Lancashire black pudding made from pig's blood but never forced it on us. She made a memorable Queen's pudding herself. I liked watching her bake. Her kitchen was my favourite refuge from the incessant warfare between my parents.

Ruby summoned Florence to the dining-room by pressing with her right foot a bump on the carpet concealing an electric bell-push; this triggered in the kitchen a flag in the wooden Servant Call Box identifying which room wanted you. That was a trick Benjamin Britten favoured; in Suffolk he enjoyed mystifying guests about how timely the servant's entry always was. Come to think of it, Ruby resembled Britten-in-drag.

Florence stayed over thirty years. Granny, who pensioned off her servants, saw to it that Florence ended in a pleasant home near Thorpe-le-Soken, where she once told me how much she had liked working for a Jewish family. Her kindly neighbour in the home, known and addressed by everyone – Florence included – only as 'Cook', had served for fifty years at Whiteladies, where our Frinton friends the Ticklers lived. I could never discover anyone who remembered Cook's real name … and I never learnt Pykle's birth name either.

6. Oundle, 1958

Bogus claims to 'sensitivity' among boarding-school memoirists exasperated Kingsley Amis: he deplored those recording unhappy school experiences and suspected they contributed to a hackneyed genre combining egotism with self-pity. *Lucky Jim*'s key scene has Dixon accusing boarding-school educated Bertrand Welch of confusing vulnerability – for Amis essentially self-centredness – with true sensitivity, which would mean being vulnerable-for-others, rather than only for oneself. These characteristically shrewd moral observations should give one pause.

Having spent four crucial years at public school seems to me to be as visible as a livid birth-mark on one's face. Some memories of Oundle, to which I won a major scholarship, are mainly happy, but survive against an absurd backdrop. We had to take a special train from Euston that was too long for the platform, then jump through the autumn mists what seemed like a terrifying five feet to the ground, holding an overnight suitcase (other luggage, including tuck box, arriving independently), wearing our navy-blue blazers from Daniel Neal. My elder brother travelled with me, helped me and tried to keep a friendly eye. This must have been a challenge. I was so often in trouble. The food was memorably awful and it was said that the house-master was saving money on his allocated budget.

Arrival was marked by idiotic rites of passage. You had to learn by heart a card-list of almost seventy names of fellow-pupils in your house and recite them all in order of seniority at manically high speed within one (timed) minute; learn all twelve house colours; and give accurate directions for getting from one part of town to another.

New boys wearing full Rugger kit including studded boots were swung from hands and feet by two prefects before being tossed into the river Nene to see if they could swim a hundred yards (those at risk of drowning were rescued by a handsome prefect in pink swim-briefs). Could this have been in March or perhaps April? The water was certainly cold. Care for our safety felt unusual: I believe that more than one boy was injured, and possibly one or two died, on school army manoeuvres during the summer holidays, when vehicles overturned. Why didn't parents protest more? Perhaps injury was seen as a lamentable tax on the essential cult of manliness, like the death of the schoolboy Tangent on sports-day in *Decline and Fall*.... I recall parents on the railway platform at Watford, many identifiable as if war-wounded with their heroic crutches, slings and limbs in plaster-of-paris from recent skiing accidents, while we offspring waited to board the special school train to take us up for the spring term.

The OTC still sported swords throughout World War II, and General Montgomery came twice to give the assembled school silly and insensitive advice: he was angry that 'so much fuss' (his words) had been created by the dropping of atom bombs on Hiroshima and Nagasaki when – as he bragged, inaccurately – he and 'Winnie' had achieved greater casualties fire-bombing Dresden.

If anyone senior to you passed you in-house, you had to stand still in silence with your back and head to the wall to let them go by unless or until they released you. Dryden house (where I billeted) had during the 1920s occupied a much older building with narrow pokey corridors. Those in our current domicile were wide but the habit of ceding precedence was itself now regarded as a noble tradition to be upheld. So was leaving the dorm windows open year-long, even in February. Bullying – systematic and often anti-semitic – appeared to be another such tradition.

What was all this designed to inculcate? Stoicism, respect for hierarchy, fair play, perhaps, together with the deliberate stripping of natural identity in order to create not an individual but a type. As Al Alvarez noted (he was at Oundle a decade earlier) 'the point was to produce people to run the British Empire: if you could survive five years at public school, there was nothing the Kalahari desert or Antarctica could throw at you'. There was still fagging, and one task of the fag – apart from shopping and running errands – was to sit on the outside loo-seat (bitterly cold in winter) near to where a boot-man lived and worked, to warm up the seat for 'your' prefect.... All of this distracted me from the sheer beauty of the town, which struck me only on much later visits.

An elaborate code governed which buttons on your grey suit could be done up, varying for each term you had been there, and it was a punishable offence to get this code wrong: on a cold day you might be tempted to do up more buttons that you were entitled to. The youngest students shared a common room with three or four tables and individual cupboards on the walls. It was an offence punishable by beating to be found *looking into* the area where the senior boys sat.

I was beaten for such infringements so often that I was eventually recommended to a child psychologist in Leicester. For important offences – such as reading a book during chapel – it was not a prefect but the house-master who beat us. You proudly showed off your impressive welts and bruises like battle-scars, which hurt grievously for a day or two. The comic writer Arthur Marshall (1910-89) was of the opinion that the 1950s saw a last return to Victorian repression at Oundle, where he had himself been happy as a school-boy and later as a master – where indeed he taught my father French – leaving not long before my arrival in 1958. In 1990 girls – wearing elegant, long culottes – were first admitted to Oundle. Their presence has so civilised the school that the experiences of those attending in 1958 belong within a different universe, closer to *Eric or Little-by-Little* in 1858.

Richard Dawkins's self-satisfied memoir makes clear he was taught by the same teachers at Oundle one year before me (I planned to be a medical student). I don't recognise his anodyne representation of the school. Nor do I recognise the reflections of Oundle I come across in novels. The heroine's lover in Margaret Drabble's *The Garrick Year*, with an impressive Queen Anne red-brick house outside Hereford, is Oundle-educated. So are some children in *The Stranger's Child* by Alan Hollinghurst, for whom attendance at the school works as a class-signifier for being patrician (a key Hollinghurst pre-occupation). It made a different impression on me. In Penelope Mortimer's *The Pumpkin Eater* the heroine Jo sends her sons off to Oundle and recounts truthfully and movingly, by contrast, how their emotional bonds with her gradually weaken, so that she figures the boys at first as if she and they stood hand-in-hand, later as if wistfully stretching out finger-tips only, and finally resigned to a full and life-long separation. That rang true.

I made myself unpopular saying how daft I found school traditions and how objectionable the class-privilege that they purchased. And my career ended in scandal when, aged seventeen, and having childishly chalked the letters O.G.P.U. – i.e. the Soviet Secret Police – on the prefect's door, I refused to be beaten for this offence. 'Too old,' I announced. The expulsion of a pupil at (I think) Bryanston for similar reasons made headline news in the broadsheets at this time. Neither the headmaster nor my Father could persuade me to get off my high horse and avoid a similar outcome.

I finally agreed to a compromise that entailed my writing 500 words on the then Common Market, but walked away that bitter-cold Christmas in the night, preparing to hitch-hike to Israel during the coldest winter since 1947. It snowed all the way from Frankfurt across the Balkans to Istanbul, and in Jerusalem too.

***

'One day I fancy he will appreciate Oundle's share in his education more accurately than now', wrote the Headmaster (Dick Knight) in his final report. More than fifty years on I take his point. The same headmaster, knowing I was about to trek to the Levant, took the trouble to introduce me to the kindly Bishop of Jerusalem, whom I hoped might help me get through the Mandelbaum Gate so that I could – despite being Jewish – visit Jordan as well as Israel.

I was afforded other concessions at school too. My refusal to join either the OTC or the scouts on the grounds that 'both were equally silly' was indulged and I and a few friends were granted leave to create a Young Farmers' Club instead, digging onions and potatoes that we fried up for tea-time, and marching facetiously past the assembled OTC drilling on parade, bearing spades in place of rifles. In a similar spirit I was let off organised games and allowed to rest or play the piano for hours in the afternoon, working off my adolescent *angst*.

Oundle had been unbeaten at Rugger for decades; and yet, despite any apparent 'heartiness' and philistinism, there was also a long tradition of powerful music teaching and choral singing, and it was there that I learnt to enjoy Alban Berg's *Wozzeck*, Stravinsky's *Rite of Spring*, Britten's *Peter Grimes*, Walton's *Belshazzar's Feast* and Bartok's *Concerto for Orchestra*. Bessie Smith, to whom we listened endlessly, too. There were memorable school trips to the Picasso Exhibition at the Tate in 1960; to Coventry to see the Belgrade theatre and the new Cathedral with its Sutherland tapestry, Piper windows and Epstein Christ-and-Child.... I also learnt to love Modigliani, Rouault, Alexander Calder's mobiles, Mondrian and van Gogh. There were terrific films: Hitchcock's *Vertigo* and *North by North-West*; *Black Orpheus*; *Breakfast at Tiffany's*; *The Wages of Fear;* the Soviet Russian *The Cranes are Flying*. And an excellent tradition of amateur theatre from which David Edgar soon profited. I played Portia; I also bought every play by Noel Coward and by Eugène Ionesco I could find, and directed N.F. Simpson's *A Resounding Tinkle*, both of whose surreal comedies struck me as true-to-life.

PC as Portia (R) with Nerissa (L), 1960

En route to my first month-long meditation retreat in summer 1985, I reflected that I had hated public school. Why did I put myself through replications of its conformism and absence of privacy, such as spending a year in 1967-68, just after the Six Day War, on an Israeli kibbutz; and, later, many long communal retreats? A Buddhist community, such as the one I've belonged to for more than thirty years, can offer company, fun and solace, but inevitably has ways of enforcing its own norms. The conformism of these communities, by contrast with boarding-schools, had a purpose either idealistic (the kibbutz) or spiritual (Buddhism) to which I could relate.

And Oundle even then had redeeming features. The History master Dudley Heesom was reported as inviting any boy who excelled to throw darts at a postcard of Graham Sutherland's portrait of a supercilious Somerset Maugham, a writer for whom he for some reason felt a lively dislike. Apart from this cheerful eccentricity there were two masters whose kindness helped save my sanity. Each provided a haven for the disaffected.

The art master Arthur Mackenzie (aka George Kennethson (1910-94)) was a left-wing, dedicated pacifist who had survived two military tribunals during World War II; his friend John Betjeman encouraged him to apply for the job of art master. The living-room at his home from 1959 in the Old Brewery was dominated by a great old papier-maché gramophone horn; bamboo needles, each requiring individually to be sharpened, played the 78 record collection; and there were wild flowers in interesting jars that his beautiful, white-haired wife Eileen painted. He sculpted his late Modernist-primitivist pieces in a 'chipping-shed' and stored the work that followed in a vast 100 foot barn, entering which famously resembled going into a Chinese tomb. Here jostled on wooden plinths many of his 400 sculptures, the busts with empty eyes resembling timeless masks from an alternative world, created in virtual isolation over fifty years. He was championed by Kettle's Yard in Cambridge, and yet his work in limestone, alabaster, marble and granite neglected current fashions and he never courted fame. Twenty years after his death, a Redfern Gallery exhibition excited enormous buyer-interest even before it opened and sold out within days. But during his life he remained a lone wolf.

He had a craggy face and was immensely strong. I admired his gentleness and innocence, and relished his vagueness and unworldliness. When asked how many sons he had, he once answered in his slow voice, 'Five, I think.' After musing for a moment about this he then added, 'Or might it possibly be six?' And when one of these children wet his pants it was said that Mackenzie, puzzled about how to proceed in his wife's absence, stood the distressed child in front of an open log-fire to dry. Eileen maintained that they couldn't have a cat in the house because it wouldn't survive his sitting on it.

He was famous for continuing to work on his sculptures for years, unanxious about selling. Yet he was willing, after persuasion, to let me buy two fine drawings, which hang on my walls, one a mother-and-child in Rouault-like thick ink, the other a finely penned young woman's face. And I was recently touched and amazed to learn from his son Jon that he kept a big abstract I painted then, under his tutelage, of which I have no memory. He and Eileen offered tea and sympathy.

The English master Pip Gaskell (1926-2001) was well-known later as librarian at Trinity College, Cambridge and for his books on bibliography and James Joyce's *Ulysses*. He came from a well-connected Quaker family that features significantly in Noel Annan's famous essay, 'The Intellectual Aristocracy'. He had just shipped his family and his Land Rover back from a brief foray to Sydney, where – happily for us – a university post had been mis-described. He now joined the staff to teach us English and reclassify the school library.

He made no secret of having hated his time as an Oundle schoolboy during the war. That made one bond. He had played clarinet in his brother-in-law Humphrey Lyttleton's first jazz band; and he now founded a jazz club at Oundle, where he introduced us to the music of Miles Davis and Charlie Parker and arranged showings of John Cassavetes's brave film about marginal New Yorkers, *Shadows*. We accordingly thought Pip super-cool. Dapper, short, wearing brass granny-specs, he seemed effortlessly inquisitive and venturesome. He had learned the alto saxophone, studied protozoa under his microscope, become a good photographer, set up the Water Lane Press and lodged his own ancient hand-operated printing press in the art rooms. He also read Russian authors that he lent us – for example Gogol's *Dead Souls* – in their red Penguin covers. A little later he learned to fly and bought for £400 a small aircraft in which he journeyed to Holland. He was a devout Christian in a silent way that was lived, never preached.

Pip infected us with his own love of English prose and poetry and was also a source of good counsel. When I gave up being a medical student in 1964 I wrote asking Pip (then in Glasgow) where he would recommend, outside Oxbridge, for reading English. A card in his elegant italic hand arrived promptly, suggesting UEA, specifying that this was because the novelist Angus Wilson enlivened that scene.

But his advice had consequences even in 1960. After I got fed up reading Agatha Christie, I sought his advice about to whom to turn. He suggested a friend of his, someone he knew from connections in Cambridge, where he was a Fellow of King's. This young novelist – of whom I knew nothing – was then, he reported, at the height of her powers. She was called Iris Murdoch and had a few years before published a novel he thought highly of, called *The Bell*. I read it and was immediately enthralled. Its leading character was gay and the novel seemed to be *about me*. And I noticed not long after this that Iris Murdoch named a character 'Pip' in *The Unicorn*.

7. Affinity, 1965

Having spent thirty-five years protecting my mother against my father, I soon graduated to protecting Iris Murdoch. In the 'Family romance' identified by Freud around 1908, the child or adolescent fantasises that they are secret children of parents of more elevated social standing than their actual parents: thus to become a disciple recalls becoming a surrogate child. I accordingly adopted Iris as an 'ideal' mother whom it took a long time partly to demythologise. Or perhaps an ideal aunt? During her 1982 Gifford lectures she gave it as her opinion that – where behaving altruistically is concerned – '*Aunts* show that the thing can be done.... Mothers have too much power.' When my actual mother in 1993 came to the Barbican to see Iris being awarded a Kingston honorary doctorate, a colleague confused them and greeted my mother as 'Dame Iris'. Mother was pleased.

Following my parents' separation in 1972 and (later) divorce a good working relationship with my father at last evolved. Although my mother, despite a second marriage to a distant cousin, never entirely recovered, the collapse of her first marriage was liberating for her children. An ancient structure of communal mistrust and blame that had seemed monolithic dissolved as if it had never been, and affection and respect grew between my father and me. Love too. We children all owed our new stepmother gratitude for so patiently and skilfully overseeing and brokering these rapprochements as also for making my father palpably contented. The 1970s after a rocky start saw my fortunes decisively change. I started teaching English literature – a job so pleasurable it seemed scandalous that one got paid to do it – and began a new doctorate on Iris Murdoch. I met Jim O'Neill, my Canadian lover of forty years, the love of my life; and bought an old secluded school-house in Radnorshire, with my old History Professor Dick Shannon, that has been lastingly important. We created what turned into an eight-acre wild garden there, with its own lake where Iris and John – later – happily swam. I decided I could be happy.

Jim O'Neill

***

I first saw Iris Murdoch in the flesh fifty years ago, when the UEA student literary society invited her and John Bayley to address them. This was in 1965. Perhaps three dozen or more students convened in a panelled room in Gurney Court, Norwich. Angus Wilson, whose good offices had helped secure the Bayleys' acceptance, joined the small discussion panel. A contemporary recalls that many of us sat on the floor and that it was our upward gaze as much as the quiet authority of her answers that sanctified Iris Murdoch as sage.

She seemed much more other-worldly than Angus, whose cheerful gossip about writers living and dead was a more open and inclusive affair. Although Bayley and Wilson somewhat hogged the action, with a lively discussion of Henry James, Iris Murdoch did – a little stiffly and shyly – discuss *An Unofficial Rose* and she also answered questions. I was already a fan by this stage, and excited that my then girl-friend, who was Secretary of the society inviting her, had been asked to dinner beforehand, where Iris's shyness was also in plain view.

I felt a strong affinity with her novelistic world. This had many sources. I liked her courage in writing fictions that were gay-friendly. *The Bell* had a homosexual hero who refused to believe that God could have allotted him a nature that He simultaneously condemned. She dealt with such questions of sexual identity with admirable compassion, confidence and even-handedness: she was one of the first writers to make being gay seem ordinary. And like A.S. Byatt, I was fascinated by the oddness of her novels, and wondered what they meant and where they came from.

I liked the opulence of her fictional world and its unashamedly bourgeois settings, with cushions made of *toile de Jouy*. I believed the assertions on her book covers that she was Anglo-Irish and had no sense how relatively humble her background was. I was fascinated by the central role she gave both in her philosophy and fiction to falling-in-love. I liked her compulsion to write about erotic imbroglio, which seemed to my generation increasingly true to life. And I found her moral philosophy, with its powerful dream of self-transcendence, compelling.

If each of us belongs inside a novel, then the novel I belonged inside was written by Iris. I felt partly at home in her very strange world for her books, as already recounted, seemed to me to be about people I could half-recognise: many other readers evidently felt this too. There were also unconscious sources of congruence, about which I was ignorant, and which it has taken me years to understand. She and I were both looking for fathers, a quest sometimes appearing strange or perverse. More about this follows. She helped me understand both my love-life and spiritual promptings, and these understandings were to help me in turn appreciate hers.

***

During the summer of 1970, when my life seemed to be falling apart, I wrote to Iris care of her publishers. She had published that year *The Sovereignty of Good*, a book that helped and inspired me greatly. The moral philosophy I had read until then was either impenetrable or so dryly reductive as to seem both repugnant and pointless. I felt I could understand *The Sovereignty of Good.* And I even felt that I might be able to put it to use. It started me on a path towards Buddhism.

Sovereignty is rightly Iris's best-known work of philosophy, a book whose influence has grown since publication. It was said to have returned moral philosophy 'to the people', those 'not corrupted' [*sic*] by academic philosophy. Lay readers gained illumination from it, as well as philosophers. It was a fiercely original and passionately argued attack on Anglo-Saxon and – equally – on French orthodoxies, both of which privileged will-power as the seat of moral change. *Sovereignty* is sceptical about the will, which – so far from being free – is often in the grip of unconscious forces that are neither investigated nor understood. Against this privileging of the will, she proposed a powerful and interesting 'rival soul-picture': it located value, perhaps unusually for so passionate a Platonist, within attention to good things in *this* life, as well as in the spiritual quest itself. Like Iris's immature philosophies – Marxism, existentialism – it was a call to action, a programme for human change, this time by the lonely individual herself, with no help from party or priest.

To illustrate her contention that 'attention' mattered above and beyond 'will-power' in the moral life, she took the example of falling-in-love. The argument runs as follows:

> Consider being in love. Consider too the attempt to check being in love, and the need in such a case of another object to attend to. Where strong emotions of sexual love, or of hatred, resentment or jealousy are concerned, 'pure will' can usually achieve little.... It is small use telling oneself to 'Stop being in love, stop feeling resentment, be just'. What is needed is a reorientation of a different kind, from a different source.... Deliberately falling out of love is not a jump of the will, it is the acquiring of new objects of attention and thus of new energies as a result of refocusing (pp 55-6).

She seemed to be talking directly into my ear and heart. I had fallen unhappily in love in the spring of that year, enduring plenty of strong emotions of sexual love, hatred, resentment and jealousy; and could see no easy way out. So I floundered helplessly and felt poisoned. My letter of thanks and appreciation for the practical eloquence of *The Sovereignty of Good* reached her safely. I had written from my flat in 27 Unthank Road, to which she humorously replied 'Thank you for your letter which so pleasantly belies your address. Such a word from a reader is always welcome'. Acquiring new objects of attention did not yet help with my largely self-inflicted misery, but a way forward now clearly existed in any case, if only I could find it.

***

This story starts in late April 1970, when I visited a gay club and found a sweet-natured Irish boy from Dublin to go home with. We were standing hand-in-hand preparing to leave, when I felt (as much as saw) someone staring with some intensity, and spotted a handsome well-set blue-eyed blonde silently willing me to break faith and leave with him instead.... He was evidently used to getting what he wanted, so that the novelty of failure interested him. He considered me and the Irish boy being together as no obstacle to his need. His stare reminded me of the wildly blazing eyes of the Miraculous Mandarin in Béla Bartók's one act pantomime ballet. This stare, I later surmised, belonged to an experienced seducer, interested both in how to conquer and how to relinquish.

One week later I was back in the same club and met and went home with him. M was an expert lover, who understood aspects of male anatomy that had been a closed book, proud of his prowess. Sex was his vocation. Twice I halted a kiss; I wanted simply to try to think about what was happening. His raw beauty hurt. After this bout he wrote out his telephone number, an honour he explained he rarely accorded, adding that he liked to have sex once a week only. That felt like a caution against the dependency that he – in equal measure – needed and feared.

Over forty years later, in Elizabeth Jane Howard's final novel, I read of her character Simon Cazalet, who found it impossible to believe that the degree and intensity of physical intimacy he had experienced with his first male lover could exist without love.... I recognised that: but intimacy without love was precisely what I had chanced upon. Someone described me that year as 'that intense and charming young chap'. I remember only the intensity, which was of no help here. Soon M wrote inviting me back for a return match and I saw with alarm that a tipping-point was approaching when I would no longer have willpower left to resist falling in love.

***

I was happy and astonished as an eighteen year-old medical student, when a beautiful young woman four years my senior took my hand in her gloved hand as we waited for an underground train and I was aroused. I told her that I had from an early age (before I was ten) believed myself queer (the term 'gay' was not yet in use) and she drily remarked that I must evidently be bisexual instead. Four heterosexual years ensued, and friendships with two women in particular have been lastingly important. I was seriously in love with BD, and suffered with and over her. Angus's short story 'After the Show' about an adolescent Jewish boy excited by the suffering of an histrionic girl – though the story stays resolutely on the surface – later rang a bell.

I was proud that two young women chose me to deflower them and wondered whether – had I been born a girl – I might not also have chosen a predominantly gay man to take my virginity, hoping that such a suitor might be gentle or considerate. During one affair we were careless about 'precautions' and my partner got pregnant; unbeknownst to me until afterwards, partly because I was abroad, but mainly because I was nineteen and shielded from fore-knowledge, the abortion she underwent by curettage had lasting traumatic effect to all concerned, myself included; recovery of balance took many years.

During my 'straight' years I never concealed my sense of marking time or of waiting for gay life to begin. One problem was that I had no idea how. The only homosexuals I knew were my old teacher Angus Wilson and his partner Tony Garrett, and they, who had been together since 1946 – though infinitely kind and hospitable – could not offer much advice about how to set about the task today. 'It takes one to know one', Angus remarked to a mutual friend, confiding his intuitive sense about my sexual preferences when he had taught and befriended me earlier, around 1965.

I wondered passionately how you could tell if you were homosexual? Surveying myself I saw that I liked as a small boy to dance round the sitting-room to Tchaikovsky's *Pathétique Symphony*, direct amateur theatre, act, and apply theatrical make-up to myself and others, and watch ballet. Listening to Shakespeare, even the Comedies, made me weep with a kind of astonishment. It still does. Was this a gay profile? Until my twenties I had no idea how to masturbate (I thought it entailed use of a cushion).

I read eagerly about homosexuality whenever I could, gleaning strange particles of dubious and silly information. One book told me that

PC by Tony Garrett, 1970s

homosexuals recognise one another by dropping key-words that they emphasise, talking in furtive code rather like Freemasons exchanging secret hand-shakes. I was interested in learning these magical phrases but had little luck. ('Is he a Member of the Tennis club?' was one…) Others said all homosexuals like the colour violet. I didn't. One text claimed that homosexuals always tuck their sweaters into their jeans to show off their torsos. I had never seen anyone so attired. A third that homosexuals are all narcissistic couch potatoes, lazing their lives away. Of course we now know that any generalisation about homosexuals is likely to be as crass and nonsensical as any remark starting 'All heterosexuals…'. But fifty years ago many so-called 'experts' generalised like mad.

My naivety today seems spectacular and droll. After reading that Hampstead was a gay part of London I sat on a bench on the High Street with no observable results: this was shortly after breakfast. Similarly in Paris in the Quartier Latin…. Finally I placed an ad in the personal columns of *International Times* – which ceased publication for a while in 1973, after being convicted for running such contact ads for gay men. Mine said something to the effect that a twenty-three year-old bisexual

PC, *International Times*, 1969

was looking for help in going gay. I had many answers, exchanged flattering photos, and had encounters during which I slowly discovered that it wasn't necessarily considered impolite to decline a proposition.

The law legalising homosexual relations between consenting adults in private had been changed only two years before. But the police still engaged in harassment and entrapment and I was accosted while cruising in Brighton on one occasion by a good-looking officer in plain clothes who sneered that I was 'queer as a clockwork orange' before taking my name and address and letting me go with a caution. Coming out was scary in other ways too: there was a constant sense of danger and uncertainty. I greatly feared the disapproval or disgust of friends and family and felt guilty about disappointing or shocking those I cared for. A banner carried during the Stonewall riots in New York – that series of spontaneous, violent demonstrations by the gay community in 1969 that kick-started the movement towards gay liberation – bore the paradoxical, neat, expressive legend 'We are the people our parents warned us against'. That expressed our longing to go beyond self-hatred, and to reject the internalisation of stigma or self-doubt, a pattern evidenced by the nasty gay habit in those days of referring to pick-ups as 'It'. We wanted to appear 'normal queers' – not obvious or camp but invisible.

When I was seventeen I had hitch-hiked to Israel during the long, desolate, brutally cold winter of 1963. To see me off my mother accompanied me to Hatch End station with a polythene bag containing two dozen hard-boiled eggs for sustenance and the following life-advice: 'Don't do anything that would make you lose your self-respect'. (The elegance of this farewell homily was mitigated by the fact that I had at once to go back to the house with her to retrieve the reading-glasses I had forgotten.) My mother's advice came back when I was making first forays into the gay world. What of casual bath-house sex for example? Gay saunas could be romantic, places where – when lucky – you found not merely physical release but an important lover for a spell, a relationship; and they could also feel sad, lonely and degraded. The issue of self-respect – together with the lack in my life of a sense of direction or purpose – nagged and prompted me to seek professional help. I entered weekly group therapy for a year in Montague Mansions. I was in a bad way.

None the less, the first gay bars were a great adventure: watching men dance and kiss was moving and exciting. Would I become camp or effeminate? I was supported and am grateful to this day to my college friends Simon and Jill Edwards, who sometimes accompanied me to a gay bar. That helped 'normalise' my change of life. It turned out to my surprise that the embrace of a male lover made me feel more manly than before, as if being desired by a man made one extra-male. Gay clubs and pubs awaited, not to speak of the romantic magic of Amsterdam, where you could walk hand-in-hand down the street with your same-sex lover.

I celebrated coming out by joining the team of friends editing *Lunch Magazine*, which preceded *Gay News* by a couple of years. We were the first such UK periodical to run stories about coming out and to engage in the now forgotten gay politics that opposed the more conservative Campaign for Homosexual Equality (CHE) to the more radical Gay Liberation Front (GLF). The latter favoured 'outing' public figures even when they wished to stay in the closet. We thought this invasive.

We appealed to various public figures. David Hockney donated a sketch and expatiated in the Deux Magots café on the wickedness of art colleges that no longer offered life-drawing; I interviewed Hockney's friend Christopher Isherwood in Santa Monica, then at the height of his fame as godfather of Gay Lib just after the film *Cabaret* was released. He wanted to see a photograph of my partner, an attractive young Swiss, and embraced me on parting. Kindly Thom Gunn, who had a poster of the Grateful Dead up in his flat on Haight-Ashbury, sent me a new poem about cruising called 'The Release'. In New York I visited the Factory and met Andy Warhol, who appeared deaf-mute, and I shacked up briefly with his so-called 'super-star' Holly Woodlawn and walked delightedly with her into Max's Kansas City, a night-club-cum-restaurant off Union Square, while Lou Reed's 'Walk on the Wild Side' played … 'Listen,' said Holly, 'They're playing my tune'…. Harold Acton, with the utmost

Holly Woodlawn, NYC, 1973

urbanity, declined to contribute. Iris wrote that she would consider contributing, adding irrelevantly that she disapproved of pornography. She told me that Angus Wilson – who helped considerably – and his partner had recently stayed with her and had evidently spoken kindly of me.

***

M had proposed coming up to Norwich to stay during his half-term but I awaited further communication in vain. So on that Friday, putting him down as a no-show, I drove down to London and went to a cinema near Victoria which was a pick-up venue. He soon materialised, walking down the aisle until spotting and motioning me out for coffee. After this he announced that he was 'very indecisive', and suited the action to the words.

A series of such farcical chance meetings ensued. I was in Hyde Park one Sunday sun-bathing when he appeared, a little short-sighted, and – spotting a bare-chested shape that appealed – made a bee-line full of his habitual resolve. At fifty yards he stalled in embarrassed recognition that he was stalking a discarded lover. We seemed doomed to bump into one another every time I came to London, spending an hour or two in a comical dance of flirtation and delay. That July I drove to Rome in my blue Mini-Cooper to collect my closest kibbutz girl-friend, whom I accompanied on a grand European tour of art galleries, in what I hoped would be a *voyage d'oubli*.

M reminded me of Mary McCarthy's Dick Brown in *The Group*, charming, handsome and dissolute, who likes to tour his old flames, undress and admire them like a wealthy man anxiously checking the value of his portfolio.... Or Brick in *Cat on a Hot Tin Roof* awaiting that moment when having just enough alcohol in his blood clicks in.... He watched you jealously with a special alert passivity, awaiting signs of admiration, fixation or desire.... This relaxed him and simultaneously put him on his mettle: he meant to hold his admirers, but at a distance.

That year we were all reading John Rechy's *Numbers*. Its hero Johnny feels compelled obsessively to return to the city of Los Angeles, to test himself anew in the arena of male love. Johnny, who is seen as an angel of dark sex, is like a retired boxer – an undefeated champion – who refuses to accept the possible ravages of time, and is led by some unfathomable force to return to combat once again. No real satiety is possible for the addict, and promiscuity is today recognised as a form of addiction.... Nothing is or can ever be enough.

***

I was looking for father-substitutes. My real father had that year tried to abandon home for his mistress. This was the moment that (as recounted) he warned my agitated and distressed mother to 'choose between Peter and me'. This turned out to be a feint or dress-rehearsal only. Mother was diagnosed with a large brain tumour and major surgery delayed his departure. Two years later he finally left, sending each of his children the same hand-written letter echoing Edward VIII's invocation of Mrs Simpson at the Abdication: 'The time has come when I feel I cannot face life and its problems without the help of the woman I love by my side'. Meanwhile he and I were still at loggerheads.

My doctoral supervisor, the writer Malcolm Bradbury, was another ineffective surrogate father. He had seven doctoral supervisees; none of us seven ever completed a thesis – let alone submitted one. He had acquired more graduates than he had time to cope with because he was seeking a personal Chair and hoping that we added to his c.v. It was also unkindly rumoured that his disappearance to Lancaster University for one weekend constituted a stratagem to make UEA authorities fear that Lancaster might create a Chair for him and UEA lose him. If so, his gamble paid off, and he soon got the UEA Professorship he craved. Here was another absent father. Meanwhile my thesis-writing was stalled and purposeless. I couldn't get the measure of what I wanted to write or why. This was scarcely Bradbury's fault; indeed it was nobody's fault. I was, in short, having some sort of breakdown (not uncommon among doctoral candidates in the arts, I later understood).

If I was looking for fathers, M was looking for sons and liked his lovers young. When he was eleven years old – a pretty blonde boy – he had been sexually used for a long spell by the prefects at his school and struggled still to make sense of this. He spoke of it often. One consequence was probably his own penchant for hunting for under-age boys, some as young as fourteen. 'It did not satisfy me', he remarked of the first he seduced. I was grateful the gods had given me no such proclivity and haunted by the idea of such youths first used and then abandoned, a condition I identified with.

If many were in love with him, he somehow conveyed that this was no less than his due. Walter Benjamin once wrote that to fall in love with someone is to intuit their essential emptiness. But the emptiness of a narcissist may be a special case, a sort of super-emptiness. M's coldness connected to his appeal. He identified with Mr WH in that terrifying sonnet 'They that have power to hurt but will do none…' where the lover's charm and corruption are secretly inseparable. 'I'm just like everybody else, looking for love', he would repeat with unconscious superciliousness. Meanwhile the arduous duty of 'plucking the latest peach' could by definition never be conclusively accomplished.

Nor was my own shallowness less than that of others. I can sometimes remember in relation to a past scene what I was wearing and little else.... The gay culture of the time was shallow too, post decriminalisation in 1967 and pre-Aids: we famously resembled children let loose in a sweet-shop, gorging ourselves to the point of sickness, hungering to be loved and paying the price with frequent check-ups in STD clinics. Of course the refusal of others to love us as we think we deserve always looks lightweight, and two lovers of mine, a Californian post-graduate at Essex and a young London architect, both more heavily invested emotionally, complained that I in turn figured as lacking in moral depth.

W.H. Auden in *The Sea and the Mirror* makes the witty, worldly Prospero say: 'I am very glad I shall never / Be twenty and have to go through that business again, / The hours of fuss and fury, the conceit, the expense.' I underwent plenty of fuss, fury, and conceit. Then there was the psychopathology that Sappho (c 630-570 BC) in a famous poem was among the first to evoke: the heart beating faster and guts turning to water, the speechlessness, sweating, trembling, turning pale, sightlessness, fainting. A tormented tenderness combines with brooding on the beloved's well-being, a longing for his approval and affection, and a plague of sexual desire and jealousy.

No modern author writes better about falling in love than Iris, who saw it as quasi-religious, the perverse parody of a spiritual experience. When we fall in love our ego – the sense we have of ourselves as centre of the universe – feels violently ripped out so that we for a spell perceive the beloved as more important than ourselves. She thought this de-centering an instructive event by which we might be taught humility or reverence. However she was also deeply aware that this first, ecstatic stage is often followed by behaving badly: a resentful fury at such apparent theft of our substance.

I did not behave badly but mislaid for a while a feeling for the comedy of life. My friend Alice Thomas Ellis described falling unhappily in love in one of her novels as like being attacked by a particularly spiteful virus. Alternatively, it is as if a noisome, vulgar and unwanted sitting tenant took up residence in your head, refusing all possible bribes and inducements to decamp elsewhere. Iris seemed among the few modern writers who understood how close to trauma unhappy love could get: and perhaps she took the condition too seriously? About the pangs of disprized love the narrator of *The Black Prince* comments movingly: 'There are times of suffering which remain in our lives like black absolutes and are not blotted out. Fortunate are those for whom these black holes shed some sort of light.'

When I wrote trying to explain all this, M wisely preached that dissatisfaction was the human lot, not just a gay area of expertise, even if we specialised in seeking the unattainable. Poor M could no more work out what to do with me than I could. He wanted me as a friend, not a partner, he declared clearly, which did not stop him flirting with me. My self-appointed mission meanwhile would be to rescue him and me alike from all our superficiality and treachery, and to ground our friendship in something deep and solid and warm. That entailed listening to him discourse on the main different types that attracted him and show off photographs of his conquests, while complaining that sex had started to seem like dealing with plastic or meat. I managed this for a year or two, hoping it helped him to watch me suffer a little.

So, claiming that they had few friends in common and that I might usefully fill this gap, he passed my telephone number on to his long-term lover, a kindly professional musician who soon made clear he too wanted a piece of the action. I declined this honour while M was in the UK. He would shortly move to live abroad, when this second dalliance started, generating joy, confusion and moral complexities I was incapable of handling: here was another imbroglio echoing those Iris spent some of her pre-married life living out, and much of her novelistic career exploring.

Iris borrowed a phrase from Simone Weil about not taking on tasks 'beyond one's moral level', a form of hubris risking disaster. My moral level was not up to such self-abnegation. The conclusion came two years later, when M came to a party I staged, stole a partner of mine and a sense of failure and grief followed. '… but this thing is sure,/ That time is no healer: the patient is no longer here' – (T.S. Eliot.)

When around 2004 he read my *Iris Murdoch: A Life* he wrote to me that he resembled young Iris. They shared a powerful and sometimes disturbing narcissism, a desire to be at the centre of the action, accumulate admirers and duel with an audience. About the 'error' of narcissism W.H. Auden memorably wrote that it 'Craves what it cannot have,/ Not universal love /But to be loved alone': a specialised source of ongoing suffering and a recipe for jealousy. M added that he regarded all his love affairs, no matter how seemingly 'casual', as 'spiritual': a convenient sentiment Iris shared about her own romantic adventures.

8. Who: Whom, 1970

Asa Briggs told me Iris believed that everyone was both innately and also indiscriminately bisexual. She thus around 1954-5 shocked him by suspecting him of having an affair with a male amanuensis in whom he had no erotic interest whatsoever. He was exclusively heterosexual; but the politics of gay sex nonetheless always interested her. And only with regard to the lives of gay men, as Martha Nussbaum has pointed out, does Murdoch retain a sense of the purely social and political obstacles to correct vision and action. She was a vigorous crusader for the abolition of sodomy laws, and in her fiction depicted gay couples as fighting an uphill struggle for love and self-respect in a society that makes fun of them, or worse.

The same summer of 1970 that she published *The Sovereignty of Good*, her novel *A Fairly Honourable Defeat* also appeared. It explores the hypothesis that all human beings are inconstant, seek substitutes, and are fundamentally promiscuous, a question Iris's life (as also mine in the early 1970s) rendered topical and urgent. 'Anyone will do to play the roles', the devilish Julius King preaches. It is remarkable and brave that Iris makes the gay relationship in the novel between Simon and Axel the only one that survives the fire-storm provided by the plot. The heterosexual relationships all fall apart. The gay one survives. And though Simon had a promiscuous past and is described as having looked for sex in Piccadilly Circus public lavatories ('cottaging'), this is depicted with a sympathy so pronounced as to approach sentimentality: 'One offers oneself in various quarters and one hopes for love. The love he had hoped for was real love. But the search had had its lighter side'. No mention of the greed, cruelty, or disease implicit in promiscuous sex.

In this novel Julius – partly inspired by Elias Canetti, Iris's early and most manipulative lover – predicts at one point that Simon Foster, who has thus far played the role of loyal younger minion or catamite to his beloved Axel, will, as he ages, learn to adopt the paternal role himself and find a younger minion of his own. 'You will find out one day that you want to play Axel to some little Simon. The passage of time brings about these shifts automatically, especially in relationships of your kind', the worldly Julius preaches. Back in 1957 in *The Bell* she had quietly transgressed conventional thinking not just by dealing with homosexuality as if it were ordinary, but also by making the fourteen year-old school-boy Nick scandalously attempt to groom and seduce his own school-teacher and senior, Michael Meade. This is a still radical, subversive and undiscussed aspect of that novel.

She places this within a broader context when Julius adds: 'No question can be more important than "Who is the Boss?"'. This question might reflect Lenin's brutal condensation of power politics in 1921 to the infamous slogan 'Who: whom?'; and important in the context of the bedroom is the question of who gets to do what to whom. I believe that if Iris knew about this at first hand, it was not just because she had women lovers.

It is a cliché in gay circles that he who plays passive in bed may well make most of the day-time decisions where he may be dominant and rule the roost. But another truism reminds us that he who bravely makes himself vulnerable in this manner may be risking and investing more emotionally than he who does not. (A truth alluded to with some coarseness in Philip Roth's *The Human Stain.*)

My lovers were – in today's gay jargon – 'bottoms' while I played the role of 'top': when M tried to 'make a girl of me' he was undoing his own shame at being so used at the age of eleven. And here is a connection to Iris Murdoch that I first noticed over twenty years ago but did not explore publicly: those made queasy by such discussions and find them tasteless might wish to skip this section. D.H. Lawrence scholars waited thirty-five years after his death before publicly explaining that, in those passages where he writes gnomically about 'seeking out', the novelist was alluding to the gratifications of anal penetration.

In her journal for 22 June 1953 she writes that [Canetti and I] 'made love with great fierceness, doing things we had never done before. Then we lay quietly'. What were these never specified new 'things we had never done before'? It was completely out of character for her to report any detail of sexual activity. It is also remarkable that she severely edited and pruned her journals – shortly to be in the public domain – and that she obliterated all mention of the name 'Canetti', who features throughout their 1953-55 affair only – ever – as 'C'. So how did it happen that – by contrast – she deliberately left unedited this passage about 'new things we had never done before'?

I believe that one clue might be found in those passages in her journal where she asks – e.g 11 December 1966: 'Q. What am I? A. A male homosexual sado-masochist.'. She also wrote to her friends – mysteriously but none the less frequently – that she inwardly identified with male homosexuals. 'I'm not interested in women. I am a *male* homosexual' and '... my ideal relationship is between two men. *Usually I play the part of the younger man.*' Why the part of the younger man rather than that of a younger female homosexual? What prompts this remarkable, very strange and oft-repeated assertion?

Perhaps another clue to this identification as also to what these 'new things' might be comes in *The Unicorn,* where we are told that after Gerald Scottow whipped Jamesie the latter worshipped Scottow, who '*took* Jamesie. That's how it was'. Scottow, it may be remembered, is thought to bear some traces of Canetti. Both use sex to dominate. Both like visiting Marrakesh. *The Unicorn* was the first Murdoch novel I ever bought on publication, when it appeared in 1963, and I remember this passage alluding to sodomy as shocking in that pre-Wolfenden year, when the act it curtly evokes was punishable with a prison sentence – and the more scandalous as the Jamesie Evercreech who is thus abruptly 'taken' is nineteen and hence under age. 'But surely things like that can't happen so suddenly?' asks the naïve outsider Marion Taylor. What exactly in her own experience prompted Iris to believe that the act of being thus 'taken' would enslave Jamesie so suddenly to his taker?

Relevant here too may be the admission of a sister of Friedl Benedikt's, who slept with Canetti for one night only, and who confided not merely how carefully un-interested he was in the satisfaction of his female partner, but how much he feared gratifying any mistress conventionally in case he aroused an unappeasable appetite that he could later neither manage nor assuage. I believe Canetti analogously took revenge on Iris by 'using her as a boy'. This – if true – might help explain their asymmetrical relationship over many decades, his notable coolness contrasting with her masochistic subjugation. She referred to the latter in 1945 when she wrote of her 'needs & demands – my great arrogance & ... great yearning to submit' (31 December 1945) and, soon afterwards, of her desire to be dominated (13 January 1946).

This leaves out of account her considerable resources of strength, which made it possible for her to 'run' other lovers at the same time as Canetti and thus resist his power-play. The effect of this on Canetti – the most important of the many wounded patriarchs, mostly Jewish, she loved and collected – will be discussed in a later chapter.

9. Son-into-Disciple

We first met at a Norwich lunch-party on a hot day in summer 1981. Iris was collecting an Honorary Doctorate at UEA, where Prof John Fletcher, an admirer, laid on a lunch party in her honour. After being ferried into the house through the garden door her immediate request was for string to tie up her suitcase, so flimsy and antique it had burst open on the journey, spilling a miscellany of items onto the floor, an image of order and privacy foregone. A scene of comical confusion ensued, following which the Fletchers introduced her to their guests, including his colleague the great Ibsen scholar James MacFarlane. We ate cold salt duck and melon, an ideal dish for such a day.

I resembled a lover light-headed at his first rendezvous, my heart pounding. Her mind did not disappoint. Talking with her was thrilling. Her gaze and her questions – I noted – 'invigorated like cold water'. I had watched her the previous evening discuss Derrida *inter alia* on a TV book programme where she now told us she had been delighted to meet Paul Theroux. On her journey up Iris had been accosted by a stranger in the train-bar who had watched the same programme, and who greeted her enthusiastically as Margaret Drabble. 'How can you *tell*?', replied the philosopher thoughtfully, 'that I'm not Doris Lessing, Muriel Spark, or Susan Hill?' The unperturbed admirer, putting a hand on Iris's sleeve, said reassuringly, 'Margaret, I'd know you anywhere'. That made her laugh. She soon discovered I was writing my PhD on Platonism within her work. She disapproved of the study of contemporary writing and advised: 'Hurry up and finish!' I feared later that I had bounded and bounced like an exuberant puppy.

***

We became friends the following year over two momentous weeks from 16 October to 9 November 1982, when I got leave to attend her

Edinburgh Gifford lectures, later published as *Metaphysics as a Guide to Morals*. I found myself lodged in the room next door to hers in the University Staff Club and we sometimes met in the Quiller pub or Milano restaurant when her daily lectures were over. I recorded her on my lecture-notes as a mixture of small girl, *grande dame*, steely-eyed don, warm-hearted mother-confessor, depressed 'liberal' who thought the human race would blow itself up, and 'lonely seeker'…. Her train from Oxford had been direct but very slow – nearly eight hours – stopping at every town and halt, and she missed John, and southern England, where she longed to return. The effort of organising her ideas dispirited her, as did the prospect of another long journey home, when she planned to travel first-class.

Her ten lectures had an over-ambitious reach, and encompassed two noteworthy weekends. I spent the first on the island of Jura in the Inner Hebrides, passing a memorable evening with Orwell's closest neighbour while he was writing *Nineteen Eighty-Four*, Katie Darroch, a surviving speaker of Jura Gaelic. She recalled how 'Mr Blair' had loved her scones and, though so ill with TB, was cheerful and uncomplaining. She did not care for his sister Avril. She read and enjoyed *Wigan Pier* and *Down and Out*. She seemed just such a good person as Iris was hymning in her lectures. Born in 1896, she had never visited England or even the Outer Hebrides. She enjoyed her own company and was at peace, watching the ocean and the weather from her window while she knitted kilt-socks with deer-heads or thistles on them. Back in Edinburgh Iris invoked the example of such virtuous individuals. She became tearful when recalling to me the courage and escape of dissident Vladimir Bukovsky, who had endured precisely the kind of abuse in Soviet psychiatric hospitals Orwell's *Nineteen Eighty-Four* had prophesied.

I took notes and identified recurrent preoccupations. She meditated upon the meaning of Goodness, a concept whose invention she ascribed to Plato…. *Phaedrus* and *Symposium* were his lyrical erotic dialogues evoking the ascent towards the Good up a spiritual ladder via the purification of Eros. 'Good is a sublimation of sex', she argued: and yet 'purified love is not entirely sexless'. She reverted often to the essentially Platonic idea that a true loving relationship could still contain sexual desire but not be dominated by it. Personal love is the most important thing in human life, she asserted, and falling-in-love the most startling experience, and quasi-religious. 'We must learn to love other people …

and perhaps dogs'. That 'chaste love teaches' was one message of her lectures, underlined when she argued that 'We should learn to fall out of love with people, and with places', by which she seemed to advocate giving up not love itself but fixation.

Plato depicts Eros as a spiritual intermediary, 'a formidable magician, enchanter, chemist and sophist'. Carnal love in *Symposium* is still love, and might be redeemed into a more spiritual form of attachment. So she lacked today's prurient preoccupation with desire as dirty and saw it as a substratum essential to the moral life, like the mud in Buddhist iconography without which the lotus of enlightenment cannot grow – an unworldly view today. Much of this was music to my ears: the title of the doctoral thesis I was writing was 'Iris Murdoch and the Purification of Eros'. 'When Plato launched his space-ship' were her gnomic final words concerning Plato's brave invention of the idea of the Good.

Buddhism was often cited: she would be happy to be considered a Christian-Buddhist, with Christ the Western Buddha, i.e. no son of God, but a mortal seeking enlightenment. Buddhism was to teach Christians to demythologise, to let go of the Virgin Birth and Resurrection, and to concentrate instead on its own inner truths.

On 8 November before giving her eighth talk entitled 'Must Religion become Prophecy?', my notes record that 'She marches in, stiffly, like a scared boy': 'We need fewer prophets and more saints' that talk asserted. It seemed to me that she touched upon the necessary loneliness of the moral agent and thinker, in her discussions of the Ontological Proof.... She appeared a solitary figure herself. Once she overslept and arrived late, dishevelled and unkempt. I was struck by her suggestion that when we are behaving virtuously there may be no experience at all. I soon had cause to ponder this.

***

My education had induced in me a certain nihilism, relativism, and cynicism, which left me hungry and dissatisfied. From this, I somehow decided, Iris was to rescue me: she reminded me of her character Guy in her recent *Nuns and Soldiers*, whose dignity, cleverness, and power were 'for [others] guarantees of stability, proofs of meaning ... a stronghold' (p 46). If human life is a pilgrimage away from egoism, then some sense might still be made of it. She pointed in the direction of possible renewal.

If her novels helped me understand my love-life, her essays helped map the spiritual life. The first question she asked was 'Are you a religious person?' I waited so long trying to decide how to answer that she shifted her ground. 'Give me a *resumé* – put me in the picture, as it were'. And soon: 'Describe your house.' I tried to oblige.

A week later I had an answer. I flew back to London the second weekend for my mother's birthday party. I was experiencing difficulties with her, and also with a close friend. In a disturbed frame of mind I plucked off my shelf Chögyam Trungpa's *Cutting Through Spiritual Materialism*, a powerful contemporary Buddhist primer, hitherto unread. Trungpa evokes what he terms 'monkey-mind' – that mind that invests in low states of emotion such as jealousy, fear, paranoia and aggression in order to perpetuate a dualistic world; and thus – at the expense of ongoing pain – convince itself of its own existence. I read it, tearfully, at a sitting. It felt as if someone had wheeled up very close an old-fashioned cannon and fired a large hole through me: the author's understanding directly transmitted, entering the blood-stream like a benign virus, starting a reaction. *Exstasis* literally means to stand outside the self. A newly created space accompanied a strange, memorable, transient state of joyous release as if I had glimpsed shedding of the burden of self. I decided to explore Buddhism, which seemed to promise a path towards absolution from the crime of existing, and towards living less blindly.

I connected this with Iris too: she had argued that the good man *literally* sees a different world: and during these days of phoney ascesis, everything felt like a species of windfall or bonus.... Nothing like this had ever happened before. It seemed as if she were the magus or impresario behind this temporary change of consciousness and I a character of hers. Her fiction abounded in characters glimpsing possible future states of being – what Dame Julian of Norwich termed '*shewings*'. The fool Effingham Cooper, drowning in the bog in *The Unicorn*, sees that with the death of the self 'a perfect love is born'; Tim in *Nuns and Soldiers* finds pain, joy and release in Hyde Park. As yet un-earned and un-paid for, these states visit but will not stay. Soon 'I' returns.

I'd found a teacher; and tried to explain to Iris a spontaneous vision whose happy motto was 'Responsible *to*, not *for* others'. I attempted to communicate this vision of life liberated from exaggerated responsibility, opened up to the possibility of mutuality. Missing the point, Iris spoke priggishly of Elder Zossima's sense of limitless obligation towards others in Dostoevsky's *Brothers Karamazov*. In Edinburgh we started a long, continuing conversation.

***

'Can anyone really change?' Iris asked me gloomily over lunch in London one afternoon.... This willingness to interrogate her own pieties impressed me. Text-book Buddhism, I volunteered, celebrated a vision of self as – in the first instance – plural and unstable, embodying different non-solid masks or manifestations. Meditation might short-circuit and exhaust the quest for a fixed identity: having no self being the state best approximating to virtue. I liked her ability to quarrel with her own position: her fictional plots often single out seekers – like Michael in *The Bell* – for punishment.

One of her characters remarks that there are friendships in which you discuss religion, and others where you talk about love (*Bruno's Dream*). We discussed religion. She could expound the Buddha's Four Noble Truths and had been taught how to meditate twice, at the Buddhist Centre in Eccleston Square, and in Japan. She had no systematic meditation practice and called herself in 1992 'peripherally involved' with Buddhism. Is self-parody intended when she makes a frivolous character in a late novel 'meditate' to the sounds of Scott Joplin? She once touched upon the possibility of my giving her meditation instruction but we never pursued this. 'Oh, something of mine!' she would remark, if I referred to an incident from a novel of hers, passing on, steering the conversation onto a different track.

So what did she make of me? I recall two references only in her journals to me or our meetings.

> March 8 1989 To see Peter Conradi at Kingston. I walked along the Thames to Kingston Bridge. Peter says he sees many cormorants.
>
> Feb. 15 1992 Peter Conradi to lunch, with Cloudy. Blue Merle Welsh collie. Talk Buddhism.

In 1989 she joined a seminar studying her work at Kingston University, where I taught. She had arrived very early (as often) and then walked along the Thames to kill time. Her Chatto editor had queried whether London really had the cormorants she claimed in the novel she was working on, and that visit provided her with evidence. The second reference connects with another novel: she was writing our Blue Merle Welsh collie into *The Green Knight*, where the dog appears as 'Anax' and she wanted carefully to check the dog's appearance. She was excited by the adventures she was devising for him, not all of which got into the published book. (On reading a proof copy, we wrote facetiously as if from the dog proposing some editorial changes, which Iris duly made, the dog evidently carrying greater weight than Chatto editors.) She gave me a salad lunch at home in Oxford while the dog spent a happy time feasting on the various scraps of old food to be found lying under the kitchen table.

We picked up our dog, which got into the novel too. When I enquired as to whether she had intended an identification between us and Bellamy James – a self-deluded ascetic who picks up his dog Anax – she fiercely rebutted it in her usual quixotic fashion.

***

Trungpa Rinpoche's teachings echoed Plato's myth of the Cave and the Sun, and Iris accordingly wrote me on 9 May 1988 that she was 'all for leaving the cocoon [of the ego] and making for the Great Eastern Sun'. The central role she gave to attention in the moral life – an emphasis derived from Simone Weil – is echoed by the supreme importance awarded to mindfulness and awareness within Buddhism. But she was disturbed to learn that Trungpa Rinpoche had affairs with his women students. 'I have committed many sins,' she retorted sternly, 'but never that one.' This claim seems accurate: her dalliance in the 1960s with her difficult RCA student David Morgan, about which journalists made much fuss when he published some of her letters, entailed nothing more compromising than some serious kissing. She introduced me to Andrew Harvey, then at All Souls, in the vain hope that he would wean me off Trungpa Rinpoche. Harvey suggested how I might stand up to her instead. In fact the taking of consorts by Tibetan teachers from among their students is not uncommon, and is associated with spiritual practice. Part of me now wonders why Iris chose to find this especially scandalous: her own belief in sublimation was not so remote from Tibetan practice. Eventually I got tired of her coerciveness and would argue that she and Trungpa Rinpoche were avatars of the same force; I also learned to change the topic.

I bought her a copy of *Cutting Through Spiritual Materialism* and her many and vigorous underlinings suggest that she read up to page 61 before giving up. The book collects talk-transcripts and she disliked what she called the 'damn-fool questions and answers' that end each chapter. When asked if there were any exchanges that she did like, she singled out 'How do you manage now that all your teachers are either dead or in Tibet?', to which Trungpa replies 'Situations are my teacher'. This she approved.

So began the first, intimidating phase of our friendship. We met on the first floor of Dino's, which she favoured because she had faulty hearing, and we were usually the only customers eating there. She liked to pay, though I was once allowed to do so; on one occasion she absent-mindedly ordered dishes for us both without prior enquiry, then, on realising, apologised. When she first came to dinner in Clapham in 1983 she talked mainly to my partner Jim. There was some cruelty here. She wrote later that she 'felt absolutely at home with him at once'; perhaps she was implicitly rebuking my taking him for granted. We made the mistake of serving a whole salmon-trout: she did not welcome food that looked up accusingly from its dish. She toyed with what was on her plate and ate little. A cool or stilted meeting could precede a warm and demonstrative letter. In 1941 Frank Thompson, who loved her at Oxford, had written home that Iris was 'as always when she hasn't seen me for a long time, full of affection'. I recognised that. It was sometimes easier for her to unbutton on paper.

That I had met Heidegger fascinated her. A business associate of my father's at the re-inauguration of the Brothers Grimm Museum in Kassel introduced us in 1964. At an upstairs restaurant over glasses of Hock, Heidegger with his little Hitler moustache had clicked his heels (in my memory) when we were introduced and asked me in German 'I hope you understood something?'. Heidegger (like Derrida) was a leading preoccupation for her: she preferred his early work while his later thinking figured in her demonology. She was accordingly disturbed when I told her some Buddhist thinkers found links between the Post-Modernism Heidegger helped spawn, and the Madhyamika teachings on emptiness. She alluded to this in a 1991 letter complaining that an un-named Buddhist friend whom she loves and respects had sent her a paper by David Loy 'proving that deconstruction and Buddhism were one and the same. And my friend seems *persuaded* by this rot!'. I could not possibly think them the same: I had sent her the paper because I found the echoes between them intriguing.

Today our miscommunications seem comical. I idealised her, and publishing her biography later partly (only) attenuated this. Iris in her turn idealised Jews as if all were instinctively wise; as she also idealised male homosexuals, whose company she found more restful than that of our straight brothers. I fitted the profile of a number of her friends: a gay seeker, spiritually hungry and confused. My reverence flattered her. (After thirty-five years I feel more equivocal about the spiritual quest, with its inevitable self-deceptions. I've spent a whole year in aggregate in group retreat which has afforded a source of joy as well as pain. However, if the planet could by magic have a collective voice, it might claim that there are simply too many human beings here, and not that there are insufficient seekers…)

I continue puzzled by the relative merits of Original Sin, a doctrine she sometimes invoked, versus Basic Goodness, in which belief Tibetan Buddhism invests. Perhaps neither premise is entirely satisfactory: Original Sin condemns us to pointless guilt, while Basic Goodness – which refers to the 'ground' of being only – might appear to overlook the horror of the world and the vileness of much human history.

The contest between these views is not abstract. Basic Goodness offers an ongoing foundation for the meditative path. While the surface of the mind may be troubled or turbulent, the deep mind according to this doctrine, like the depths of great Tibetan lakes, is always calm and at peace. I'm not sure, after decades of meditation, how this helpful hypothesis might actually be 'proven' – though the lives of great teachers suggest the powers such a belief can unlock. I thought that a belief in goodness accorded better with the Christian mystics she so loved and valued – Dame Julian, whose waking vision promised that 'All shall be well', and Meister Eckhart's invitation to 'find God within'.

In 1987 she left a voice-mail inviting my partner and me to join John and her for Christmas lunch. Since this invitation arrived on Christmas morning itself, she may have been, in Bayley in-house parlance, 'shooting us down' – winning social credit for an invitation declined, thus unattended by the bother of having actually to entertain. This invitation was perhaps triggered by publication of my study of her work that year. In 1988 I spent three months meditating in the Rocky Mountains, after which I lost some of my fear of her so that we met more as equals.

Our friendship started a-symmetrically. She would catechise me about the details of my life: respect for her privacy caused me not to reciprocate; she twice vouchsafed that she was off to see Tom Phillips, who was working for years on her National Portrait Gallery portrait, once (I deduced) to see Brigid Brophy. The painter Harry Weinberger, I later learned, struck a bargain whereby he required her to divulge one story about herself before exchanging one about himself. Andrew Harvey would get her well-oiled to encourage disclosures; he was important to her and contrived to introduce her in Paris to HH Dalai Lama.

Perhaps there were two Irises. The writer Rosemary Hill declares her 'frequently demonstrative to the point of exhibitionism. There simply could not have been so many later revelations had she not revealed so much of herself'; while the philosopher Martha Nussbaum saw her as guarded to the point of aggression, 'desiring to mystify and prevent people from finding her where she was'.... These are perfectly compatible. Both seemed true. She veered between being guarded to the point of invisibility, and 'demonstrative' when – as so often – she fell in love. I experienced the first of these *personae* and witnessed the second.

***

For more than two decades I would buy each new novel in hardback as it appeared and devour it fast: her fiction helped me negotiate both my sexuality and my spiritual urges. Once she and I became friends in the 1980s, Iris sent me advance proof copies with the little *putti* that were Chatto and Windus's trademark on their covers.

The sibling rivalries and oedipal dramas in her novels helped me recognise the politics of my own family and understand something of how these got inherited and lived out. I now see how my life-story distantly reflects hers: both bisexual outsiders hunting for father-figures.... She liked to catechise her friends about their lives and, after one such session around 1985, said enthusiastically, 'You come from a particular world: why don't you write about and celebrate it?'. To this task – before returning to the topic of discipleship – I now turn.

Part Two: Family History

Father's Family

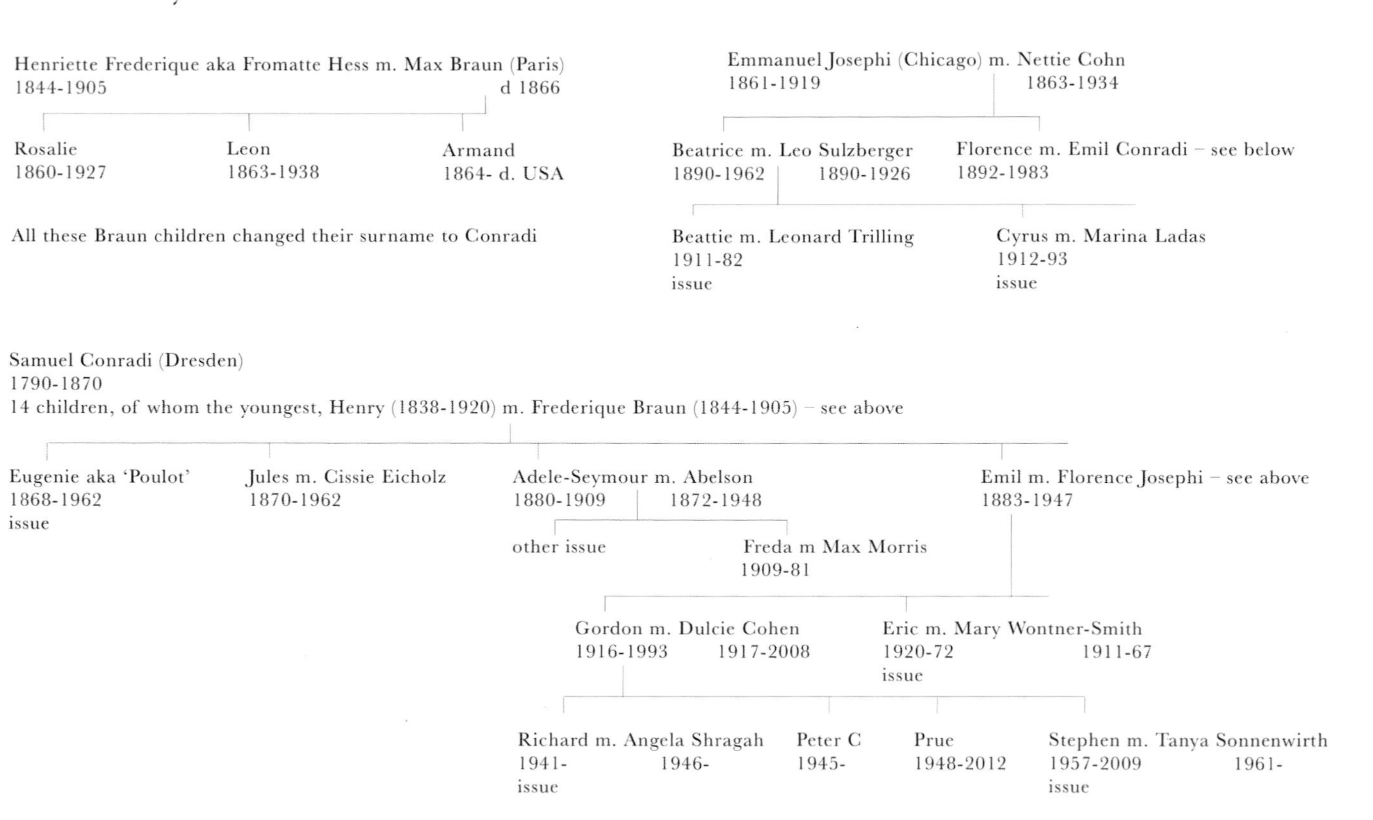

Father's Family:
10. Quitting Paris, 1870

In 1870 the American legation in Paris was a gloomy apartment 'finished in the most bourgeois manner' with a green carpet worn almost black, situated between a grocery and a laundry and up two flights of stairs at 95, rue de Chaillot, just off the Champs Elysees and not far from the Arc de Triomphe.

There are a number of curious features about my great-grandmother Mme Fromatte Conradi's visit to this legation on Monday 4 July. Congress had for the first time that year designated Independence Day an American *jour de fête* for federal employees and the Minister – impercipiently expecting no international dramas – accordingly left by train that same Monday for a Karlsbad 'cure'. He would soon be summarily recalled on the day France declared war on Prussia (15 July), 'like a clap of thunder in a cloudless sky', as he recorded. One mystery is that she obtained a Pass '*pour se rendre à Londres: Mme Conradi avec cinq enfants*': she had as yet four children only, while her fifth (Jules) would not be born until 28 July: and indeed the figure '4' has been scratched out before 'cinq' was superposed. *Enceinte* and under one month away from her *accouchement*, she was evidently prescient, guarding her growing young family against approaching misfortune: international tension between France and Prussia had increased alarmingly over the previous four years and war between them now looked inevitable. The main question was 'When?'.

Born in Paris of humble Jewish Alsacien stock (her mother Sophie Levy from Soultz-sous-Forêts in the Bas-Rhin, her father Moise Hess from the Grand Duchy of Hesse-Darmstadt) and given a first name that in both German and Yiddish signified 'pious', Fromatte Hess's habitual prudence was encouraged by her first husband, Max Braun.

Although the 7th arrondissement where she was born includes the

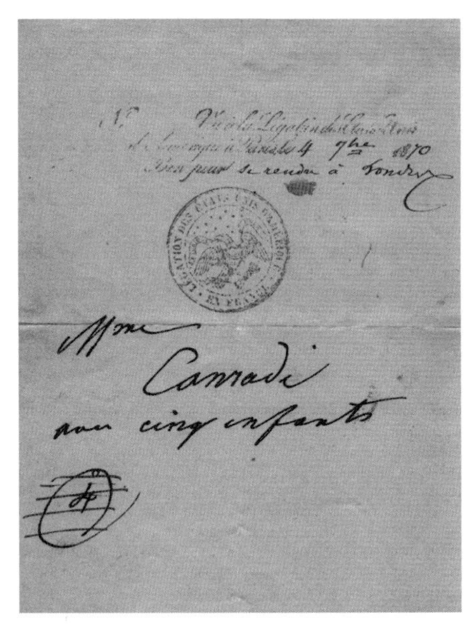

Mme Conradi, Laissez-Passer, Paris, 1870

aristocratic Faubourg Saint-Germain, much frequented by Marcel Proust, her father was a *colporteur* – a hawker or peddler – while her uncle Samuel Santschi, who lived with her family, worked as a *lythographe* – a printer or engraver. Before Baron Haussman created his Grands Boulevards even smart Paris arrondissements like the 7th had their local poor living under the eaves of many-storeyed buildings or in modest alleys at ground level. Fromatte and her family surely inhabited one of these.

Among French-speakers she called herself Frederique, but 'Fromatte' is often used of her, and she may have spoken German to both her husbands. Her second spouse preferred Heinrich to either Henri or Henry, and the ancient Alsacien patois and Saxon German were mutually comprehensible. My great-aunt Poulot and my great-uncle Jules spoke fluent French like their parents; and of course English, in Poulot's case with a strong French accent. Theirs was a tri-lingual household.

She was married in 1859 in the 4th arrondissement, in a synagogue in that old Jewish part of the *Marais* centring around the Rue des Rosiers, to an Attaché at the small Saxon legation in Paris, Max Braun. Fromatte was only fifteen. Evidently not uncommon at that time: the poet Paul Verlaine married his child-wife Mathilde Mauté de Fleurville when she was sixteen. Fromatte gave birth the following year (1860) to her first daughter Rosalie, who – their age-difference being so relatively small – always reminded outsiders of a younger sister.

After they decamped to London in 1870 Fromatte's family struck their few new friends as poor (initially) and yet cultured. Max Braun's career helps explain this. He was born in Frankfurt-an-der-Oder – which is to say in Prussia – but changed nationality to work at the Saxon legation in Paris, where he served both as Consul, and also as attaché-cum-private secretary to the Saxon Minister, Baron (later, Count) Albin von Seebach. The Baron's family were evidently philosemitic, and he was an interesting man to work for. He had married Princess Maria von Nesselrode, daughter of the famous diplomat who led Russia's delegation to the Congress of Vienna and whose Russian estates he inherited.

Von Seebach, once Chamberlain to the Saxon King, showed kindness to the Royal Saxon Court Conductor Richard Wagner, after the latter participated in the May 1849 Dresden revolution and so was forced into exile. In 1860 von Seebach, working through the wife of the Austrian ambassador to France Princess Pauline von Metternich, persuaded Napoléon III to order Wagner to produce a new version of his *Tannhäuser* for the Paris Opéra. Despite a warrant for his arrest, von Seebach also gained for the composer his first and partial amnesty: incompletely rehabilitated, Wagner soon had his access to all the many different German states restored to him, excepting Saxony. For this default Wagner blamed von Seebach's timidity.

Max, a first-hand witness, must have made Fromatte aware of this bigger, cultured world even if – burdened with babies in their apartment on the Rue d'Artois in the 8ieme, and indeed underage – she only occasionally entered it directly herself. Richard Wagner haunts her story. She brought to London and so evidently treasured a hastily written invitation, dated '*Le Mercredi 27 Avril 1870*' from a certain Mme Fould, to join her for tea at 22 Rue Bergère. This little paper puzzled me: why and how had it survived nearly 150 years? No other notes or letters whatsoever to or from Fromatte have surfaced and nor – she having died in 1904 – are they now likely to. I thought its rapid flourishes and curlicues suggested urgency and came across the Fould trail quite by chance through a reference in Richard Wagner's *Autobiography*: Wagner, who hated Achille Fould (1800-67) as a champion of his enemy Meyerbeer, called Fould 'Napoleon III's unapproachable and terrible Minister of State'.

Fould was 'terrible', in Wagner's eyes, because of his hostility and his attempts to stop this new production of *Tannhäuser* for the Paris Opéra. Both *Fould, Oppenheimer and Co* (his family's bank), and L'Hotel Fould (his home), were situated on Rue Bergère, today in the 9th arrondissement.

Fould, like Fromatte of Alsacien Jewish origin, was four times minister of finance, taking a leading part in economic reforms. Fould was also President of the Council, from the start of the Second Empire, and in charge of the general administration of the revenues of the crown, and of cultural institutions such as theatres, museums, libraries, archives, refurbishing the Louvre and overseeing institutions like the Legion d'Honneur and the Institut. He directed the 1855 Paris Great Exhibition, was a close friend of the princes of the Orleans family, a great horse-lover and a founder of the Jockey Club. In Napoleon's confidence, he became *de facto* the single point of interaction between ministers and the sovereign and was arguably – after Napoleon III himself – the second most important citizen in the Second Empire. Fould's mistress, known as 'Skittles', was later *grande cocotte* to Edward VII. And L'Hotel Fould at 22 Rue Bergère, where Fromatte took tea on 27 April 1870, had been a hub of Parisian life since 1830.

Fould was also the first Jew to be elected to the French Senate, in 1852. The anti-semitic Wagner doubtless also hated him for being a Jew. Anti-semitism does not seem to feature during the Second Empire, whose favourite composers after all were Offenbach and Meyerbeer, in quite the way that it did during the Third Republic with its agonising Dreyfus Case.

Achille Fould was also one of the so-called Banquiers Nouveaux who financed railway (and canal) building, helping lay the foundations of France's rapid industrialisation so favoured by Louis-Napoleon, through the family bank Fould, Oppenheimer, and Co, whose origins dated back to 1795. It is a reasonable guess that he might have funded Henry Conradi's engineering company, which was engaged in tramway and railway construction in Liege, Berlin, Paris itself and notably north Spain, where Fould, Oppenheimer, and Co was involved in numerous transactions. Here Henry helped survey and construct the North of Spain Railway, engineering its bridges, amongst much else. The Second Empire, with all its authoritarianism, debts and inefficiency, invested in modernisation.

Inconvenient to this otherwise neat theory is the fact that Mme Fould's note is addressed to Mme Braun rather than Mme Conradi. This means that Mme Fould's and Fromatte's acquaintanceship went back at least four or five years. During 1867, the year Fromatte re-married, Mme Fould had been distracted first by Achille Fould's retirement from office, by travels between her homes in Paris, Trouville and the Hautes-Pyrénées, and then by his retirement to his villa in Tarbes, where he suddenly died on 5 October. A grand ceremonial funeral at the Temple de l'Oratoire – Achille having nominally converted to Protestantism without wholly abjuring Judaism – followed.

Mme Fould – née Henriette Goldschmidt – had been born in London, eldest daughter of a banker and as a girl thought 'well educated, pretty, and fascinating in her manners'. She was now in her seventieth and last year. She was also an Englishwoman, and may have described her native realm to Fromatte, perhaps commending England as a country hospitable to refugees. The survival of Mme Fould's invitation suggests that their meeting mattered to Fromatte. By the spring of 1870 Fromatte evidently had at least one well-informed friend to counsel her, which might go some way to explaining her sensitivity to the growing international tension between France and Prussia as early as 4 July.

***

Max Braun fathered Fromatte's first three children (Rosalie, Leon and Armand) while simultaneously encouraging her to train as a midwife as 'you can never tell what the future may hold'. This prescience reads uncannily some 150 years later. Fromatte's diploma as a Paris midwife 1st class is dated 30 August 1865 and the following year Max stumbled under the wheels of a carriage and the hooves of its terrified horses and died in the street. She received damages for Max's death and £200 pledged for each of her three children on reaching twenty-one. Fromatte was herself only twenty-two that year.

Two years later she married her late husband's closest friend, the civil engineer Heinrich or Henri (and soon, Henry) Conradi, who had his own engineering offices in Paris. It was evidently a traditional orthodox ceremony: her *Ketuba* (marriage certificate in Hebrew) shows the date as 1st Tamuz 1867, which translates as 4 July 1867. The official ceremony was held in the Mairie du Louvre in the 1st arrondissement, before the synagogue wedding that followed later the same day.

Her new husband was not a Prussian but a Saxon: a distinction

Parisians might at that historical moment be excused for overlooking. In Bismarck's war of 1866 Saxony not merely fought Prussia but actively helped Prussia's enemy – Austria – instead. But the Prussian route to Austria lay through Saxony. So Prussia simply invaded and over-ran its recalcitrant neighbour before defeating the Austrians at Königgratz in Bohemia. Despite Austrian insistence that defeated Saxony be spared annexation, it was now forced to pay an indemnity and to join the new North German Federation, its independence under attack as Bismarck legislated the unification of the northern states. Even though Saxony as late as July 1870 still maintained its own separate legation in Paris, Prussia had *de facto* taken over control of the Saxon postal system, railroads, and foreign affairs. In particular, Prussian military laws now replaced local military regulations so that Saxons in their light blue uniforms accordingly contributed to the 1870 war with France; as also to the siege of Paris itself.

No doubt an ancient Saxon fear of their bullying Prussian neighbour gave extra force to Fromatte and Heinrich's determination to flee on the latter's approach towards Paris. It puzzled me that Fromatte on 4 July went for a safe-passage to the US rather than the Saxon legation: both her husbands were Saxons, by birth or naturalisation, and her first husband moreover had worked as legation Consul and attaché until his death four years previously. As it turns out, although the Saxon legation was that week and also the next still (precariously) open for business, their Minister had during that July officially invited the American legation to take charge of the well-being of Saxon citizens, as of Saxon affairs and archives. All these commissions were accepted.

There was a further irony: the devastating speed and efficiency with which 400,000 German soldiers mobilised and reached the French border by the end of July before the French were ready, was enabled by the new railways, which allowed troops to arrive within days at the theatre of war not exhausted by weeks of forced marching. Henry's father Samuel had helped build the first railways in Saxony: the privately funded Dresden-Leipzig stretch had opened in 1839. Moreover Henry's brother Adolf was a railway engineer in Berlin, where Henry had worked too. If the Franco-Prussian war was indeed the first 'modern' war, Henry's family played their part in contributing to its Blitzkrieg technology and to the bitterly humiliating defeat France was about to suffer.

In any case France's 15 July declaration of war ignited and inflamed

Henry Conradi, 1865

Parisian hatred for all Germans, regardless of their origins. Both the Saxon legation and Prussian Embassy soon closed and their staff sent packing; the French government proclamation on 28 August ordering the immediate expulsion of all nationals of German origin resulted in their arriving in desperate shoals at the American legation as their last hope, seeking protection and assistance. By 7.30 each morning there were up to five hundred German nationals already waiting, corralled by half a dozen police, so that Minister Washburne expanded his staff to eleven to cope. Fromatte's 4 July visit may have constituted, as it were, an individual advance-guard.

The Prussian government gave 37,000 US$ – in today's money $600,000 – via Rothschild's Bank to Minister Elihu Washburne and his legation, to help Germans leave the country. Washburne, one of only six Ambassadors or Ministers to stay, was a quiet hero in his own right. He opted to remain both through the Siege and the Commune despite being given discretion to leave. The bolting of the British Ambassador by contrast caused anger both at home and among the 4000 Britons stranded in Paris.

From 15 July no German was able to get work; many were turned out of their lodging, without money or friends and – even before the Siege started on 19 September – they were begrudged or denied food. German women together with their babies slept in the streets. Washburne did all in his power to visa passports and provide safe-conducts, buying railway tickets to the Prussian border for 8000, and giving small sums of money or food to others. He did what he could, too, for the many Germans arrested as spies and thrown into prison, often without any legal or logical pretext. Some of these were none the less executed.

The second day of the disastrous battle of Sedan (Friday 2 September), Fromatte obtained from the Préfecture a copy of her parents' marriage certificate. The French Army after suffering ignominious defeat was now in chaotic retreat, Napoleon III a POW, his Second Empire collapsing, while his Empress fled Paris and escaped to England in disgrace. The gates of Paris were shut on 19 September for four and a half terrible months of siege, rocketing food prices and starvation.

Possibly Fromatte was hoping this certificate would show that she was – even if married to a German – French by birth? If so that was her last gambit to avoid eviction. It is of course also possible that she had already left for London by 2 September, after requesting a friend to procure this copy and then send it on to her; but no mail was permitted out of besieged Paris from the 19th except for those letters that made it out by balloon flight. I favour the dismaying theory that she was still in Paris on 2 Sep and that she and her family got out during the ensuing first two weeks of September. By that date just under 30,000 panic-stricken Germans had already left in great confusion and amidst many scenes of suffering. The plight of the few thousand remaining was becoming daily more desperate.

It is true that Henry's eldest son recorded that that they had to quit France within twenty-four hours. But some family mythologising may be at work here. Fromatte acquired her Laissez-Passer on 4 July while the final edict ordering the immediate expulsion of all German nationals was not made law until 28 August. The interval between these dates is nearly two months; and the dozen or so documents I have in my possession – many copies of earlier certificates of birth, of marriage, and of midwifery – must have taken time to accumulate.

Even if not 'kicked out within a single day with their babe-in-arms', as family legend maintained, the family of seven – Heinrich, Fromatte, her three children by Max, and her two by Heinrich – did leave precipitately none the less, forfeiting their belongings, and arriving in London relatively impoverished. Although I note that within eight months of arrival they could afford to hire a young live-in maid-of-all-work called Ellen Burgh, they were careful to save the expense of producing any further children for the next ten years. This was an intelligent and (with hindsight) even a propitious flight. Washburne subsequently recorded pitiful vignettes of the starving and desperate German families who did not manage to escape, with whom he often divided and distributed his own rations.

It is worth sketching what they were saved from in more detail. In mid-October, Washburne had seventy-four German women released from imprisonment for no other offence than their ethnicity, and properly fed. By November rats, cats and dogs are being sold, cooked and eaten. During that brutally cold January Washburne, driven out of his own home by 'military operations', counted 1753 Germans who had failed to get out 'coming out of their holes like starved woodchucks' and starting to die of hypothermia, typhus and starvation. He fitted up one whole floor of the US legation just to house impoverished Germans, and bravely withstood the Parisian fury that resulted. It was impossible for the legation to do any other work. Crowds were also flocking there simply as the main source of accurate news as French newspapers were both censored and mistrusted and Bismarck allowed London and US newspapers to be delivered only to the US legation. 2,810 Parisians died in Christmas week, a further 3280 by New Year's Day, and 4000 each week thereafter while the Prussians started their month of bombardment to hasten the city's surrender. By armistice day of 29 January Bismarck had presided in front of the Princes of the German states over the formal unification of Germany into a politically and administratively integrated nation state at the Hall of Mirrors in Versailles. King Wilhelm I of Prussia was now German Emperor and a triumphal march down the Champs Elysees followed on 1 March before their quiet departure on the 8th. The Conradis also missed the terrors of the Commune that followed, when many further thousands perished: Washburne wrote that the Commune was guilty of 'unparalleled atrocities', followed by 'awful vengeances' as government troops retook Paris.

Father's Family: 11. Settling in London, 1871

Even if Uncle Jules's story that they had only twenty-four hours to pack and leave France is apocryphal, time for rational discussion of the future was limited. Since Henry had engineered railway bridges in Spain, Belgium and Berlin, he must have had contacts in those countries. One question is: why choose London? From 1849 the German states saw a sharp rise in emigration as thousands left for political reasons, and Henry had siblings scattered over half a dozen cities.

Henry's brother Sigismund had served as a surgeon during the Crimean War before leaving for Sydney, Australia with his Swiss bride and children; he died after falling from a pony-and-trap en route to see a patient. Another brother Joseph was a watch-maker in Hamburg where a sister also lived. A third had taken poison after years of paralysis.

But Henry also had two brothers and one sister based in England, and may have expected their succour. In ascending order of importance, these were his sister Clara (aka Klara), governess to the children of a Lord and Lady Smilie and after they grew up a valued house-keeper to their parents, who left her a handsome endowment. But Clara – inconveniently – may have been in Ireland.

Henry's architect brother William, six years his senior, had lived at least ten years in England, marrying an Essex farmer's daughter in 1863, naturalised as British and converted to Christianity. Of his six children, one (a boy called Julius) would grow up to be an engineer like Henry. It is hard to estimate how much help William could have given Henry. Missing from the 1871 census, by 1881 he and his family were living in Christchurch, Hampshire in a street where their immediate neighbours were in humble employment (e.g. postman, tailor, dress maker, clerk, labourer, school-mistress).

Uncle Jules recorded that William helped build both St George's

Anglican Church in Paris and the mausoleum for Queen Victoria's haemophiliac son, Prince Leopold, in Menton or Nice – and Nice is indeed where Leopold died, aged 31, in 1884, from a cerebral haemorrhage caused by a fall. Though the Prince of Wales brought back Leopold's body to St George's Chapel, Windsor, it is entirely possible that Leopold's widow commissioned a memorial for him on the Riviera when during 1892 she inherited the house that he had loved. By the time of William's death by fire (1894), he is living in Brompton in London; if he was by that date in easier circumstances Henry was by then no longer in need of his help.

The brother best placed to give Henry and Fromatte assistance was Moritz Conradi (1830-87), resident in Marylebone, eight years older and a successful painter who exhibited between 1865 and 1876 at the Royal Academy and whose fine miniatures of Queen Victoria and Prince Albert, copied from daguerrotypes in the year of the latter's death (1861), were bought by Victoria three years later and still feature in the Royal Collection today. His portrait in oils of Fromatte herself, which my brother now has, is said to have hung in the Royal Academy in 1875 where it attracted the admiration of Empress Eugenie ('*Qui est cette belle bourgeoise?*' she is supposed to have inquired), herself by then exiled in Chislehurst and a widow. Fromatte, who had named her second daughter Eugenie after the Empress (though in the family we called her only ever by her French nickname 'Aunt *Poulot*') would have been flattered by the Empress's interest. A placid, embonpoint Fromatte wearing a black and gold outfit, perhaps a shawl, her hair beautifully braided with a flower, looks out and languidly holds our gaze, three-quarters face, dark-eyed, enigmatically beautiful. Moritz painted Fromatte's daughter Rosalie in 1880.

In 1859 Moritz had arrived at the Port of London from Calais on board the ship *Triton*, writing down his profession on arrival in the register of aliens as 'Peinter' [*sic*], a mis-spelling that suggests he was trying to arrive at the English word from the French 'Peintre', rather as in the 1861 census when he briefly metamorphoses German 'Moritz' into English 'Maurice'. The titles of his paintings are also polyglot, from *Nach der Ernte* (After the Harvest: a water-colour of a pretty peasant girl relaxing on a hay-rick, hands behind her head, an earthenware jug in foreground) – to *Fillete aux chatons, dans un jardin* (a pretty smiling girl in a garden holds two kittens in her apron while a third, perched on her shoulder, rubs itself against her cheek) and the self-explanatory *View of the River Aar and Interlaken with Jungfrau beyond, Switzerland.*

These titles suggest a certain facility and a willingness to flatter conventional bourgeois taste and pieties. He was occasionally capable of real power, as in his self-portrait that now belongs to a cousin, and of using brilliant colour in the manner of the Pre-Raphaelite Brotherhood. I possess, as well as his 1833 Hebrew Bar Mitzvah prayer-book printed in Sulzbach, a marvellous pencil drawing, dated 1845 when he was only fifteen, of his and Henry's devout looking mother, wearing an elegantly laced bonnet and pelisse, exquisitely detailed and truthful.

Moritz's Mother, 1845

But he was also an Academic (in the derogatory sense) or Biedermeier painter, portraying a sentimental and pious view of the world in a realistic way. Painting titles such as *After the Catch* (oil on canvas, 1856), *Off to School, A Little Girl on a Doorstep*, *Homewards from Shopping* and *Bent on Mischief* say it all: many of these are stilted *genre* paintings, anecdotal vignettes that eschew political and social commentary in order to reinforce feelings of security, *Gemütlichkeit*, and picturesque simplicity.

Although Christie's sold Moritz Conradi's small 1870 water-colour *The Fruit Seller* for £1763 in 2001, his pictures rarely command high prices nowadays. That he was in his time an international figure is attested by both Jules and Poulot, who recalled his being attached in some official capacity to the Russian court, probably from 1880, when he disappears from RA records, as from the 1881 census. If so he painted briefly under the liberal Alexander II and then (after his assassination in 1881) his son Alexander III, during whose reign terrible pogroms occurred, which might also explain his re-appearance in London, where he died in Marylebone in 1887.

Moritz was in Glasgow during 1870-73 when they first arrived, but his London studio address at 23 Berners Street might help explain Henry and Fromatte's settling – after docking in the Port of London and staying in Woolwich (5 West St.) – at 18 Golden Square, fifteen minutes walk away, in multi-lingual Soho, then hospitable to political refugees and artists. Their immediate neighbours included two Italian-born sculptors. Life was hard for him, his son Jules recorded, as a German living in London.

It is no accident that one surviving tale about Fromatte in London concerns her being shocked at how spoiled English children were and how indulgently brought up, compared with those in mainland Europe. No doubt Henry's rigidity gave added thrust to her sense of shock. The other tale is that she herself – Parisian born and bred – shared the French fashion for dipping her sugar-cube into her tea or coffee, calling the habit '*faisant le canard*': the strictness belonged mainly to Henry, not to her.

***

Once in London Fromatte's three Braun offspring changed their surnames to Conradi to mark their step-father's protection; and Fromatte, as well as bringing up seven children in all, occasionally practised her trade of midwifery. Uncle Jules recorded that this profession held a higher status in Paris than in London, where it was long associated with Dickens's comical caricature Sarah Gamp, symbol of an occupation in dire need of reform. (Jules's claim about the status of French midwives was not wishful thinking. Although the Goncourt brothers' mistress Marie Lepelletier became a Paris midwife and thereafter furnished the brothers with salacious low-life tales for use in their fiction, in France in this period midwives were recognised as part of the educated elite and even provided with houses and land.)

The social status of engineers in France and the UK also differed. In Paris, as in Germany, engineering was a gentlemanly profession, traditionally produced in the *Grandes Écoles* together with most of France's high-ranking civil servants, politicians, scientists, writers and philosophers; in Britain alone it was closer to being accounted a mere 'trade'. Henry doggedly worked on steam tram-lines in Lille, Paris and Sunderland and gave worthy-sounding papers to the Society of Engineers ('Stone Sawing Machinery' 1876; 'Clear Tramway and other Rails' 1893; 'A History of Mechanical Traction on Tramways and Roads' 1908), after which the Society presented him with two gilt-embossed calf-bound presentation books, *Water – Its Origin and Use*; and *Eminent Engineers*.

Golden Square : Leon, Henry, Rosalie, Emil, Fromatte and Adele Conradi

The Conradis' years of early hardship in London passed. Armand became a diamond-setter and left for the USA, Leon a jeweller's apprentice, Rosalie and Adele teachers.

Their circumstances changed around 1900. Fromatte's prudent first husband Max had invested in Saxon Government Lottery Bonds whose unexpected maturity brought his widow a largish windfall. My grandfather Emil, youngest-born, was remembered as a result for having 'Great

Expectations', and being spoiled, strong-willed and opinionated. Henry naturalised as British during 1879; his stepson Leon preferred to stay German and to wait to naturalise until he was sixty-nine years old, in 1932. And so in the Great War there would be Conradis fighting on both the German and also now on the English side, cousin pitched against cousin. Henry's two surviving letters show him courteous and circumspect, a little florid in his manners and fluent, if stilted, in English: 'Following the French custom of social courtesy, I beg to greet the incoming New Year, after the five terrible and unfortunate years of the war…'.

A big file of Emil's papers survives, concerned with how – during the first weeks of hostilities in 1914 – he travelled arduously from Interlaken, with many trials, back to London. Memory of this little exodus was surely itself haunted by his parents' considerably more traumatic flight from Paris to London nearly half a century before. Emil had not yet been born in 1870, but was evidently brought up on the legend of this exodus, with all the hopes and fears that must have accompanied it.

Father's Family:
12. War, 1914

The week that the Great War began, my grandfather Emil Conradi – together with 8000 other British citizens – found himself stranded in Switzerland with no foreseeable means of returning home or obtaining credit. Swiss banks – later to profit spectacularly from the coming conflict – declared themselves unable to cash English cheques with the result that visitors, willing as they might be, could not settle their hotel accounts before departure. Moreover the Swiss, struggling to mobilise an army of 300,000 within a few days to protect their neutrality, had commandeered all telephone and telegraph communications. For a week Emil had no contact with his family in London. Civilian travel by train almost ceased for the same reason: the amount of rolling-stock available for through transit was extremely limited. Clearly many of these visitors would have to remain in Switzerland for a while. The financial situation was further complicated by the fact that ready money was practically unobtainable: H.M.'s Minister himself, Ambassador Evelyn Grant Duff, was only allowed by his own bank in Berne to draw frs. 50 – about £2 – per week.

Emil, now aged thirty-one, kept a file of diaries, letters and telegrams from that alarming and annoying week, detailing how he eventually contrived the journey home, taking much longer than in peace-time: seventy-seven hours instead of the more usual twenty. His future wife, a much younger American girl called Florence (aka Flo) Josephi, whom he had first met in St Moritz in December 1912, was staying, accompanied by her mother, in the same hotel and this attenuated his present distress and added a private poignancy. She was due to celebrate her twenty-second birthday in Switzerland that 20 August.

Flo later typed up and sent him from New York her August diary on sheets of Swiss Hotel letter-heading that she had carefully safe-guarded and travelled home with, thinking to please him. She never refers to Emil

Emil Conradi, 1914

in this diary by name: only as 'The Englishman'. Probably their recent engagement did not yet have her father's sanction: when he learnt of it, he advised the couple to await a time of peace before considering marriage. Their shared trials that August will have bonded them more closely: 'How absurd were the majority of reports on which we were fed!' she wrote to him later that year, 'Always – dear heart – your Florence'.

Emil's troubles – in the apocalyptic scale of human suffering now unfolding – were trivial. He suffered twelve days of uncertainty and inconvenience, and he married Flo the following spring in New York, returning to London to father two boys and enjoy a prosperous career.

He was the youngest of his mother's seven children. Photographs show him a handsome, dapper, somewhat dandy-ish figure in spats, probably playing the part of the spoiled child used to getting his own way: the youngest in the fairy-tale, destined to prove himself by surmounting obstacles.

In 1908 he had set up his own electrical engineering company specialising, like his father before him, in constructing tramways, in Edinburgh and in Croydon, and in supplying parts and advice to various government departments, railways and municipalities. His later treatment of his gentle older brother Jules, whom he unceremoniously kicked out of this firm, showed considerable ruthlessness. A few years earlier he had visited Brussels, staying at the Palace Hotel while drumming up custom, and he had probably been doing the same now in Switzerland, before granting himself furlough to meet his fiancée.

The legendary, luxurious Regina Palace Hotel, Beatenberg, where they met for a holiday, was huge – 180 beds – situated at 4000 feet with spectacular views over the Jungfrau and the Bernese alps, famous for attracting wealthy Americans and Russians. Renewed and enlarged in 1907, no other Swiss hotel at that date boasted so many en suite bathrooms or private apartments. Emil's adventures there lasted nine days. On Friday July 31 1914 the British Consul in Berne, a Mr Hill, writes to Emil accurately warning that if surrounding countries mobilise they will likely requisition most available rolling-stock and horses and it may be difficult or impossible for private persons to leave Switzerland.

An anxious weekend followed, during which (2 August) the hotel owner Herr Fritz Brunner writes a letter attesting Emil's character, as '*une personne d'excellente famille et de toute honorabilité et mérite*'. Hotel employees and shopkeepers were being called up to defend the national frontiers, border towns were over-crowded and food shortages caused distress. In spite of a crippled domestic force and the difficulty of obtaining food, Mr Brunner continued to give good service and sustenance and to greet each guest with a cheery word and smile. Those guests totally without funds, or any means of obtaining them, he generously kept on credit.

The only open frontier was with Italy, whither musicians were returning: some feared that Italy – which had nominally declared neutrality – might invade Switzerland. Emil looked into the chances of escape on a train to Milan followed by a boat home, making a note of the address of the Italian Embassy in Berne and sending a cable of enquiry to Thomas Cook. That Sunday saw an exodus of Russians, while the doorways framed tearful women and children playing at being soldiers. Swiss mobilisation notices were posted along all roads and on trees calling for a complete muster by 3 August. One Englishman decided to go home via Berne: this would take him a week. Alarmist and extravagant reports soon circulated, of great naval battles, the sinking of many ships and the bombardment of Belgian towns.

A Major Nuttall stranded there was also anxious to return home and he and Emil decided to combine forces. They accordingly travelled together the sixty-five kilometres – one hour by train – to Berne the following Monday to visit both British and French Embassies where Emil's fluent French will have come to their aid. The French Embassy supplied letters of recommendation. On 3 August he acquired from Consul Hill a single sheet passport from Berne for Mr Emil Conradi, 'a British born subject travelling on the Continent'. It seems that Emil was considering enlisting to fight. If so, he later had second thoughts: by the time conscription began in England in 1916 he had a wife and child and he never joined up.

Raising money had become urgent. He wrote home that 'All Letters of Credit from English Bankers are cancelled due to the European troubles'. Finding himself awkwardly placed as a result, his 3 August wire home, saying he is 'detained', requests £20 to be sent to any Berne bank or post office. This telegram had not arrived by the end of that week and even if it had, wiring money from England was still impossible. His anxious brother Jules wired unhelpfully 'Advise immediate return, Jules'. Easier said than done. 'Up here' Emil is 'entirely cut off from all connections and relations'. Such English or French newspapers or mail as were getting through could be one month old.

Emil wrote to a local business contact, one Mr Hauser, apologizing both for his temerity and for the urgency of his situation that left him few other options, to find out whether he would accept an IOU for a 'nominal amount', say 100 to 200 francs. On 5 August an electrical wholesaler in Geneva – *Appareillage Gardy* – who, since they misspell his surname Conrady, cannot have known him well, sent him a postal order for 200 Swiss Francs. Then on the next day Jules wired again 'Are you safe? Jules'. 'Quite safe,' Emil replied. 'Wired Monday last [3rd]. Hope return shortly, [or, in his French version, 'next week'] on a special train under Embassy protection'. The Consul had assured Emil that trains would be available to ship English people home, albeit not for some time. The previous day, 5 August, Ambassador Evelyn Grant Duff in his final posting (1913-16) offered Emil his services for the carrying of dispatches – i.e of the diplomatic bag – and wrote pleading, to Whom it May Concern, for Emil's journey home to be facilitated.

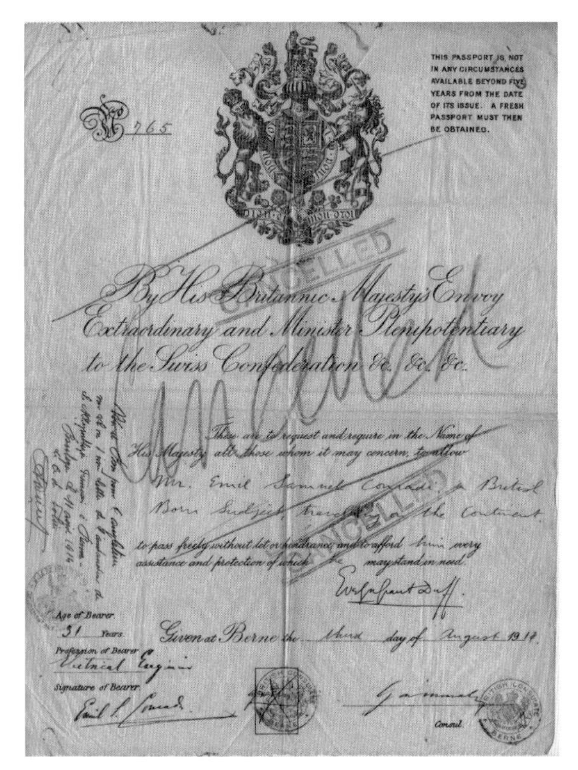

No. 765

THIS PASSPORT IS NOT IN ANY CIRCUMSTANCES AVAILABLE BEYOND FIVE YEARS FROM THE DATE OF ITS ISSUE. A FRESH PASSPORT MUST THEN BE OBTAINED.

CANCELLED

By His Britannic Majesty's Envoy Extraordinary and Minister Plenipotentiary to the Swiss Confederation &c. &c. &c.

These are to request and require in the Name of His Majesty all those whom it may concern, to allow Mr. Emil Samuel Conrade a British Born Subject travelling on the Continent to pass freely without let or hindrance, and to afford him every assistance and protection of which he may stand in need.

CANCELLED

Age of Bearer 31 Years

Profession of Bearer Electrical Engineer

Signature of Bearer Emil S. Conrade

Given at Berne the third day of August 1914.

Consul

Emil's passport, 1914

Emil finally left the Hotel at 5am on Saturday 8 August by char-à-banc to Interlaken, then train to Berne. The Swiss army, in a state of high excitement, was monitoring all trains so that a journey of 120 km took one whole day, arriving at Pontarlier in France at 18.35. The French customs officials gave his luggage, pockets and person alike very close inspection – ladies were taken aside to be searched in private rooms. The last train for Paris having already left, he stayed overnight, acquiring in advance yet another permit to leave the town. Then a Safe-Conduct in French guaranteed his place on a special train – packed and with 24 coaches – to Paris, changing at Dole and at Dijon: Emil counted forty troop trains leaving at five minute intervals from Dijon and thousands of soldiers mobilising at the various towns through which they passed.

At Verrey the train was stopped and intensively searched for a spy who proved unforthcoming. Emil arrived in Paris 04.30 am on Monday 10 August after the hottest journey he had ever experienced; the Gare de Lyon was deserted apart from Italians sleeping on their luggage. He took a cab to the Gare du Nord, where the train left 06.44. Changing at Amiens brought further delays, and they arrived at Boulogne after another passage of eleven hours, at 17.45. Emil noted in passing that two transport steamers had already brought the first British troops to France, now quartered in Boulogne.

There was no boat that night so he stayed over at Packham's Hotel du Louvre, the nearest first-class hotel to the Paris terminus which took its clients to the steamer for free. Here he and his new friend Major Nuttall were by chance re-united: the cable Emil had sent Nuttall in Berne detailing journey-plans had never arrived, and Nuttall as a result had detoured to Lausanne looking for Emil. They were delighted and amazed to meet up again by sheer serendipity after three days.

Emil's passport had to be vetted by the Boulogne police, who scribbled their visa on to it. Before boarding there were further stiff searches, of papers, luggage, and person, and at 05.44 the steamer finally left Boulogne. Of the six submarines in Boulogne harbour, three plus a second-class gunboat accompanied them across the Channel. At Folkestone at 07.30 he had to wait patiently to get off the boat until his name and particulars had been called out and double-checked; their train reached London Cannon Street at 10.15 am on Tuesday 11 August.

He had been travelling for more than three days. The only fast train had been from Folkestone to Cannon Street, and this was the first train he had boarded without military protection, which only put in its appearance once they neared London. On arrival he cabled Flo in Beatenberg, who daily joined the knots of anxious Regina Palace Hotel guests – about fifty remained out of some two hundred – hovering near the office-desk at meal-times awaiting news. She followed his journey closely: a card from Neuchatel showed he had arrived there safely despite missing Major Nuttall in Berne; a letter from Verrières immediately after crossing into France; a cable announcing arrival at Boulogne; finally a telegram from London on Friday 13 August that took three days to arrive showed that he had arrived safe home the previous Tuesday.

Emil will soon have told tales of his escapade to his brother Jules, his sister Eugenie, his half-brother Leon and his father, all of whom had some recollection of fleeing Paris nearly half a century before, in far more dangerous circumstances and leaving their possessions behind. Jewishness played no role in this exile, which happened because Emil's father was German, but it fed a potent sense of insecurity nonetheless. His parents kept their own file of papers generated by that violent rite-of-passage too, and something of the inherited trauma of this event, and of his parents' exemplary fortitude, seem to haunt Emil's 1914 odyssey.

Perhaps there is a half-conscious tribal resonance also: Jews have by tradition been accustomed to 'keeping their bags packed', resented and feared for the 'rootless cosmopolitanism' that followed their expulsions from England (1290), Spain (1492), and the thirty years of pogroms in Russia which were still in 1914 hitting the news. As for Flo Josephi and her mother, they too reached Boulogne after many rigours, on 26 August. The Christian name given Emil – like those of his siblings Jules, Rosalie, Leon and Adele – was evidently selected for fitness in three languages: English, French and German. Conradis and Josephis were thoroughly cosmopolitanised.

I vaguely assumed that everyone had foreign cousins; indeed that the word 'relative' probably signified someone from abroad. My father had cousins living in Rome, Athens, St Jean Cap Ferrat, Paris, the Greek islands, San Francisco and Washington DC; my mother boasted relatives in Geneva, Rotterdam, New Jersey and Johannesburg.

Father's Family:
13. Brothers and others, 1938

My parents met in Frinton in 1938. A stout forty-five year-old American matron in a summer frock, plastic rain bonnet and flat shoes stopped on the famous beach to admire a school-boy building a sand-castle with a moat to capture the incoming tide: 'What an imaginative child!' Ruby Cohen thanked Mrs F.J. Conradi for this kindly praise of her youngest. She invited her together with her sons around for sherry that evening at 'Chesterford'. She observed that Mrs F.J. was American and thought this accounted for her being showy and eager to 'drop names' but never told her so.

Mother's name was Dulcie and she was twenty and beautiful despite what she termed milk-fat, and also wilful, over-protected, and immature.

Dulcie, 1939

She had persuaded her parents – on the strength of reading Angela Brazil's school-girl stories – to let her board at Micklefield school near Seaford in Sussex. That rescued her from the purgatorial drive to Queens's College on Harley Street, where she made Cubitt the chauffeur stop two streets away, so that she could pretend to arrive on foot. Her family's wealth embarrassed her. She next persuaded her parents to move from their Reform synagogue – where she had to sit in the gallery separate from her boyfriends and admirers – to the Liberal Jewish synagogue in St John's Wood, which operated no such sexual apartheid and which seemed 'more English' in offering a regular prayer for the health of the royal family and also group confirmations like Anglicans, rather than a singular Bar-Mitzvah. A year at Villa Brillamant, a finishing school near Lausanne in Switzerland, learning passable French, hopeless cooking – her notebook survives with its instructions in French to '*ratisser les asperges soigneusement*' – and how to 'goff' lace onto pillow-slips was followed by a year training in social work at the LSE; some of the men, whom she recalled wearing Sloppy Joe sweaters and Oxford trousers, fled to fight against Franco in the Civil War. She had recently joined the Red Cross as a VAD nurse working at UCL Hospital.

Gordon was an apprentice electrical engineer at British Thomson-Houston (BTH) in Rugby and had joined a Territorial Army unit. She was soon invited to visit his parents' comfortable flat in newly-built, Art Deco Fairacres in Roehampton, decorated with the help of White Allom and with Margaret Lockwood – fresh from filming Hitchcock's *The Lady Vanishes* – their immediate neighbour. Mother was shocked to discover that he had no room of his own. The four bedrooms were occupied respectively by his mother's favourite child Eric, by the housekeeper Mrs Noone aka Noonie, and by his parents who each had their own room, in those days not necessarily signifying a *mariage blanc*. Gordon when home from Rugby slept on the sofa or a camp-bed.

That exclusion symbolised much. An invidious distinction was always made between the boys. His father had taken Gordon out of school in 1933 where he was doing well, boxing and debating. This was before he matriculated, and done on the grounds that they could not afford to maintain two sons at Oundle, doubtless chosen originally because of its scientific bent. His dandy-ish parents did not stint themselves however: they continued throughout the 1930s – with the astonishing egoism of the pre-war bourgeoisie – to have their shoes hand-made. I have Gordon's copy of Charles Lamb's *Essays* that, in the year after he left school, he read and annotated assiduously, paragraph by paragraph: as if he were trying on his own to compensate for and complete his truncated education. He bought an early edition of T.E. Lawrence's *Seven Pillars* and listened on his wind-up gramophone to Paul Robeson and Florence Desmond.

Gordon's father Emil took Dulcie out to dinner at Kettners restaurant in Soho to show her off to some business associates. The restaurant had been started by Napoleon III's chef who, like Emil's father, decamped to London from Paris around 1870. My mother – instinctively Tory but also a determined democrat annoyed by ostentation – stung his vanity by remarking after the meal with what she considered simple directness 'I should have been just as happy with a soft-boiled egg'. (When she finally inherited she gave half away to us children, saying 'Pointless waiting for me to die first'.)

It was also headstrong, in her parents' view, for her to fall in love with Father, a man whose prospects they considered unsure. They therefore stipulated that the engagement – which started in January 1940 – should last until peace was finally declared, however long that should be – in the event five long years. Dunkirk was to change everything.

***

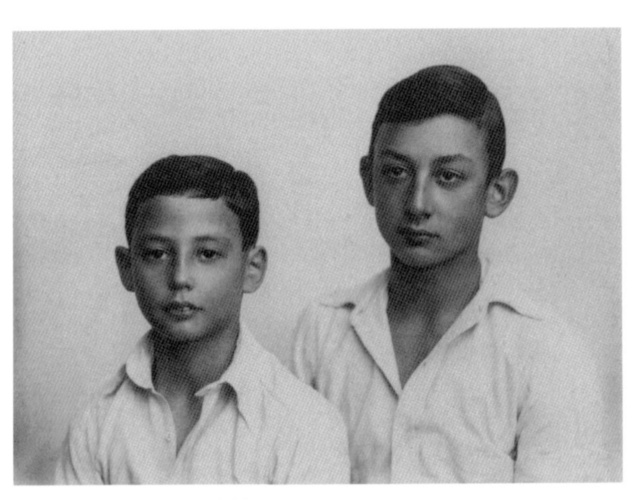

Eric and Gordon, c 1930

My father was set up from infancy to be jealous of his younger brother; and the fires of this jealousy were stoked and fuel added during young adulthood. 'We fought bitterly and regularly', he recorded later. Eric was a weak baby demanding special care and attention for years, an imbalance that stuck. He was nearly blinded as a child after a teacher threw a book hitting him just below the eye. As already recounted: when Eric went up to Oundle, their parents – unable, they claimed, to pay for both boys at once – made Father leave before he matriculated; and he had no bedroom of his own. When Eric developed into a notably strong young man, his current strength – like his earlier weakness – meant that he continued to gain the lion's share of parental love and attention.

Eric grew up excelling at all sports, especially cricket. When around 1997 I wrote to Hugh Lloyd-Jones, ex-regius Professor of Greek at Oxford, soliciting his memories of Iris Murdoch, he enquired whether I was related to the Eric Conradi who was, in his words, such a star at cricket, and in 1937 scored 121 not out at the Oval. He was chuffed to discover that he was my uncle. *Wisden* records Eric as 'a lefthander [in fact ambidextrous] of strong build, who made many runs … and often hit with great power'.

Eric won a major scholarship to Oundle and became the first Jewish head boy there, no mean distinction (Al Alvarez was the second); an all-rounder who won prizes for French and Maths, he was also Captain of Cricket, Rugby, Football, Fives and Squash. After this he won a major entrance scholarship to read Mathematics at Cambridge. Eric was charming and much-loved and the first of my surrogate-fathers. Father was proud of Eric and also jealous of him. This had a big impact on all of us, not least me, much later.

Letters from both brothers survive from the last week of May 1940. Eric's are superbly upbeat and confident, my father's often anxious and fretful, needy and demanding. True, Eric is nineteen and safe at Gonville and Caius College while Father at twenty-four is in the front-line in Normandy and writing just before and during the Dunkirk evacuation of 26 May to 4 June. So Father had plenty to worry about, not least his own possible death or capture, let alone a rapid German victory.

Father's letters start calmly enough, after a crossing that was 'uneventful, long & excellently organised'. Mother, though rather upset, took their separation 'v bravely' – more than he did. Due to his proficiency in spoken French, he is deputed the task of shopping for his unit and gets fresh daily social contact, which is welcome. He had acquired French when, as a school-boy, his parents sent him on annual month-long trips to Normandy and Belgium. Both French locals and soldiers congratulate him on his fluency…. And he is at this stage impressed by the spirit of calm determination among the French: '*Ils ne passeront pas*', he quotes, from a famous song about Verdun.

The weather is glorious and they are all as dark from sunburn as from dirt. They drink white wine at meal-times – 9d per large bottle, and even Cointreau and three star brandy cost only 2/9d, while champagne is a mere 2/2d a bottle. They rise at 4am each morning and compensate for lack of sleep by snatching cat-naps when they can…. There are for now quiet days behind the lines which afford time to sleep, do one's washing, catch up with correspondence. They are camping in a dense wood like gypsies.

When he argues conventionally enough that he and his unit constitute 'one big happy family' or that – despite anxieties – 'Worry is not part of our make-up on the whole' this is gainsaid by his own letters. These display both deep uncertainty and a certain obsessionality about concerns that might – in the light of the scale of the military disaster about to unfold – be thought disproportionate. He worries again and again that he had been due on 30 May, so he believed, to report to an RAOC (Ordnance corps) Officer Cadet Training Unit or OCTU, where he would have had the chance to train as an Officer. The personal drama of this missed opportunity looms as large as the national drama of Britain's devastating impending defeat. Eric sympathised, and wrote to their parents that Father's departure at *that* particular juncture – i.e. just before his OCTU – was a most unwelcome surprise…. 'He *does* seem dogged by ill luck'.

In the event Father would complete his Officer Training on 14 August 1940 and be commissioned 2nd Lieutenant by 18 October. Meanwhile he frets about forfeiting this May deadline, and fusses about arranging travel home for it, and establishing what is going on. 30 May was to have been his 'big day'. The W.O. was to have written a letter to the Colonel. Has the letter got lost? Has a further hitch happened? …The Major reassures him 'Don't worry! The Battery is not lost! – they know where to get you when they want you & will then get in touch with you…'.

His 1 June letter is the last to survive. That day – when the final daylight evacuation occurred of Allied soldiers (64,429) from Dunkirk,

200 miles away, after which increasing air attacks prevented any further – he notes verbosely: 'I have still no news at all of my recall & as we are expecting to get "back to grips" – we are now a few miles behind the lines – & I am naturally a little anxious to do all I can to expedite matters but fear I have now done all it is in my power to do in my modest position in the army & having regard to our complete isolation by all known means of communication (except an irregular post).'

He had not had 'one single letter since leaving England' and also worries 'If only I knew my letters were getting through to you'. Was this silence due to his outfit continually moving around? A rumour was circulating that a large consignment of mails had been lost. His sense of isolation was assuaged later that day: 'Hurrah yr welcome letters arrived – 1 from Mother, 1 from Father, 5 from Dulcie, out of the 10 letters she makes clear she has sent…'.

They had travelled a lot and were nearing the front, where there were 'no telephones, electricity, water or wireless at all'. He is filthy dirty and starting a new moustache. He now confesses to Mother that 'we have had a very "hot" time, and are lucky to have a very low list of missing – I only hope to goodness our luck continues'. The roads were covered in the tragic and pitiful sight of tens of thousands of refugees. Fortunately they shot down four Dornier German aircraft the previous day, but two more attacked that morning until British guns opened up. He finds time – touchingly – to lament the abandonment of live-stock: 'there is no-one to milk the cattle who are ill for lack of milking…'. And they were constantly under fire.

He makes importunate requests: 'Cd you please send me immediately: 1pr pants & vest 1. Unbreakable shaving mirror about 6" x 4" i.e metal-chromium plated & polished. & 2 or 3 *Readers Digests*, or *Lilliput* or *Men Only* to read'. He twice requests his khaki gloves and brandy flask from his wardrobe.

***

Eric sounds a very different note. He was about to gain a First in the Mathematics Tripos that summer, and already knew this was likely. Moreover, at a Cambridge cricket match on 23 May 1940 his score (136) was broadcast on the 6 pm BBC news. There were seventeen separate occasions when he scored four runs while the ball reached the boundary,

On his 21st birthday Gordon got news of Eric's record Oval score

and his average match score that term was 99.5. However he is to miss the next match owing to an interview at the War Office in Whitehall at 3.30 pm on 4 June; at the recruiting board he had been awarded the unusually high score of alpha plus – the plus being given for his cricket.

His parents have discomforted him by offering to gatecrash and support him at the interview in Whitehall or – alternatively – to invite the interviewer out afterwards for tea. Embarrassed and alarmed by this mixture of well-meaning pushiness and smothering Eric skilfully scotches an idea he clearly finds ridiculous. 'I'm not worrying a hoot about this interview on June 4th. I shall *walk* it, provided I go alone & am left to my own devices.' He reiterates, 'I know I'll get through the interview as I know I have the ability to impress people.' This was a justified swagger… 'I should not be at my best if I was with anyone else.' He was due to play at Lords on 22 and 24 June and offers his parents this as a booby-prize instead: 'so you shall come to that.'

Father's Family:
14. Cousin Cyrus, 1943

Sibling rivalry is a slippery entity that can be displaced or transferred. Father was jealous of Eric, and he was also jealous of their American first cousin Cyrus, whom he thought life had rewarded beyond his merits. Cyrus had lived in London before the war, and returned there three years after it started.

On 23 March 1943 Eric found himself seated on a log in a field with a biscuit-tin on his knees in lieu of a table, writing to my father in London. Eric was training African troops in the Gold Coast (now Ghana), where he would contract bilharzia, an infection caused by a parasitic worm that swims in fresh water in the tropics, at that time nightmarishly diagnosed via a metal cystoscope pushed up the urethra, an indignity he suffered many times. Eric's airgraph congratulates my father on a photo of his baby son, my elder brother Richard: 'He doesn't look Jewish', he declares. And he also professes himself very jealous at missing their mutual first-cousin Cyrus Sulzberger 'yet again'.

Cyrus had arrived in London in 1938 working for the *London Evening Standard* and other newspapers. I imagine that – although notoriously 'un-family-minded' – he none the less at that time cultivated his cousins both because they might be useful to him and also to give his mother Beatrice first-hand news of her English relatives.

In mid-February 1943 Cyrus and his new wife Marina came to lunch in Roehampton with my grandparents and parents. That busy week Cyrus and Marina also gave a dinner party for the exiled Czech leader Jan Masaryk, then the Czechoslovak Government-in-Exile's Foreign Minister, in a vast, empty *New York Times* apartment at the Savoy Hotel overlooking the Thames. Even the Savoy suffered food shortages and they sometimes ate omelettes made from swan's eggs stolen from the river. They also lunched that week with King Peter II of Yugoslavia and his

Marina and Cyrus Sulzberger, Emil, Dulcie and Florence Conradi

fiancée Princess Alexandra in Grosvenor Square.

Cyrus had his own painful experiences of British 'red tape', which he records finding arrogant and obstructive; he is likely to have proven sympathetic to Father's war-time troubles. This was the month when Father re-enlisted as an acting unpaid Sergeant in R.E.M.E., eight months after being court-martialled, a tale that belongs a little later in this narrative. Everyone appears smiling and relaxed in surviving photos. Yet my father was determinedly unimpressed and critical of Cyrus, whose career he always claimed evidenced nepotism.

Cyrus protested that he was independent-minded. He felt an irritable pride that his uncle Arthur Hays Sulzberger (1891-1968, until 1961 publisher of the *New York Times*) twice during the war actively prevented him for reasons of *realpolitik* from gaining the Pulitzer Prize when he was shortlisted. (He won it in 1951 in any case.) He had graduated *magna cum laude* from Harvard in 1934 and, though he wanted to go into journalism, chose to start elsewhere to establish his name, reluctant to call upon family connexions. He joined the family paper only on the outbreak of war as their Balkan bureau manager, covering seven countries from Hungary to Turkey. He soon travelled 100,000 miles through thirty states, writing so many provocative articles that he was successively banned from Hungary, Romania, Bulgaria and Italy. In 1941, he was arrested by the Gestapo in

Slovakia and accused of being a British spy; he was later released without a trial. Moreover post-war he always refused honours from any foreign state, lest his status as objective witness be compromised.

Much evidence today favours Father's view. From the time that Cyrus's father died of pneumonia when he was twelve, his uncle Arthur had acted as surrogate father. In 1943 Cyrus requested and got seats paid for by the *New York Times* on a Pan Am clipper from Cairo to New York: each ticket – for himself, Marina and also one for his wire-haired fox terrier Felix, who required a daily cocktail – was worth $1300: around £35,000 in today's currency. In August 1943 he secured Arthur's help releasing Marina's brother from sentence of death as a spy by the Italians; and, arguably most useful of all, Arthur helped Cy receive a draft deferment so he could continue to cover the war rather than have to fight in it. In 1944 he was made chief foreign correspondent of the *New York Times*, one of the best jobs in U.S. journalism; and *Time Magazine* that year dubbed Cyrus the paper's crown prince and heir apparent.

The family connection loomed large. Cy came to epitomise the privileged high-flying foreign correspondent who viewed his job as becoming intimate with powerful foreign leaders, needing to secure maximum attention for their views. The official history of the newspaper paints a picture of him as a power-or-rank-snob focussing exclusively on the most important people in whichever country he happened to be, a man who came to feel he deserved to be treated himself like visiting royalty. 'He adored rank', as the paper's historians noted. His office walls were plastered with photos of the famous power-brokers he accounted personal friends: De Gaulle, Tito, Krushchev, Castro, the Duke of Windsor, Eisenhower and Churchill. If he was not much liked on the *New York Times* this was because he traded on his relationship with it and editors had to treat him gingerly.

He spoke French and German well, and three Balkan languages passably. But he was not a team player, unable to share his sources with anyone. He was also reputed to be greedy, 'rarely spending a penny of his own money'. Though he saw himself as a victim he was in reality crusty, irascible and notoriously insensitive to the feelings of others, receiving a degree of attention out of proportion to his talents. His over-detailed memoirs are of great interest to historians of the period: he met everyone and was an observant witness. But they simultaneously show him a careless dandy and show-off: septentrional, obnebulate, fulgurous, urticarial, deodand, heteroclite and chthonian are not words in common use.

Small surprise, perhaps, that he was twice passed over for the top job in favour of cousins, in 1961 of Orvil Dryfoos then two years later of Arthur Ochs Sulzberger, aka 'Punch', who brutally forced cousin Cy, of whom he was jealous and whom he hated, to retire, aged 65, in 1977, one year after Marina's sudden death. She was much-loved and made their Paris home a salon for the illustrious and the powerful; without her no-one invited him socially. He had now to address allegations of links with the CIA, and soon wrote that he realised with horror that in all his long life 'I had never done a single thing of which I could be genuinely proud: no act of true courage, generosity or sacrifice or even pure kindness. It is appalling to contemplate'.

Father was not the only family member antagonistic to Cyrus, who in 1982 published *How I committed Suicide, a reverie*. In it, he lamented his loneliness after Marina's death, his departure from the *New York Times* under a mandatory retirement programme, and recorded that he had outlived his era. He was a time-warp American, who last lived in USA in the 1930s so that even his children seemed a little foreign and were ill at ease with him.

***

Neither Father nor Cyrus was family-minded. Father was a home-body, while Cyrus – living in Paris and summering on the island of Spetsai – had the excuse of geographical distance. Whenever we visited the USA in the 1960s and 1970s we Conradi children always stayed with Cyrus's thoroughly admirable and philanthropic sister Beattie Trilling in Washington DC. She was full of good works, and quietly self-effacing. Cyrus had no time for her or for anyone else much in his family. He had bigger fish to fry.

Father would denounce his American first cousin Cyrus Sulzberger when his name cropped up, for having been spoiled by fortune. Perhaps he was also in this way displacing his jealousy of Eric. '*Cousinage, dangereux voisinage*': Iris Murdoch quotes the French adage in *The Sea, the Sea* to point to this slippery aspect of our secret emotional lives. The transferability of sibling rivalry is one burden of this essay; Cain might well have displaced his jealousy of Abel onto a third party. Father's jealousy of Eric was a moveable feast. He was not only jealous of Cyrus, but also of me, for gaining more than our talents warranted.

Mother's Family

Morris Isaacs m. Phoebe Levy
1857-1926 1866-1920

Katie m. Fritz van Zwanenburg
1884-1979 1883-1938

Ruby – see below
1893-1962

seven others

Moss Cohen m. Sarah Hart

Amelia m. Lawrence Levy
1827-82 1823-1907

George Cohen m. Sarah Isaacs
1828-1890 1826-1890

other issue

Lewis Levy m. Hannah Cohen
1847-1913 1851-1932

Moss Cohen m. Isabella Solomon
1857-1900 1861-1942

other issue

Lawrence Levy m. Cissie Phillips
1876-1950 1884-1956
issue

George Moss Cohen m. Ruby Isaacs – see above
1886-1954 1893-1962

other issue

Dulcie m. Gordon Conradi
1917-2008 1916-93

Eileen m. Arthur Cohen
1919-84 1908-

John
1921-41

Micky m. Annette Cross
1931-2011 1934-
issue

Richard m. Angela Shragah
1941- 1946-
issue

Peter J
1945-

Prue
1948-2012

Stephen m. Tanya Sonnenwirth
1957-2009 1961-
issue

Mother's Family:
15. George Cohen & Sons, 1834

My mother's family business – buying and selling scrap cast and wrought iron – had been developed by my great-great-grandfather 'old George Cohen' at 44 Goulston Street, off Aldgate, from at least 1834 and possibly two decades earlier. My mother joked that old George had probably walked around London with a pram collecting discarded metal like Nicodemus Boffin, the new-rich 'Golden Dustman' in Dickens's *Our Mutual Friend*. Certainly he would often wield the sledge hammer himself when old plant was to be demolished. He was known as Farmer George and habitually dressed in square bowler, black frock-coat, Gladstone collar, wide cravat and high Wellington boots. 'Call him dead!' he would pronounce of anyone who returned a kindness with an injury.

His well-attested policy of offering 'cash on the nail' paid off and by 1869 he moved the firm first to 209-11 Cable St., then in 1876 – momentously and shrewdly – to 600 Commercial Road, which gave directly onto Regents' Canal Wharf or Dock from whence metal could be shipped directly. Coastal sailing vessels could be used for transporting scrap and the wharf also accommodated ocean-going steamers, a new access greatly facilitating the speed of trade. This opportune address much later afforded a new and durable name: his business would post-war be known as the 600 Company.

On a single summer's day in 1879 (19 July), eleven ocean-going ships are registered as loading for the firm, travelling to Rhode Island, Copenhagen, Durham and elsewhere; and the Belfast office opened the following year. Sales of 1000 tons of scrap were by now common. George also acquired a large depot at Canning Town for trading machinery.

George's many dependents included his mother, two sisters, two aunts plus his wife from 1844 Sarah Isaacs, five sons – three of whom became partners in the firm – and six daughters.... They had at first lived in terraced houses which appear to have had outdoor privies, in Goulston and Cable Streets close to the family business. But by 1875, a year when he employed twenty-five labourers and four clerical staff, he bought Coborn House in a still elegant 'almost rural' part of Bow, just off Tredegar Square: such fine Bow houses were owned by City men who drove each day to their offices in town. And in 1880 he persuaded his nephew

Coborn House

Lewis Levy (who was also married to his daughter Hannah) to buy adjoining York House. These two houses shared a garden, stables and coachman. As well as the friendly carriage horses, one of which, 'Snowdrop', was evidently a favourite, there was a small zoo of pets, an ancient climbable mulberry, and beneath it a fountain with fat golden carp.

Since these gardens famously sported a cannon of Nelson's (that still fired) from one of Nelson's ships they had broken up at Blackwall, it would be pretty to imagine them breaking up the 98-gun 'Fighting Temeraire', which had played so heroic a role in Nelson's 1805 victory at Trafalgar, and whose final voyage from Sheerness to Rotherhithe occasioned Turner's famous painting. But in 1838 (the year in question) the scale the firm was trading on was still modest. By the 1870s, by contrast, ships were indeed being eagerly purchased for breaking up, including Queen Victoria's yacht, *R.Y. Osborne.* A summerhouse that had once been a ship's deckhouse caused great excitement when it arrived at

Coborn House for the children to play in, towed by eight horses, and complete with lanterns, ship's furniture – shiny brass things – and even portholes that opened and shut.

Soon the company's dealings start to shadow successive phases of the national story. They broke up Pimlico Gas Works in 1900 and the Earls Court Exhibition's Great Wheel in 1906. During the Great War the firm furnished the War Office with one and half million tons of scrap at a state-controlled price (i.e with minimal profit); then post-war twenty-five U-boats that had surrendered in 1918 and a number of ironclads were also broken up at the Regents Canal Dock and in south Wales. They decommissioned half a million tons of ordnance with the approval of the War Office, employing 7000 workers to carry this out. They scrapped the towers of the Crystal Palace after it burned down in Sydenham in 1936, and the Skylon and the roof of the Dome of Discovery from the Festival of Britain in 1952. By my youth in the 1960s the 600 HQ in White City – immediately opposite the BBC – was roughly as big, one cultural icon facing another.

***

Lewis Levy, who had bought York House, was on the move for most of 1892 to Bournemouth, New York City, Washington, Chicago, Canada, Swansea, Belfast and Scotland, building up the business. In January of that year, and aged only sixteen, Lewis's son Lawrie was sent to live in Paris to learn good French (and some German). This schooling was evidently designed to help him represent the family firm in these languages: on his return eighteen months later he is doing business from the Grand Hotels in Paris and in Stockholm. Surviving letters afford a glimpse of Anglo-Jewish mercantile life at this period.

Photos show Lawrie dark and handsome. He was evidently intelligent, in one term, aged nine, winning three prizes at school: (Lamb's *Tales from Shakespeare*, *Westward Ho!* by Charles Kingsley, *English Circumnavigators*). His uncle Phil (10 March) wrote from Bournemouth, 'I suppose when I get to see you again (DV) you will be quite the Frenchman'. Indeed, by April, after only three months, his French was already good enough to follow plays in that language. His hobbies included stamp-collecting, fishing and cage-birds – and his adoptive mother in Paris Stella Tucker gave him some of the latter, together with millet,

Lawrie with three siblings: courtesy of the Jewish Museum London

groundsel, and hemp seeds to feed them.

He had to leave behind his dog 'Tiny', given to eating reels of cotton and feathers off ladies' bonnets and thriving 'wonderfully… a very good digestion'. Tiny would not let the family cat into the house but liked to play games of 'touch' in the garden with the family horse, Snowdrop. (Lawrie's Papa observed that it was like watching the Griffiths brothers – who made comedy out of wrestling – at the music hall.) Tiny was succeeded by the larger dog 'Bang', who took a dislike to aunt Bella, flew at her, and had alas to be returned by train to Sheffield, a city doubtless visited by Lawrie's father for its steel.

Lawrie's four sisters all write to him as 'My Darling Lawrie'. This reads in part like a family in-joke, but also as if each sister were competing to be his favourite. Most surviving letters come from his mother Hannah, who in photographs looks short and dumpy, and in print comes across as wry, smart, full of realism and solicitous about his health. She bore thirteen children between 1875 and 1894 of whom ten survived.

At the close of his first week in Paris January 1892 Hannah writes, 'Your father would like to know how you spent Friday evening and Saturday' – i.e. whether he observed the Sabbath. The family was observant without being '*From*', strict or devout. That meant they held High Days and Holy Days, fasted for Yom Kippur and celebrated Purim with some dressing-up. Letters are peppered with token pieties: DV, TG (Thank God), PG (Please God), GRHS (God Rest his Soul).... Male babies were circumcised – which they facetiously call 'getting shortened'.

Upright and even staid as the family was, they often adopt a tone of pleasant worldliness. 16-18 April: 'You know there is no harm whatever in drinking claret during Passover...', Hannah tells Lawrie, advising 'Do as you like for Tisha B'Av' – the annual day of fasting and mourning to commemorate the anniversary of the destruction of the First Temple by the Babylonians and of the Second by the Romans. 'There are few who keep it now...' she notes without regret. When George Cohen died in 1890 he desired his family to observe mourning for one month only – not one year. He 'wished they should not cloud their happy and cheerful lives even for a few months out of respect for his memory'....

The family did not neglect worldly pleasures. A 12 June dance in the garden at Bow entailed a large party plus a marquee and they 'kept it up till 5 am'. On 19 March Hannah went to the Tivoli Music Hall in the Strand, built 1889, with Uncle Moss and Aunt Bella. Dan Leno, George Robey and Little Tich all played there. They had a pleasant evening 'tho should not care for *that sort of thing* often'. Hannah preferred straight theatre, and there are few weeks that she does not record some theatre-going (albeit not on Friday nights). April 26: 'I went to see *Niobe* at the Strand last Saturday evening. The week before I went to see *The Magistrate* ...at Terry's Theatre [also in the Strand]. I have also seen *The Vicar of Bray* and *Lady Windermere's Fan*...'. This was a few weeks after Wilde's play opened. 'On Thursday evening I am going to a Ball at Cannon St Hotel'.

They rented a hideaway on the edge of Epping Forest, to which the children could be sent with their nurse for short breaks. The Thames offered further recreation and escape. My great grandfather Moss Cohen, with whom Hannah went to the Music Hall, joined the firm in 1873, loved the river, and loved his tug, also named *Coborn*. This tug – doubtless useful for accompanying ships that were either laden with scrap or in transit before being broken up – doubled up at weekends for family use. On 6 April 1893 ten family members boarded the tug for an outing to

Gravesend on the Thames estuary, twenty-one miles out of London: 'the 4 girls & George [my granpa], 2 of Aunt Bella's children, Sarah Cohen, your father and Uncle Moss'. Three days later Hannah again travelled on *Coborn* to watch the Oxford and Cambridge boat race, meeting up with her four daughters near their boarding school at Kew Bridge. Since one nephew had passed just below Senior Wrangler – Cambridge's top mathematics award – they probably cheered Cambridge, the losing team that year.

Moss – short for Moses – and his brother Barnett both loved horses and were considered good judges of 'form'. Barnett bred race-horses with dashing period names: 'Jarvie', 'Jaunting Car', 'Urgent', 'Golden Brick', 'Disposals' and 'Hope' and, among other big prizes, won Ascot's Victoria Cup. He never married, and my mother, who dimly remembered him towards the end of his life (d. 1927) thought that he was probably gay.

Moss's sister Amelia married (confusingly) yet another Moss, this one Moss Harris the antiquary, art expert, and founder of the renowned furniture dealers. If the family were moving up in the world, her rise to easier circumstances left Hannah unimpressed by rank – illustrated by her reaction to that winter's *cause célèbre*, the trial (14 Feb 1892) of a Mrs Ethel Osborne. This lady had stolen pearls belonging to her lifelong friend and indeed hostess in Torquay, Mrs Hargreaves. Ethel then sold the jewels on to Messrs Spinks in Gracechurch Street for £550, and compounded her felony by accusing Mrs Hargreaves of lying. Mrs Hargreaves herself pleaded for mercy for Ethel, who must have been mad when she took the pearls because she herself had loved her all her life.... This pleading won Ethel a lighter sentence of nine months' imprisonment with hard labour, the judge intimating, however, that owing to her ill health she might be kept in the infirmary.

The public expected theft and perjury among the so-called criminal classes: they were accordingly shocked, enthralled and fascinated when such crimes were exposed among the genteel. Hannah, however, comments, 'People have a great sympathy for her because she is a lady, but I fail to see why she is to be studied and made a great fuss of any more than a poor person who steals for their starving children'. She sounds resolutely egalitarian, displaying an admirable dislike of snobbery. If she was unimpressed by rank, she was also independent-minded where gender politics was concerned, maintaining that boys – just like girls – should be taught sewing skills.

Charitable work was an arena where the this-worldly and the religious met and are inescapably interlinked, exemplifying the natural poise or balance that is (to me) an admirable feature of the Jewish faith. Obituaries of family members in the *Jewish Chronicle* make clear how committed they all are to this: as one cousin commented, 'such works are not optional extras but Mitzvot or commandments which we are not free to ignore'. When Lawrie's grandfather (another Lawrence Levy) died in 1907 aged eighty-three, the long list of charities he was associated with included Friendly Society work; work for the New Synagogue, founded 1761 in East London; the Society of Independent Friends; the City of London Benevolent Society for assisting distressed tradesmen; the Loyal and Independent Lodge of Goodfellows; the Jewish mutual Birmingham Benefit Society. He also worked as Overseer of the Poor and for an Old Widows Home which was founded in the 1820s and which was ultimately, after many changes, incorporated into the Home for Aged Jews on Nightingale Lane. I used in the 1970s to drive a mini-van taking residents on outings to take tea with other kindly volunteers, though I had no idea until now that family had been linked to this place for two centuries. I and my siblings were all brought up under the same compulsion and I spent a dozen years prison-visiting for the New Bridge.

***

Lawrie's surrogate mother in France, Mrs Stella Tucker, who lived at 14, villa Bellenot, Colombes, a suburb of Paris, was witty, worldly, well read – she quotes Dickens – and polyglot. She admired good needlework and indeed may have worked as a seamstress: she had a notable client in Dreyfus's wife Lucie Eugénie Hadamard who, accompanied by her two children, Pierre (6) and Jeanne (4), visited her often. She writes to Lawrie on 26 June 1897: 'We are, as you suppose, much interested in the Dreyfus Affair; his poor wife is a client of mine. She often comes in with her two children but of course I never speak to her of her husband. We fear that even if he is innocent, he will not be allowed to appear so. It is a dreadful injustice but Government seems to hush up all that transpires or may transpire in his favour.'

Lawrie had evidently asked Stella Tucker about Dreyfus, and was interested in the issue of anti-semitism. One way of assimilating was to leave the old Jewish East End behind. The family soon outgrew their home there. When they first moved to Bow in 1875, the twin houses displayed Bow's Regency elegance, albeit contrasting increasingly with much neighbouring poverty. It was convenient for what Stella Tucker called, with light irony, 'you business gentlemen' since a carriage could take you to work in a matter of minutes. On 9 April 1893, returning from a jaunt to Hyde Park, Hannah laments wistfully – 'what a different world it [i.e the West End] seems!' Hannah regrets the absence of parkland in the 'poor East End', while reflecting 'though if one has their health, it doesn't matter much where we live'. Stella Tucker asked Lawrie on 16 Aug 1894 'in which neighbourhood do you think of settling? It will be very nice, in many ways, you living West.' Indeed in 1896 the Levy family moved out of Bow to Hawthorn Lodge, 155 Finchley Road, London NW.

A classic English-Jewish trajectory runs from rags to riches, from Stepney peddler to Hampstead prosperity via Highbury or Golders Green in a few generations. Lawrie Levy, who had started out in Bow in the East End, finished his life in 'Glen Chess', a big house whose rural Hertfordshire estate was tended until World War II by six gardeners and where he lived in style, wearing tweeds, plus fours and matching hat, striding around the grounds followed by several dogs (corgis?), and – more English than the English – fishing for pike in one of the two lakes or the river Chess, while his wife Cissie, large, generous, beautiful, would invite any callers to stay for lunch, 'just boiled cod, darling!'

Mother's Family:
16. Parvenus and Pariahs, 1920

In 1890 the Isaacs' neighbours and closest friends were the inter-related Cohen and Levy families, with their adjoining houses and interconnected gardens and stables off Tredegar Square, the sons of both families working for George Cohen & Sons. If all three Isaacs daughters married well, my grandmother Ruby Isaacs scooped the pool by marrying the founder's grandson, another George Cohen.

It remained for over a century very much a family-owned and run business, with more than a dozen uncles and cousins on the Board, many of them from 1864 Freemasons (Lodge of Tranquillity) just as they were often also members of Regents Park Zoo with (when I was a child) private keys for Sunday access. The Cohen founder had adopted his Levy nephew around 1851 before he succeeded in producing a son himself, and these Levys – cuckoo-like – seem still to me the smarter and stronger of the two branches and the more cohesive: an annual Levy country walk today still attracts a hundred Levy-related cousins, and fewer Cohens.

One cousin who worked for George Cohen & Sons after 1950 recalls that the firm was 'highly paternalistic, and looked after its employees wonderfully, even visiting the sick, and way ahead of its time in personnel policy and conditions. The many staff were well-disposed to the family. There was a real warmth.' In 1947 it became a public company with numerous branches, acquiring engineering subsidiaries and diversifying to suit the stock exchange.

Upward mobility is a theme of much recent Jewish family history. Fromatte on my father's side had risen in nineteenth-century Paris from peddler's daughter to legation Attaché-and-Consul's wife; while in 1920 Ruby progressed from Bow via Highbury to a huge pebble-dashed Edwardian house on Frognal Lane that is nowadays divided into two and where there were during my early childhood still six or seven live-in servants: cook-general, daily-woman, gardener, house parlour-maid (who cleaned upstairs) and housemaid (who cleaned downstairs and waited at table), nanny, nanny's help; the chauffeur Cubitt lived three miles away in a Hendon mews flat, tending the black 1936 convertible Buick Roadmaster, drivers in those days being required to perform as mechanics too.

Hannah Arendt divided all Jews into either Pariahs or Parvenus. She preferred the Pariah stance for (by a simple paradox) its nakedness and brave self-empowerment; but I guess Frognal, if forced to make this comfortless choice, surely belonged to the Parvenu, which is to say the assimilationist. My Uncle John, in an essay in 1941 meditating on anti-semitism, starting 'I am a thoroughbred Jew and proud of it', recorded his distaste for brash Jewish wartime wide-boys, writing of the two to three generations needed to transmute a foreign Jew into an English gentleman, a journey he saw that his family were undertaking, but which could never by definition be fully accomplished. Not without foreswearing your Jewishness. And the house aped a particular patrician English style: the big stair-case I remember with embarrassment for its stuffed alligator – or crocodile – hanging on the wall. This Pooterish or Parvenu touch

3 Frognal Lane

was probably the memento of a trip to South Africa, where some cousins lived: I cannot imagine my gentle grandfather handling a gun on safari, or indeed hurting a fly. I remember this with a mix of amusement and discomfiture, for it seems like a gambit to appear *plus Anglais que les Anglais*, and to bespeak insecurity.

That said, a discussion about whether Mother should follow her Lausanne finishing-school friends by 'coming out' as a debutante in 1937 was short-lived: no one – and she least of all – had much interest in her so doing, and the good opinion of the family loomed larger than that of any wider world.

The house's middle-brow atmosphere recalled something between *The Forsyte Saga* and Mr Pooter in *The Diary of a Nobody*. A further 'touch' was a blue glass bowl containing a toy-scale enactment of the dramatic fable supposedly depicted on Willow Pattern plates. This bowl, sitting on a table in the hall, contained the statutory elements:

> Two birds flying high,
> A Chinese vessel, sailing by.
> A bridge with three men, sometimes four,
> A willow tree, hanging o'er.
> A Chinese temple, there it stands,
> Built upon the river sands.
> An apple tree, with apples on,
> A crooked fence to end my song.

A bronze version of the three wise monkeys ('See no evil, hear no evil, speak no evil') sat insensibly on another side-table, together with potpourri.

Granny, who called her parents-in-law Mater and Pater, was infinitely generous and hospitable and hosted non-stop clan gatherings. Her drawing room featured from 1937 four of Edward VIII's elegant walnut bergère chairs on their cabriole legs, which arrived via a London antique-dealer and friend (Edward Lehmann) who after the Abdication helped sell off Fort Belvedere furniture. (I own two of these, tapestried in mother's meticulous and beautiful *petit point*, which now, after *The King's Speech* – confusingly written by my name-sake – elicit interest.) Fresh-cut flowers were delivered and displayed everywhere; there were unmemorable paintings and a display-cabinet with fascinating netsuke, like the Hare with Amber Eyes Edmund de Waal famously writes about, albeit with a less dramatic provenance. I was ashamed that among the papers she had delivered was the *Sunday Express*.

Although without care for the accoutrements of wealth, she kept up a conventional starched style that nowadays seems as remote and absurd as ancient Tibet: her four children parading on the Heath in matching sailor-suits with their French Nou-Nou, and her staff on Christmas Day filing into the drawing-room in afternoon uniforms for presents the children had saved up their pocket money to buy, to cries of 'Three cheers for staff! Hip hip Hooray!' A maid attended during meal-times.

Dulcie, John, Eileen, 1924

The decade of a woman's prime can mark her for life: Ruby's carefully angled hair-style, slanting hats and round shoulders all seemed as redolent of the 1930s as picnic baskets, cocktail shakers, plucked eyebrows and deck quoits. She was advised by her naturopath, who commended a polemic called *I Accuse the Doctors*, to eat melba toast and the bitter interior parts of apricot stones. She loved to make extravagant birthday gifts that irritated my mother because she thought – probably accurately – that Ruby was buying affection. Her bed was tipped backward, a precaution against haemorrhoids.

The most durable aspect of their Jewishness was charitable work, which everyone took seriously. After her death the Royal Free Hospital kept up for a while an Auntie Ruby Memorial garden in her name to honour her fund-raising – with Enid Blyton's support – via something called the Auntie Ruby's Jig Stamp Club: we hapless children had to beg for money to pay for stamps to fill each page – though Ruby habitually spoiled us by giving us the money at the same time as the stamps. The cash went to purchase toys and other items for the childrens' wards at the RFH. I liked the injunction at synagogue to give away 10% of one's income to charity (though less bothered by the annual recommendation of two charities to give to, one of them in Israel).

My earliest memories date from the late 1940s when at Christmas thirty or so relatives (so it seemed to my young eyes) sat down to lunch and a different set to dinner and there was constant movement and bustle. I doubt that they had celebrated Chanukah (the Jewish December Festival of Lights) since the previous century and they wore their Judaism lightly. Lily Smith, the London house-keeper, meek and shy to the point of near-invisibility, served everyone *à la Russe*, manipulating spoon and fork, from the right.

On my fourth birthday, to cries of 'Speech! Speech!' I clambered onto my dining-room chair but got no further than the precocious opening words 'I remember when I was very young…' at which point the room dissolved in gales of laughter. Then Ruby, to console me while I sulked, cuddled me on her lap. While her rhinestone necklace and red beetle-like fingernails distracted me, she accidentally brushed her lighted cigarette quite hard into my neck so that I cried and concluded that love was dangerous. Neither of my grandmothers really liked small children and both sensibly employed a servant when a grandchild came to visit.

Granpa had spent two years before the Great War studying at a Technische Hochschule in Germany. Wearing a single pink rose in his silver boutonnière, he liked to retire to his library to listen every evening to the six o'clock news. Here he showed me the little guillotine he used to cut his best Havana cigars, which fascinated me. It was called the library, and the shelves were made of some pale wood, probably maple, but some of his books languished behind glass-fronted cabinets, that sure-fire badge of philistinism. It seemed a house given to smoking more than reading. Everywhere were cigarette boxes of different shapes and sizes made from chased steel or smooth silver, malachite and onyx. Their hinged tops, when opened, caused galleries of cigarettes to offer themselves ingeniously in fan-shapes, or like musketry in different lines and angles of defence, and one was a musical box too which, each time

I opened it, played the opening bars of Lily of Laguna ('She's my lady love, she is my dove, my baby-love'). Cigars were stored in sweet-smelling cedar boxes. Everyone smoked and the stage business of offering a light was still an accepted aspect of flirtation.

Smoking apart, the house saw a good deal of whisky-drinking and bridge-playing. My uncle penned a facetious doggerel about the dangerously competitive rubbers played in that house, a poem Ruby had framed. Card-tables abounded. 'Say what you like about the Chosen People,' says Billy-Pop in Angus Wilson's *No Laughing Matter*, 'they do play a damn good game of bridge'.

During the war the billiard-room, big enough to double as a hall for dances, was reinforced with steel girders to make a shelter where everyone slept together in hospital-style beds through the Blitz, family at one end, servants at the other. The most formidable was Miss Binnings aka Binnie, the snaggle-toothed and Scottish nursery governess who, come to think of it, resembled a pocket version of Hannah Arendt herself. Binnie was intelligent and, when she visited Anna Freud (who was wearing a hand-sewn dirndl) in Maresfield Gardens in 1939 to discuss my then still young uncle Micky, she held her own.

She knew German from working for the Rosenthal family near Selb in Bavaria and I was greatly impressed to learn that Binnie could (or so I believed) also address you when in the mood in Latin. I waited eagerly for this to happen but only ever heard Kelvinside. She had a vigorous moustache and the (to me) charming habit of calling our middle-aged mother 'Darling' in her Glasgow accent. She had after all known her since she was a small child; but this struck me as stylish and positively Russian, like something in Tolstoi or Chekhov. She came to my mother later as our house-keeper and taught me how to cook field mushrooms (butter, garlic, black pepper) and pheasant (chestnuts, stuffing, game chips): cooking was one of the ways in which I tried – with some success – to appease my Father. But Binnie strongly disapproved my habit of staying late in bed. She had a propensity for filching my father's whisky and on my twenty-first birthday came down the long stairs of our Pinner house with tipsy unsteadiness carrying a suitcase in either hand, wearing a battered hat and Granny's discarded fox stole, and left our employ for good: 'Goodbye Darling, I've had enough', she said. But she kept in touch with Mother none the less, who stayed 'Darling' for the rest of Binnie's days.

Mother's Family: 17. Parents-at-War, 1940-45

Father, a gunner and 2nd Lieutenant in the Royal Artillery, found himself trapped outside St Valery-en-Caux in Normandy ten days after the general BEF evacuation. He reported in a letter home that 'the infernal Huns, were up to their devilish tricks: machine gunning cattle, horses, & refugees – any living thing that moves – *la Guerre Totale*'. Over twenty thousand soldiers, some of them Seaforth Highlanders, were marooned in this part of France, and half of these would be captured.

Gordon in uniform, 1939

He survived one night in a small cave with sixty others, with no food and little water. The Germans threw bodies over the cliff top to lure them out. This was followed by a bombardment during which many were killed and large numbers wounded while others drowned trying to swim away. Then the remaining able-bodied waded out chest high in the water to climb a rope-ladder into the overcrowded life-boats. His account of this escape – which does not conceal that the British behaved better than the French – was published first in the *Sunday Express* and later in an anthology by John Murray. On arrival in Southampton he phoned Dulcie, who at his request rang his mother to tell her both that he had been rescued and that he had indeed survived. 'Don't *ever* give her a shock like that again' Emil came on the phone to foolishly direct.

Dulcie liked to remember the meeting that followed because – despite all that went wrong later – they still loved one another then. Gordon's mother insisted on accompanying Dulcie to this rendez-vous, like the mother in the comic song ('And her mother came too'), thus delaying the meeting – through requiring to have her hair permed first – by five hours.

They had been lovers, unbeknownst to their parents, since the beginning of that year, when he had been stationed at Bovington and Dulcie had come down to stay in Bere Regis. Now on 11 June 1940 they met on the platform of Winchester station. My father put down his kit-bag. They ran into each other's arms.

Considering the circumstances of this narrow escape Dulcie's parents relented: they must have learnt from him in person the full horror of this episode which, given war-time censorship, his written account necessarily downplays, as it does his undoubted and necessary courage. Yet their doubts were still unallayed and they had him sign a last-minute deed protecting her inheritance whose implications caused offence to Florence and Emil. They married the following week, Thursday 20 June. It was a war wedding, and she accordingly dressed not in white but a colour she called gas-blue. There were two hundred guests.

They stayed in love through the war. In November 1941 Gordon arrived back at their small Mill Hill house unexpectedly in the middle of the working day. Dulcie was surprised but went on bathing and then nursing her one month old baby while he sat patiently in his uniform waiting for her to put the baby back to sleep in his cot. Then he took her to the neighbouring room to tell her that her nineteen year-old brother had been killed. John had joined the RAF in defiance of their father (who

Wedding photo. Florence in the background.

wanted him to learn accountancy) and had survived one crash before. On his last flight as a trainee navigator/observer in a night fighter, during a so-called tip-and-run raid off the Lincolnshire coast, he was – as already noted – shot down and killed. He had his wings in his pocket ready to be sewn on after that flight. Gordon feared that the shock of this news might distress their baby and cause Dulcie's milk to dry up; his patience and kindness were remembered later as proof that their marriage had once been based on something real.

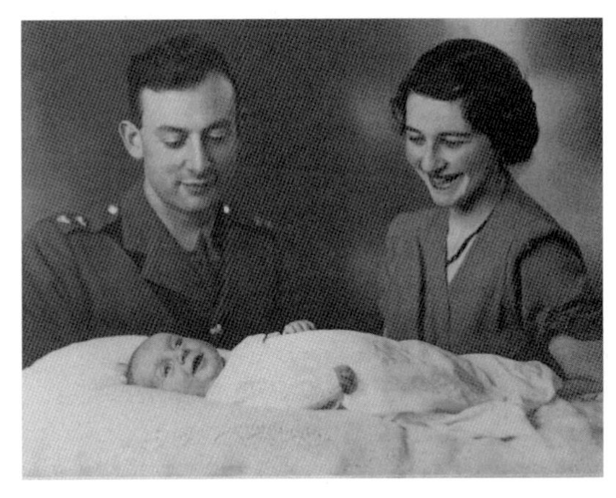

Gordon, Dulcie, Richard, 1941

A further test came the following summer when Gordon was court-martialled. At Chelsea barracks on 4 June 1942 eight charges were levelled of which five 'stuck': having his car (an old Morris 8) repaired at Aldershot during working hours; claiming that this was an army vehicle; stealing army property, mostly car-related, including one 6 volt bulb and one tail lamp; causing a soldier under his command to construct for his private use a table, stool and book-cases from army timber; and lastly permitting coal to be delivered for his private use. Possibly his parents' making a favourite of his brother had left him feeling cheated, and this was his unconscious way of redressing the balance? Mother held her head high each time she visited him in detention. Eric wrote to Gordon: 'In your time of trouble again and again I took my hat off to Dulcie for her bearing and self-control under the most trying conditions'.

An expert on the period tells me that these amounted to 'technical infringements' that, in another time and place, might have been overlooked. Father's batman, who carried out his commissions and subsequently turned him in, bore him malice. Perhaps this batman was a CP member and bore class resentments – or racial ones? A second factor was the atmosphere of fear before the tide of war turned in our favour after El Alamein: who or what was to blame for our succession of humiliating defeats? That same summer Father's younger brother Eric was subjected to a Court of Inquiry for having supplied incorrect measurements when the German battleships *Scharnhorst* and *Gneisenau*, early in 1942, dashed through the Channel back to Germany without mishap. Happily it was proved that the errors were not within Eric's data – which were wholly accurate – but were made by the clerk who mis-copied them. Eric was both exonerated and, in the view of his commanding officer, 'vindicated'.

Captain Gordon Conradi was cashiered on 7 June. Cashiering or dishonourable discharge – the infamous fate suffered by Alfred Dreyfus – entailed public humiliation with no possible return to military service. For three black days this was his lot; then, by dint of special pleading, this sentence was commuted to 'dismissal for one year' – in the event eight months – after which he re-enlisted as an acting unpaid Sergeant in R.E.M.E., demotion to the ranks being evidently thought too harsh. Sentimental rhetoric about the Dunkirk-cum-Blitz spirit overlooks both how widely resented war-time loss of civil liberties was, and how many rebelled: Ivor Novello went to prison for fiddling his petrol ration, and others falling foul of war-time regulations included Lady Astor, Lord Donegall, Noël Coward and the army's provost marshal: as one historian of the period recently put it, in kindly extenuation, 'After all, everyone was on-the-fiddle'.

Father's court-martial was never mentioned and I found out about it only recently. To me he described his war in an odd foretelling of *Dad's Army* simply as 'Being bossed around by bank managers'. Perhaps ten years after the war he startled us by announcing one evening that he had just hired a man who had served time in prison, adding kindly: 'Someone has to see their side of things'. He would also often say that it was not enough if you were Jewish to behave well: you had to be above reproach, always better than gentiles, since any small lapse might be punished. His twenty-four page pamphlet entitled 'British Jewry in Battle and Blitz' (1942) survives, with its long list of Jewish soldiers mentioned in dispatches, designed to encourage *esprit de corps*.

His eight months in civvy street cannot have been comfortable. He was not in a so-called 'reserved occupation' like coal-mining or farming, which indemnified you against call-up. My parents had to give up their Mill Hill house and move back to live with Dulcie's parents in Frognal while he worked for Emil on £3 per week. There were further humiliating consequences. The court-martial surely exacerbated the doubts Dulcie's parents had about him. And it probably played a part in sealing his own mother's animosity.

***

Emil suffered heart attacks towards the end of the war and afterwards, followed by a period of such intense anxiety and depression that – in the barbaric custom of the time – he underwent a lobotomy. This was the procedure called by Ken Kesey in *One Flew Over the Cuckoo's Nest* 'frontal-lobe castration', a form of punishment and control following which 'There's nothin' in the face. Just like one of those store dummies … his eyes are all smoked up and gray and deserted'. It indeed rendered Emil quiet and biddable and probably led to his death in 1947.

Father was discharged in 1946 with an 'exemplary' military character: a 'very keen and conscientious soldier who does his utmost and is most co-operative. Good disciplinarian and well-liked generally'. After this Major Flockhart adds the strange phrase 'Quiet but rather excitable'.

There was much at home to be excited about: even though he was now Managing Director, Emil's shares in the family electrical wholesaling business went to his mother, not to him, resulting in years of post-war legal wrangling, and anxiety.

***

A lasting riddle in my childhood went: 'Shall we ask the great-aunts?'. You could not invite one great-aunt without inviting – from different quarters – all, in which case you catered for up to a dozen extra guests. Dulcie occasionally found this large extended family claustrophobic.

They were worldly and not unduly censorious when it came to sex. Although a Politzer cousin was gaoled for homosexuality, Granpa George Cohen's gay first cousin Harold Cohen lived openly with a boy-friend and my mother believed Uncle Barnett Cohen, who owned race-horses, was also gay. A mistress (aka 'a bit-of-fluff') was a fact of life, as were lovers for some stay-at-home wives during the war. 'I had a very good war' my great-aunt Betty once said; and when I asked what she meant, she replied 'What do you think I mean? American GI's!'. From 1942 she ran three London flower-shops which did a brisk trade in re-cycled corsages: an American soldier would buy a bouquet for his date, who, if (unbeknownst to him) 'a good time girl', would after a few hours sell the flowers back to Betty, and so forth.

But such tolerance did not necessarily extend towards other forms of transgression; and perhaps tongues wagged over my father's troubles. In October 1946 her father bought my mother a house in Hatch End and she was relieved to escape the Hampstead gold-fish bowl, the world of hand-me-down clothes and gossip. I found the north London suburbs in each season wan and sad, and (foolishly) envied her the intimacy she had enjoyed with a big extended family. I felt I had missed out on that closeness and did not appreciate its claustrophobic price-tag of knowing-better and minding others' business.

My family's history meant that I grew up with an embarrassing love for England, a simple-minded gratitude for its striking physical beauty, its civilisation, its old traditions of tolerance and decency and for the strange certainty of the English about their place in the world. Few English friends will nowadays admit to both Anglophilia and Europhilia in tandem together. Such love brands me an outsider; and perhaps this condition in its turn helped pre-dispose me towards Iris, another outsider: an Irishwoman displaced in England, and a London-lover exiled to Oxford, about whose charms she long felt equivocal.

Part Three:
Iris Murdoch

18. Disciple into Biographer

I felt a growing kinship with Iris, and in 1995 my friendship with her and with John changed tempo, and became a good deal closer. Early that year, having met John at an exhibition of Harry Weinberger's paintings, I plucked up courage to invite him and Iris to a big birthday party we were hosting in Wales. He replied that they would love to come – straight from Charleston – and would stay two nights. 'Iris is very enthusiastic too.... It would be wonderful to see your country place', he wrote. While there he indicated that they would like to return. I duly invited

John, Iris, PC and Cloudy, the model for Anax in *The Green Knight*.

them for a weekend and they stayed for a week: another friend observed that the Bayleys were experienced 'cuckoos'. That pattern soon got repeated and we worked out that they spent an aggregate of eight months with us in all. Iris was happy with us, and distressed when she had to go back to Oxford.

Her confusion had been increasingly clear since I lunched with her in 1993, when she sometimes repeated sentences and lost the thread of what she wished to say. This was now palpably worsening. Appeals to John – some by mutual friends – to get professional help in looking after Iris were dodged. We tried, he resisted. A long letter in September 1997 from John acknowledges that Iris feels lost at home in Oxford, and continues 'I can't tell you what a difference it makes having you & Jim in support … you are … just what is needed … I can't imagine what I should do without you'. The situation gradually became *fait accompli*, then choiceless. We had to learn some necessary new skills. Happily, other friends rallied and helped too. And friendship with John came to matter a great deal: he was an extraordinary man, brilliant, wayward, loving and generous in equal measure.

This situation was also – in a strange way – beautiful. We satisfied each other's need for rational converse; Iris's joy and relief at being with us, and at being helped to bathe and wash her hair, were palpable to everyone; we soon felt like family, with an uncanny ease of communication, and essential to one another. 'Each of the four of us gives the other three the space to be exactly who s/he is', John observed. And he added, 'I've only ever had one friend before this – Lord David Cecil'. When I enquired, 'What is a friend?', he memorably replied, 'Someone you *don't have to bother about at all*' (said with emphasis). My partner Jim O'Neill brought her clothes from the British Legion shop in Knighton. If John and Iris Bayley were surrogate parents to me and Jim, we tried in our turn to return the favour and meet their needs. When it was hot, we all went swimming in our pond: Iris sat regally in an ancient white metal chair by the water's edge, dragonfly darting and hovering around her head, while Jim acted coiffeur. John stripped down to an astonishing vest that had so many loops, strands and holes you could no longer tell which were the arm-openings. His index-finger to his lips, he whispered owlishly, 'Mustn't let the moths think they're winning'.

***

In a long 2003 letter to an army friend John Bayley recounted the story of his friendship with A.N. Wilson – how much the Bayleys loved him, and so consented to his writing Iris's Life. 'Well why not – if you want to…' But, John wrote, 'she soon found he was gossiping & passing on things she told him in confidence. She then dropped him.'

In Ménerbes, May 1997

While on a trip together to stay at a friend's house in Provence in May 1997, John invited me to write Iris's biography. This would be a commission eased by the time we were spending together, and I accepted. I had recently taken early retirement, at fifty-one, from university life. Turning to this new task resembled moving through a looking-glass. It was intimidating to experience vicarious intimacy with someone who had been for decades a source of awe. I suspected that I had in some sense never known her and felt spooked. Michael Holroyd once remarked that any biography-writing can 'put one on the rack'. But it must surely be unusual for a biographer to be acting simultaneously as one of his subject's principal carers: the sense of being eaten up by another consciousness became doubly overwhelming. I tried to make light of this when I wrote 'As she gradually forgot her past, I rediscovered it'. One reviewer commented acidly, 'So that's alright then'. I sympathised: yet the alternative to sounding glib would have meant baring my soul – a boastful distraction. When – no doubt appearing haunted – I ran into Michael Holroyd he would quip pleasantly, 'I'm glad you're looking like that: it augurs well'. I felt ambivalent about the idea of biography. At its best it belongs to high literature and can paint a whole age. But such manifestations were rare and there seemed few depths to which it could not stoop. I sympathised with those – like E.P. Thompson's widow Dorothy – who felt distaste for so-called 'instant biography' before the dust has settled, and while there are survivors to be offended and hurt; not necessarily by scandal, but simply by reading an alternative narrative about someone you loved. (Dorothy nonetheless gave me permission to write a life of her brother-in-law, Iris's Oxford suitor, the poet and Partisan fighter Frank Thompson.)

Diffidence about invading privacy was not the whole story. When an old friend asked whether my bias in her favour might cause me to suppress the uncomfortable, I determined never to do so. I would try to evoke someone multi-faceted, and celebrate contradictions and discontinuities. Much that in her work had appeared romance or fantasy, I now came to understand for the first time, had roots or echoes within her own strange and eventful life. If I felt overwhelmed by the task it was doubtless in part because of my identification with her: to traduce her would be to betray myself.

'Was it terrific?' asked Natasha Spender, going on to explain that she meant 'Was terror involved in the writing?' There were indeed memorable panic attacks during the writing and run-up to publication: in Dublin, Belfast, Oxford, London and elsewhere. I tried to explain my fears to my mother, who briskly riposted that there was no point in my worrying since – if the Queen Mother were to die in the week of publication – no one would pay the biography any attention whatsoever. The Queen Mother survived: but the Tuesday of publication week saw 9/11 instead. The National Portrait Gallery launch went ahead nonetheless, where my mother was charmed by Denis Healey kissing her hand. Few copies of any book were selling, for many weeks, in New York.

My wish to be a good apprentice was also complicated by proximity of every kind. Jim (a psychotherapist) was one morning seeing a patient who had for years been obsessing about Iris's novels when she wandered by mistake into his therapy room: the patient looked appropriately shell-shocked and ruminative. On another occasion, after visiting Leo Pliatzky, I got into a District line underground carriage and found myself sitting exactly opposite John and Iris, en route for lunch with Audi Villers. Astonished and delighted by a happenstance that would have been deemed improbable in an Iris novel, we joined forces.

***

In 1981 I had published an article dealing with a woman character in Iris's fiction who conducts numerous emotional intimacies simultaneously: Anna in *Under the Net*, charged with 'emotional promiscuity', whose character is 'not all it should be' and who yearns for love 'as a poet longs for an audience'; Antonia in *A Severed Head,* who when told 'It turns out everyone is in love with you', comically replies 'I am rather good at it'; Lady Millie in *The Red and the Green* visited by four different suitors on the same night; Morgan in *A Fairly Honourable Defeat.* The long sequence of vamps came to an end in *Nuns and Soldiers* (1980) where Anne Cavidge enters a convent, having lived a wild youth conducting two, even three, affairs at the same time, keeping the victims happy by lying before wholly going beyond this. She regards her youth as what she terms 'a teaching, something laid down from the very start'. Iris, as we have seen, condensed all her Platonism during the Gifford lectures into the phrase 'Chaste love teaches', a slogan by whose truths she tried to live: no accident that her most detailed attempt at depicting a good man – Stuart in *The Good Apprentice* – is given the quality of sexual coldness as one token of his virtue.

Iris was clearly invested in these vamp-figures herself, and yet I do not believe she considered herself 'promiscuous'. The narrator in *A Word-Child* pronounces early on (p.3) 'There is nothing like early promiscuous sex for dispelling life's bright, mysterious expectations', and she stood behind this judgement in interview with Adam Mars-Jones. John commented to me that an unconscious vamp might be deadlier than a conscious one; he also suggested that there is nothing that cannot be said or written, if one can only find the right tone and style.

So, how should a biographer write about his subject's faults? About Plato's predisposition towards envy Iris observed that 'Philosophers attack their own faults'. Since she for her part repeatedly attacked egoism, romanticism, vanity, solipsism, fantasy and the will-to-power, it should not therefore surprise if she shows evidence of all of the above, especially before her marriage in 1956. Indeed part of her intellectual legacy is a revival of the importance ceded to the inner life, an entity divided and at war between low, half-conscious motives, and higher ideals. Without having pondered her own frailties, she could not have argued this with clarity or force; and her writings would lack their charge of truth.

A related idea was expressed by her old friend E.P. Thompson: 'I have no objection to reminders that persons of genius share all the infirmities of other mortals. Their particular infirmities … often help us to understand their genius. But it is, in the end, the plus of genius, and not the lowest common denominator of infirmity, which gives their lives importance'. I believe that Iris might have shared this view.

To write the biography of a recently dead writer carries risks in a way that commemorating someone who died a century or more ago does not. Richard Holmes confided that he could not have done the former: the risks of causing offence, albeit unwittingly, are much greater. I agreed that the biographer may not use privileged information when this could hurt survivors – one of many dangers of 'instant biography'. There was so much in Iris's story that to delay disseminating some of this did not damage the coherence of my account. Nearly twenty years after Iris's death, some stories I held back can now be told. I was scarcely in a position to sit in judgement on her or anybody's promiscuity. I did not stop loving her, but my devotion became less fantasy-ridden and a little more grown-up.

In Wales with Jim

19. Strange Beginnings and Endings

The purpose of this section is to explore my own discipleship: the biography's back-story, and also those matters that I either edited in the biography or 'smoothed out'. Some stories I omitted because they would have disturbed John Bayley, Philippa Foot, or others. Revisiting such matters now that the survivors have gone is both a selfish pleasure and an attempt, for the historical record, to resolve some contradictions. Moreover the 'learning' entailed in writing biography does not always end with publication so that the work is in some sense never finished: some matters have only recently come into focus.

That the husband of my subject was sometimes inaccurate raised problems for me both as biographer and as friend. I took it as axiomatic that a biographer may not knowingly cause hurt to the living, especially when the principal witness concerned is a close and deeply admired friend. John's brave literary criticism, with its lonely and unfashionable championing of 'character', had long mattered almost as much to me as Iris's novels. The belief that the biographer may not wound survivors caused quandaries in writing, which I coped with by skating over or minimising some contentious issues.

***

John has recorded that Iris and his mother Olivia Bayley met for the very first time at Iris's and his civil wedding in Oxford in 1956. As if to emphasise both the novelty of this situation, and her own innocence, Olivia is evoked comically congratulating Iris's youthful-looking mother Rene on having married John, mistaking her for her daughter. This boasts a fine and picturesque disregard for conventional behaviour. It is amusing and bohemian; it also suggests that both courtship and its end were carefree.

It offers a simplified narrative, shorn of ambiguity, contingency and the messiness and unhappiness of real life. However this incident never happened and significantly misrepresents what did.

It was in fact Aunt Florisse (aka Flummie) Bayley, flying in as she did fresh from Chicago and thus knowing few of the main characters, who mistook mother for daughter. If John's fiction implies that Olivia and Iris had yet to become friends, then – for reasons that will become clear – it carries, unwittingly, some uncomfortable reality. But John is sometimes an unreliable narrator.

A careful reader might feel confused when, some pages on, John Bayley asserts that Olivia had *barely* met Iris before the wedding. Had the two in fact met? Or had they never met? What might constitute 'barely meeting'? Might it be that John feared being caught out in a fabrication and offers this 'barely meeting' as a sop to those in the know? Christopher Heywood was a Rhodes Scholar from South Africa writing his B.Litt on the history of the novel under Lord David Cecil's supervision in 1952-4. John and he during their toil at the Bodleian Library had tea most days in Joe's café in the covered market. He remembers a small party for Iris and John in the latter's room in St Antony's, with both his mother Olivia and Iris present, probably during the summer of 1954.

Evidence for Olivia and Iris being known to one another before the marriage comes from another source: Gloria Richardson had known John from 1941 on and sufficiently well to accompany him to Britten's *Rape of Lucretia* at Glyndebourne when it re-opened in 1946. Olivia and Jack approved of Gloria, a cavalry officer's daughter from a landed Scots family. By around 1954 Gloria considered John a significant part of her life and she was often invited to Nettlepole, his parents' house, by John's parents, who might perhaps have welcomed her as a future daughter-in-law. Although she and John were not engaged, they took successive holidays together, the first on the French Riviera, the second a week in Rome and Sicily. Though never lovers, they sometimes shared a bedroom simply to save money. On one such occasion John's bag upturned and condoms fell out, items on whose use he claimed Iris insisted together with pessary and spermicide.

Olivia was – in a striking phrase of John's – 'insanely ambitious' for her three sons to marry well and accordingly never made any attempt to hide either her deep disappointment with Agnes Whatmore, who married her eldest son David, confirming him in evangelical Christianity, or her initial disdain and hostility towards Iris to whom, when John tried to introduce them, she at first took a deep dislike. John's reference to a 'bare meeting' encompasses this snub. Gloria was put out when Iris appeared on the scene, as also when she took lodgings near Ashford, five miles from the Bayley home in Little Chart, so that John could 'sneak off' for occasional liaisons with her. John would pretend to be meeting Gloria when his rendezvous was actually with Iris: Gloria was being used as a smoke-screen.

Iris did not fit the bill. She was six years older than John, by no means in 1955/56 yet a household name and Olivia would complain bitterly about Iris 'hanging around'. Iris was in her turn long-suffering and patient. Olivia had been equally put out when in the 1940s her favourite child Michael formed a strong attachment that turned out life-long to the wife of his commanding officer, and only slightly appeased when by a series of chances she became Duchess of Norfolk.

Tangential evidence about how Iris may at first have been perceived by the Bayley family as by other Little Chart villagers is to be found in a novel by H.E. Bates. John's father Major Jack Bayley liked watching cricket on his neighbour H.E.'s TV and also organising the annual village cricket match with him, a match in which Michael Bayley (John's beloved middle brother) always batted early. Bates and the Bayleys were good friends and Jack appears in many Pop Larkin novels as the comically down-at-heel Brigadier wearing absurdly moth-eaten tweeds.

In *A Breath of French Air* (1959) a dowdy bluestocking named Iris Snow, 'the oddest female [Pop] had ever seen in his life', has a walk-on part. This parody of Murdoch is painfully funny: she sports school-girl socks, a rough school-girl bob and an air of bloodless surprise, and is given to words like 'ossuary' that Pop thinks *très snob*. She alternates silence with sententious speeches. She experiences difficulties aligning her breasts and is mad about relics, saints, and France itself. Bates rewards her francophilia with a French waiter. Bates's satirical view was probably not a million miles away from Jack and Olivia's.

There was a further reason for Bayley family disapproval. Gloria at this time worked as private secretary to publisher George Weidenfeld at his small firm Weidenfeld and Nicholson on Cork Street. She was understandably curious about Iris, with whom she knew John to be romantically involved, and asked Antonia Fraser, an editorial assistant with knowledge of Oxford life through her father Frank Longford – then teaching at

Christ Church – about her. Antonia reported Iris's then 'notorious' reputation as lesbian, something Jack and Olivia were, Gloria believes, well aware of. Nor was Iris perceived as the passive recipient only of the affections of other women, as in John's memoir, a kind of 'unmoved mover': she was quite capable, in the opinion of one witness, of instigating same-sex romances. She had moreover acquired a reputation for being a woman either indifferent to or unmoved by convention: in the word memorably used in this connection by Philippa Foot: 'ungovernable'.

John's memoir simplifies their courtship. He omits mention of his first fiancée, Katherine Watson, like Iris six or seven years older than him, who broke off their intense relationship in late 1953 by running away to become a Catholic nun. But he was not by 1955 simply the wholly inexperienced creature he pretends. There are other omissions or sleights-of-hand. He claims that Iris in the 1950s was 'mildly in favour of country sports' including fox-hunting, albeit admitting that she hated and protested at a fox being killed near their house. The Iris of 1989 befriended Roger Scruton, a champion of fox-hunting, and if she had – conceivably – by then relaxed her hostility towards that sport, it is unimaginable that the passionately Left-wing Iris of 1960 felt the same way. Change is being smoothed out here and simplified in the name of some sort of radical innocence.

That their marriage became in the end legendarily happy needs also to be emphasised. John provided Iris with a much-needed emotional stability: he offered unconditional love and simple common sense. He thereby grounded her as probably few others could have done and was within a decade of their marriage indispensable. Moreover his influence on her cannot easily be over-estimated. They shared common views on many matters, starting with the history of the novel. Even her changing views of Ireland owed much to John, grandson of an Irish builder, and whose middle brother, working in Intelligence, was stationed for two years during the Troubles in Ulster.

***

John's exposure in his three memoirs of Iris in her last illness made him enemies. Together with the film that followed, they ensured that Iris is nowadays remembered not only for her novels and her brave pioneering philosophy but for her love-life and final illness. Some thought he could have channelled his grief and evoked some of the complexities of his (in the end) notably happy marriage by writing his account and then banking the draft for posthumous use only. The first memoir was published during Iris's life-time and seemed to be an act of appropriation, and a seeing-off of rivals for her affection. Iris had formerly belonged to her readers and friends; now, finally and unsettlingly, she belonged to John, and he was marking this change of ownership. That he made my partner and me dedicatees was partly gratitude for our roles as carers, partly propitiatory.

There were tears and heated rows when John left papers lying around the house in Wales that made clear a second – then a third – memoir was on its way and we confronted him. 'I don't see why I should be silent', John once said. Silence is not a charge that will stick; nor will strict adherence to the truth. John told the *Oxford Times* that few had been present at Iris's cremation. In fact no friend or relative was there: 'We will have none of this charnel ground stuff,' John said with some passion, when I asked about attending.

If his memoirs provoked resentment, his exposure of Iris to immediate public gaze was – at that point – a source of more urgent shock and alarm. In 1998 she wandered unscripted on to live camera in Charlbury Road dishevelled and distraught – and thus onto the 9 o'clock ITV news, with the entire nation as potential audience. The affront, grief and fear this caused marked a nadir. Taking Iris out to parties at a stage in her illness when this distressed her caused further bewilderment. A party for her in Lanzarote in spring 1998 offered an early clue that such gatherings could now be a source of suffering. Later that year she was none the less present, visibly upset, at the launch party of John's first memoir in Blackwells in Oxford. These public events won him a little breathing space, but were gratuitous and unkind. Not many months before Iris's death the novelist Anna Haycraft found herself seated at the same table at the Dorchester Hotel, at a gathering to celebrate a literary prize, and was bemused that John had Iris – plainly disorientated and in mental pain – in tow. Although he appeared deaf to criticism, we at that stage probably censured John more for these public abductions and displays than for the memoirs, which she was after all beyond reading.

Tony Quinton's close friendship with John went back over fifty years: when in 1955 he and John were both elected fellows of New College in the same week, so bad was John's stammer that Tony Quinton gave the speech of acceptance for both. His *Spectator* review of John's first memoir contrasted Iris, 'unworldly all the way through', with John who 'is unworldly by choice'. This contrived to suggest that he was not – deep down – unworldly at all. Quinton ends '[The Memoir] should perhaps be seen as John Bayley's way of keeping himself going as Iris Murdoch's devoted custodian.' That is also barbed: 'keeping himself going' implies both a way of surviving and also a way of presenting himself, a way of appearing.

There were strict limits to his worldliness, however. When we watched Princess Di's funeral on a neighbour's TV in Wales in 1997 Iris declared how moving she found it and John alone was dry-eyed, irritated by so much emotionalism. He sat up only once, when the coffin was wheeled on: 'Good Lord, that's a 1916 gun-carriage', he announced '13-pounder if I'm not mistaken' and then, after 'Candle in the Wind' was sung, 'Who exactly is this Elton Jim?'

The second review that John took to heart was by another old friend, Katherine Duncan-Jones in the *TLS*. They had known one another since 1959, when he sent, to the wrong city, the postcard telling her she had been invited for an interview at Oxford. He later encouraged A.N. Wilson and Duncan-Jones's courtship and the Bayleys attended their wedding. John was always accident-prone, she recounts, given to 'sweetly babyish, naughty-child gaffes' and getting away with them, so that potential misfortunes often came out right. This might imply that he was, in Irish parlance, 'a bit of a chancer', an opportunist.

When asked on *Woman's Hour* what she thought of these memoirs, Iris's oldest and closest friend Philippa Foot replied wryly, 'I could have lived without them'. If there are breaches of good taste in the memoirs, there are also incidental half-truths. One photo is captioned 'Iris taking her mother to the ceremony at which she was made a Dame of the British Empire'. Iris became DBE in 1987 two years after her mother's death. The photo in question records her CBE award in 1976. That is of little consequence. His claim to have tried 'to keep the house clean' is silly: after his second marriage rats had to be evicted or poisoned in the outhouse. His assertion that Iris never slept with a woman either before or after marriage is stranger. Leaving aside the uncertainty about her exact relations with her St Anne's colleague Peter Ady, Iris's relationship with her St Anne's colleague Margaret Hubbard, which came close over two to three years (1959-63) to destroying the marriage, was undoubtedly sexual and widely known. And Philippa Foot recorded a brief physical affair with Iris in 1968.

When challenged John replied disarmingly, 'Why should *I* tell the truth?'. Others concur that John simply 'could not be bothered' to disagree with most people, though he had often secretly strong opinions. Gloria Richardson agrees that John was privately a person of strong views, which he was often 'too lazy' to disclose. He had a habit of agreeing slavishly with his interlocutor, whoever that was: he was 'very, very quaint'. But he also had always, she added, as well as brilliance, a kind heart. If caught out John liked to quote Parolles's bleak maxim in *All's Well That Ends Well* IV, iii: 'Simply the thing I am shall make me live'.

20. Organised Innocence

Moral questions are – and should be – raised for the biographer as his knowledge increases in the process of understanding his subject. When we first became friends in the early 1980s the attraction I experienced to Iris appeared to me to have a physical element – for all that she was my mother's age, a topic we once touched on obliquely and then permanently put aside. Andrew Harvey, pre-dominantly gay despite sharing Caroline Blackwood's life for a while, experienced the same. Iris's propensity for romantic friendships or *amitiés amoureuses*, which somehow carefully blurred the line between ordinary affection and desire, is very strange. She told Philippa Foot in 1964 that she was 'sort of quasi in love with about ten of my friends' and Georg Kreisel a little later that 'I can't divide friendship from love or love from sex – or sex from love &tc If I care for somebody I want to caress them...Sex is something very very diffused for me'. That did not necessarily mean going to bed; it could mean serious kissing.

As my researches revealed their extent, I had difficulties understanding Iris's extra-marital relationships. I could imagine being in love with two people but, the idea of being in love with ten mystified and confused me. Something other than appetite, as Philippa Foot observed, was at work: perhaps power? The fact of the matter is that she fell in love with people's minds first, and almost incidentally and later, sought to give that some diffuse physical expression: love was often an aspect of discipleship. Her lovers were not famous for youth or good looks, to which she seemed indifferent. Many were on the contrary, in the American sense of the word, homely and some considerably older than she was.

Was the reviewer accurate who proposed that Iris in the end loved nobody but herself? That is neatly reductive but – blessed by her love myself – I don't recognise this description. Her friends felt held by her in a gaze that was – if in some ways unaccountable – none the less always steady and compassionate and full of good will. A letter from her was always a thrilling event; a meeting more so. Her presence calmed you down and cheered you up. I agree with another writer who wrote that Murdoch was determined to be a force for good in the lives of those she loved, and the overwhelming sense from reading her recently published letters, as from talking to many friends, is that she managed it.

***

In my biography of the soldier-poet Frank Thompson, I recounted how his suicidal decision to enter Bulgaria in May 1944 may have been influenced – *inter alia* – by his receiving Iris's news that she had been bedding his old school-friend and rival M.R.D. Foot. That this news influenced Frank's end still seems to me possible. Though my book was well received, some saw Iris as Kali, goddess of destruction. 'Destroyer of men', one reviewer called her. This downplays Frank's own remarkably self-destructive romanticism. It also ignores the fact that Iris's letter-cards arrived after a period during which Frank and she had not set eyes on one another for over three years of war, years when even my staid and conventional mother confessed that the old rules governing sexual morality were in suspense or irrelevant. Finally, when Iris wrote to Frank about her love-life, she was also evidently (both from the tone of her surviving letters and also from the letter that he wrote her in reply) appealing to his wisdom and seeking his guidance, which he duly attempted to give.

Despite decades of feminism, a double standard still obtains: men are forgiven their wild oats and women condemned or punished. Lara Feigel's *The Love-Charm of Bombs: Restless Lives in the Second World War* shows how tolerant war-time sexual morality was: Graham Greene at one point ran three women as well as visiting prostitutes, but he stays un-rebuked by critics. Kingsley Amis's promiscuity is tolerated with good humour. The same charity is not extended to Dame Iris, whose life example was belittled by a *LRB* woman editor in 2010. (A number of young women dons have nevertheless written, from Oxford and London Universities, to declare how important a model to them Murdoch has been.)

This tendency towards harsh judgement was no doubt given momentum when A.N. Wilson published *Iris Murdoch as I Knew Her*, with its centrepiece discovery by John of Iris and Eric Christiansen making love on a 'black leather sofa'. This, Christiansen wrote to me, is 'not to be taken seriously. [Wilson] and John did call in on me after dinner on 18

March 1974 but all the rest is Andrew's novelistic imagination … I thought he was a friend and still can't work out what made him write this stuff or for what purpose'. John did not read Wilson's book, limiting himself to the quip that Wilson's malice was, after all, 'quite impersonal'.

After I wrote that Iris, despite her busy love-life, 'rarely forfeited the regard' of past lovers, only M.R.D. Foot protested, pointing out that 'a lasting coolness' supervened in his case. Foot, his third wife and Iris lunched together on one occasion but his point is accurate and his hurt at her cruelty to him during World War II was still vivid to him when he spoke of it in the Savile Club in 1997. He is one of two great exceptions. Her sometime lover Fred Broadie would ring me from Massachusetts fifty years after his affair was over to safeguard her reputation; her ex-fiancé Wallace Robson came to see her in Edinburgh when she gave the Gifford lectures in 1982 and, shortly before his death in 1993, reflected that 'Iris was always so mysterious'. The other great exception to this rule is Canetti, whose lasting malice towards her for somehow plundering his very soul and then exploiting this theft in her novels merits special consideration in a separate chapter.

For Galen Strawson, Murdoch was always disabled by her self-insulating and self-denying power. 'Lost in the vast selfishness of her odd lack

Iris with Tom Phillips's sketches of her (c. Leo Phillips)

of ego', as he brilliantly puts this, she was destined to squash more sensitive creatures, partly because she failed to recognise her own weight. There is truth in this, and Foot was just such a victim; and yet when John Bayley says each relationship was innocent, he also knew what he was talking about.

***

Innocence is a leading theme of John's first book about her, *Iris, a Memoir*. He uses it variously to mean harmlessness or guiltlessness, unworldliness, and to evoke situations lacking complication and given to simplicity. 'Shared innocence', he tells us, is what brought them together. 'One reason we fell in love and got on so well, is that both of us have always been naïve and innocent, at some deep healing level…'. They were ideal co-children sharing a world of play. He also argued that Iris desired that each of her relationships should be 'special and separate, as innocent as in the garden of Eden, …what she felt about each of them was totally genuine and without guile'.

John's willingness to manage his own jealousy was one *cost* of this innocence. He had agreed the price in advance. He wrote to Iris two years before they married: 'Darling, … I could live in any contradiction indefinitely with you, and never mind the mornings when one wakes early & alone.' This leaves no doubt about his consent to an 'open marriage': to her continuing to have lovers and to the complexities that must ensue. He repeated this assent in 1956 with a conceit about being turned into a bat so that he could 'hang inconspicuously upside down in the corner of your ceiling while you did your work or entertained your lovers.' He agrees, bat-like, to be a mute witness to her creative output and to her infidelities alike.

Watching him closely over some years, I felt that there *was* a cost. John often had little certainty about who had and who had not – after marriage in 1956 – been a lover of Iris's. Tact was necessary when this became clearer, in working out what (if anything) to say. When Iris started her *amitié amoureuse* with her RCA student David Morgan, she wrote, 'I have, by the way mentioned your existence in general terms to John, who trusts me absolutely and never wants to hear details. All that side of things is OK.' Some matters he did not need to know about; others he decided not to know about. He had to repress his own natural curiosity; and this became harder once big alterations to Cedar Lodge were completed during 1964. Moving a staircase and knocking down internal walls enlarged the hall and produced a larger space for entertaining. It also meant that Iris was very rarely able to make private telephone calls. She apologised to Brigid Brophy in 1966 for her 'slightly crazed air' on the telephone: this was due to John standing beside her asking 'Who's that? What do they want?' She felt solicitude about John's 'tendency to mope like a dog in kennels' when she was absent. Iris's patience on the telephone sometimes maddened him and I remember him – a propos Sir Malcolm Williamson, who was capable of talking with her for more than one hour – quoting some words from a comical song he had learnt long ago in Occupied Germany in 1946, '*ich liebe dich… aber nur telefonisch*' [I love you but only telephonically].

Brophy, who was in love with Iris, planned in the 1960s to write to John to request his agreement to allowing Iris to spend more time with her. 'No, don't write to John.', Iris advised. 'He is on the brink of being jealous of you, and if it's formally stated that you and he compete for my time I think this would just annoy him. Things are much better left vague and nebulous'. She avoided overtly deceiving John by simply not confiding in him and keeping her liaisons 'in the dark'. This was not always easy. He was evidently divided between a desire to be in-the-know and an equal desire to rest in ignorance.

John had other causes for jealousy. Perhaps the stark choice between a noble-and-heroic love-narrative – the verdict greeting his first memoir – versus a jealous-revenge-script, the judgement of many reviewers on his third, is a false one. The opposition itself is a simplification: John deeply loved Iris *and* was jealous of her. The two conditions were – as with most of us – interdependent. It may be relevant that he started writing a second novel after publishing his first – *In Another Country* – in 1955. In a January letter the same year to his old friend Michael Howard he says 'Publishing date Feb. 7th approx. Hope the next one (just starting) will be better'. Penelope Lively, reading modern history at St Anne's, thought he finished this second novel. If so, exactly like Iris, he had good reason to conceive himself an apprentice novelist. Yet he abandoned fiction-writing for the next forty years until Iris stopped writing, when he published a further four novels, none of which fulfilled the brilliant promise of his first. When asked why this long pause he would reply sadly that Iris's career had been 'simply too meteoric': he wished not to appear to compete.

***

It is hard, when reading her letters, not to regret that she spent so much time and energy on friends perhaps unworthy of her solicitude. Brigid Brophy wanted a physical relationship that Iris refused and emulated the frustrated lover in Sonnet 129: 'murd'rous, bloody, full of blame, / Savage, extreme, rude, cruel, not to trust'. She would dismiss both Iris and her novels as rubbish. Iris was patient and resourceful in meeting Brophy's insults with calm affection. She charged Brophy in 1964 'You are the one who advocates *promiscuity* and ergo lust. I am, austere puritan, against it.... And of course I also commend seriousness'. About this time her RCA student David Morgan's deep insecurities rendered him treacherous. She could see this, and was capable of fury with him, but nonetheless wrote to him 'I am very steady in my attachments'. And so, on the whole, she proved.

If there is a moral ambiguity here, it is one well-focussed when she describes Tom in *The Philosopher's Pupil* as either relaxing or – alternatively – expanding his ego to accommodate others 'according to one's point-of-view'. The result in any case is a healing one, and what she terms 'a movement of salvation'. If there is an element of healthy narcissism in Iris's ability to accommodate her friends' grossest faults, there is equally an element of altruism, and it is not always easy to distinguish these two. She practiced magnanimity, the single virtue said by Buddhists to entail recouping power by surrendering it.

***

In 7 April 1956 Iris wrote, 'And every day feel deep deep relief at being free; and joy at all the freedom & simplicity of my love for JB. Back again in a world of simplicity & truth. Truth bought at *that* price.' What price? It is unlikely that by that date she meant relinquishing Canetti, a matter by then settled; more likely that she meant renouncing a satisfactory love-life. I never broached this topic, but noted that talking to me on three successive occasions John tried out, as it were, contradictory accounts, rather like someone trying on different hats in a hat-shop before making a purchase. Firstly he claimed that, like Iris's parents, theirs was a *mariage blanc*, unconsummated; next that their love-life was first-rate; finally he opted for somewhere between these last two, which was probably accurate.

Close friends – as has been noted – attested how unsteadily the Bayley marriage started out. John confided his unhappiness to Gloria Richardson, to whom he wrote around 1957 saying he wished that he had married her instead; Iris confided separately in Leo Pliatzky and in Philippa Foot, to whose flat she around 1960 envisaged fleeing. The period 1959-63 probably saw a succession of scenes, some brinkmanship, and a showdown or two, especially when Iris threatened to leave John and live with her colleague Margaret Hubbard instead. Iris methodically edited her journals around 1990 to conceal (or even rewrite) much of this. Careless traces remain: marital conflict is implicit when she wrote in July 1962 (or 1963) 'I wish I were not so decisively and hopelessly divided from my chance of ordinary happiness. Yes, yes, exiling myself from it'.

Richard Wollheim recalled how much Iris liked compartmentalising her friendships and affairs and characterised her love of intricate dissimulation as 'Shakespearian'. One chill example survives in her letters. Her friendship/affair with the Treasury civil servant Leo Pliatzky went back to pre-war Oxford days. Although she did not finally lose her virginity until three years later, Leo remembered their time alone together in her bedroom in her parents' house in Chiswick in 1939. They were briefly lovers in 1946, and picked up their affair after Iris started teaching at the RCA in 1963, when she spent Tuesday and Wednesday nights in term-time at her newly rented flat off Redcliffe Square. On Sunday 24 October 1965 Iris wrote, 'Leo dear, am I to dine with you and Jean on Tuesday? ...I *did*, officially, have lunch with you recently. Didn't I? And I *have* read your novel? Please brief – best RSVP to 59 Harcourt Terrace SW10'. Jean and Leo Pliatzky had been happily married for seventeen years. Iris quizzes Leo in order to get their stories straight so that they don't incriminate one another or arouse the suspicions of Leo's wife that they are lovers and that Jean is an injured party. This dissimulation is methodical if not cold-blooded. She ended the affair a little later.

***

In *A Severed Head* Martin, the narrator, early invents a striking and perfect phrase to describe the 'idle thoughtless happiness never to come...ever in my life again' while he is two-timing his wife Antonia with his mistress Georgie: 'I was happy ... with [the] particular quality of a degenerate innocence'. The phrase 'degenerate innocence' bears contemplation: it wonderfully proposes that innocence in and of itself can be guilty. Iris's novels often show how false innocence must be transcended so it can be recuperated as understanding or wisdom. Thus Otto in *The Italian Girl* says, 'Sin is a sort of unconsciousness, a not knowing', instancing the 'dreaming, swimming, dazed Eve of Ghislebertus at Autun' as an iconic depiction of this unconsciousness. This theme of degenerate innocence flowers memorably in *The Black Prince,* where wickedness is often 'the product of a semi-deliberate inattention, a sort of swooning relationship to time … we ignore what we are doing until it is too late to alter it'.

Like Martin, Otto and Bradley – and like all who account themselves seekers – Iris wanted to discover what lay beyond 'degenerate innocence'. From this stand-point the myth of the Fall belongs *inside* the spiritual quest; and the best innocence might be what Blake termed 'organised innocence': the innocent vision of a child informed by the wisdom and experience of an adult.

Iris in Lanzarote, 1984

21. Philippa Foot

The name of Philippa Foot – the distinguished Oxford philosopher – recurs far more often over half a century in Iris's journals than that of anyone else; and she was arguably Iris's closest as well as longest-standing friend. Philippa soon said to me of Iris's biography, 'I'm so glad it's you'. If she, like others, confided in me, I don't flatter myself that this was owing solely to my own shining qualities of character. She explained that she could not have cooperated with A.N. Wilson: 'He would have made us all feel dirty'. Fears of being maligned or traduced, as of Iris's strange and eventful history being cheapened or short-changed, brought new friendships about: Joanna Kilmartin, Anne Wollheim, Natasha Spender. But I learnt that almost everyone wished their story to be heard, and to understand how this story intersected with that of Dame Iris.

Through writing the biography I forged a friendship with Philippa that was both personally important and also vital to me as biographer. I first met Philippa – I use first-names for brevity's sake – at a lunch party for eight at Iris and John's in Charlbury Road on a sunny day in December 1997; Iris beamed with palpable delight that she was helping bring us together, a happiness Philippa and I were warmed by. She was witty, tall, elegant, she wore trousers and she stooped a little. She resembled one of those lofty cartoon English patricians Mark Boxer evoked on the covers of Anthony Powell's *Dance to the Music of Time* novels.

Philippa played the role over some sixty years of Iris's elder sister, both stalwart yet unconsciously judgemental. Iris in 1945 had described 'brilliant and darling Pip' as 'very tender & adorable, yet morally tough and subtle, and with lots of will & self-control'. So she proved half a century later. This chapter explores some effects of her will and self-control in encouraging the writing of the biography and proposing ways in which it might be shaped and edited.

Philippa and I were soon close, meeting often in London, Oxford, at our weekend house in Wales, and travelling once to Bulgaria. 'Come at a *relaxed* four-o-clock', she would write, in her own distinctive idiom. If I returned from a trip abroad when my partner was away, I would find a post-card from her welcoming me back: 'I know these moments of slight desolation as one arrives alone', she wrote. This was, she explained, a kind habit her and Iris's tutor Donald MacKinnon had taught both of them: to attenuate the sense of alienation and loneliness that can overtake the soul in transit. It was also quixotic: it went with the Philippa who helped pioneer Oxfam and looked after Hungarian refugees in Oxford from 1956 on. Such gestures were touching.

Around 2000 I started to recognise how Iris had borrowed aspects of Philippa to create Paula in *The Nice and the Good*. It shocked me to see that – contrary to her frequent claim that drawing from life was 'taboo' – Iris had done precisely that. Paula is described as 'foxy-faced': an exact evocation of Philippa's long aristocratic face with its expressive air of high intelligence verging on shrewdness or craftiness. She thought carefully before speaking quizzically.

Paula has the same letters – P and A – as Philippa at the beginning and end of her name. Paula's pronouncement 'Everyone invites a divorced woman' is a recognisable echo of Philippa's own brave wit after her husband abandoned her in 1959. The account of her relationship to 'Mary', who has some character and physical traits of Iris, recalls their real-life friendship. The fictional characters Paula and Mary have like Philippa and Iris been friends since college. Paula is said to be an uncompromising person whom Mary experiences at times as an unconscious prig: the strength and clarity of Paula's being, her meticulous accuracy and truthfulness 'reproach' the mediocrity and muddle which Mary feels to be her own natural medium. At other times by contrast Paula's coolness, her detachment and peculiar virtue soothe Mary's nerves.

All of this recalls in a very literal manner some of the ways Iris experienced Philippa, who recognised this evocation when I pointed it out. She wrote: 'Perhaps she saw me as someone she could never quite seduce like all the others. I think that I did present myself as an immovable object; which would fit with your idea that I was Paula the unconscious prig.....'

***

Iris had noted wryly of one of Philippa's letters 'order of legibility one out of ten btw' and Philippa apologised for her eccentrically elongated and spidery hand-writing. Another philosopher friend, Mary Midgley, Philippa vouchsafed, once told her that a graphologist would simply infer from this style of writing that she was 'a very secretive person'. She did not dispute this. Indeed she told me that the philosopher Heinz Cassirer, probably in love with her, once called her 'pathologically discreet', a phrase Iris appropriated to describe Mrs Tinckham in *Under the Net*. She made clear why she would stay away from the launch of my biography in the National Portrait Gallery in 2001. Although she was the biography's co-dedicatee, her privacy was none the less to be safe-guarded.

Philippa of course had lovers, could discuss these relationships and once discoursed briefly about 'recreational sex'. Although she had an upper-class upbringing, it is wrong to see her merely as a 'lady': her disclosures could be as striking as her reticences and she was always interesting and unexpected. It had been Philippa who in 1944 brought Iris the news of Frank Thompson's death; and she astonished me at Frank's grave in Bulgaria in 1998 by opening a bag she was carrying and handing me a single red carnation to place there, as if from Iris. She enjoyed taking centre-stage on occasion. Perhaps from living so much in the USA she took a common sense, pragmatic view of psychotherapy, which she relished and could speak about freely. She liked to be in therapy and was so at the end.

In July 1999 I sounded her out to consider being interviewed for the forthcoming BBC *Omnibus* on Iris that I was to help anchor: 'I am essentially a back-room person, so No. There are many people who can do it. And better'. Similarly, when approached to ask whether she would accept an Honour – possibly a DBE – she declined. As a fiery radical, her disdain for the English establishment and its Honours system was certainly one motive; mistrust of becoming visible may have been another.

She spent weeks carefully destroying quantities of her correspondence and yet prized Iris's letters, keeping them safe and inviting me to make use of them. Having destroyed a suitcase full of Donald MacKinnon's letters, she found a handful remaining and handed these to me on the day Iris was – we knew – dying. We were taking tea together in the state rooms of Magdalen College, where I was Visiting Fellow, when Pip remarked, distraught, that with each death you lose a voice that says your name in a particular way. She had visited the Home the previous week, when Iris had kissed her hands; I had visited that afternoon, when Iris was unconscious yet in evident physical distress, and yellow from liver failure. I went up to my rooms and rang John, who told me Iris had just died. Philippa remarked, 'She was the light of my life', and added 'A good number of people will feel that'. Three months after this death grief was still wearing her out. 'I just get exhausted', she wrote me. An acupuncturist helped her. One year later she wrote that anniversary dates did not usually mean much to her 'but I can't forget this one. It seems to me years since you came downstairs from your room in Magdalen with your eyes so very red.'

In 2004 the film *Closer* came out, with Julia Roberts and Jude Law. Near the start a huge black-and-white close-up of Philippa is on display. This photo belonged in a series of snapshots supposedly taken by Roberts's photographer character: in fact all photos of prominent contemporary philosophers were taken from a revealing series by Steve Pyke and Mick Lindberg: Karl Popper, John McDowell, Peter Geach and G.E.M. Anscombe together, and Philippa. She made things hard for the film company which had omitted to secure her permission: she was not to be 'walked over', or displayed to the cinema-going public. She was not an easy touch.

Her attitude to her own secretiveness was interesting. Discretion partly belonged to her class-conscious yet irritable awareness of having been brought up a 'lady'. Her mother, daughter of President Grover Cleveland, had been born in the White House, the only time a First Lady has given birth there; her father was an industrialist in Kirkleatham, where she was brought up in typical upper-class fashion by governesses who – she quipped – left her ignorant about whether the Romans came before the Greeks.... She and her sister Marion, fox-hunting with local grandees, recalled the hunt in full rig entering Raby Castle hall on horseback. In adult life she used hunting metaphors to illustrate discussions of philosophers: who fell at the first ditch, who were the front-runners. Her gift for philosophy mystified her: believing that she lacked other kinds of intelligence or knowledge, she could not account for it. Yet she knew she was a front-runner all the same. Around the age of eight Philippa suffered abdominal tuberculosis followed by the then 'cure' of sleeping for a year on an out-of-doors balcony in North Yorkshire. That included the winter months. This cruel treatment taught her a hard-won self-sufficiency. Her main source of love and care was their Nanny, whom their mother threatened to sack: the ten-year-old Philippa and her eleven-year-old sister

Marion packed their infant bags to leave home. The death of this good woman in 1976 was a deep loss to her and when, on her ninetieth birthday, she was herself approaching death, Philippa announced that Nanny was waiting for her and that it was time rejoin her. While the product of this background, she felt contempt for its political conservatism and its treatment of women alike. When she won a place at Somerville in 1939 one of her mother's friends had remarked consolingly, 'Never mind, dear: she doesn't *look* clever!' She invented her own adjective – 'dementing' – to describe the vexatious irrationality of the world.

Philippa, California, 1980s (c Norm Schindler)

***

She minded how Iris was represented. She early wrote to me that 'As you say the important thing is to convey an impression of her work, her special charm (not quite the right word) and above all her goodness. Even now it is wonderful to see the old Iris in her total lack of the usual touches of malice & pettiness & self-absorption that most people have. I love to be with her & see her apparent happiness with me....'

A bank statement of Iris's left open and floating around in our house in 1996 in Wales shocked me by having so few monthly direct debits or standing orders: I recall one only, to the NSPCC. I had been brought up to think that giving away a tithe of one's income was what ordinary adults do, a defining characteristic of grown-up citizenship. This account had well over £100,000 in it. Probably Philippa was correct in observing that Iris never had much grip on her finances but – whenever asked directly for help – could be relied on to be generous.

Philippa felt that I must find a way to include 'a good bit' about Dame Iris's confused and confusing early love-life – 'because if you don't other people will.... Yours must be a definitive biography. It should be. But of course there will be many difficulties'. Again, two years later, 'I think it very important that you do not at all gloss over her many affairs, so that no-one can discover a "seam" to mine when the letters become available...'. We agreed that the truth about her 'slightly bizarre tendency to fall in love with half the world' should appear in the context of my admiration for and appreciation of her seriousness, and the way she lived the life of the spirit as well as the flesh. This, she hoped, would 'cut the ground from under the feet of her detractors'. Our views converged. She wrote that 'You know how much I loved her and would guard her reputation. If I allow myself to see something comic in quite so many lovers, I wouldn't want anyone else to be disrespectful'.

She was disgusted, as was Stuart Hampshire, when the distinguished but amoral mathematical logician Georg Kreisel was reported as giving public readings from Iris's letters to his students at Stanford: she was teaching herself then at UCLA. That the architect Stephen Gardiner left piles of her letters stuffed in the glove-box of his Mini so that others could read them bothered her too. She was also alarmed when Iris's letters to David Hicks were bought by the Bodleian: I had added to her fears by warning her that one or two outspoken letters vied with Hicks in their sexual frankness and worldliness.

A dramatic instance of her care came around 1999 when Iris's agent Ed Victor wished to have Iris's journals photocopied. Philippa feared John Bayley's desire to please everyone, or his apparent addiction to the oxygen of publicity, might make him agree to this copying, with its risk of premature dissemination. So Philippa offered to store them in the basement of her house on Walton St. There they lived for many years, safe from public scrutiny. She knew John to be a great literary critic who therefore must care about the truth – and yet, as she put it, 'he doesn't mind what he says' – or, by implication, what he does. If there was something cold-blooded about this appropriation, with which I colluded, there was also relief. John appeared complaisant about this move.

She appreciated that while writing the biography 'there will be many challenges'. When I felt overwhelmed she suggested wisely and wittily: 'Write the biography *without curiosity*': a tough yet helpful proposition. I did not tell her that researching and writing were causing me to suffer panic attacks. She picked up a good deal of my mistrust of my own voyeurism without having to be told. In January 2000, she wrote 'I know those mood swings and jitters myself … and my task [writing her book *Natural Goodness*] is much easier than yours. But I am sure that Iris would say affectionately but understandingly "Don't be afraid Dear Peter"'.

She delighted in one story I passed on to her. André Malraux's friend, a Catholic priest in his nineties, when asked what he had learnt about the human heart from listening to nearly seventy years in the confessional replied: 'There are no grown-ups'. Philippa included this in her monograph.

***

When our friendship began, Philippa later told what became a famous joke: that around 1943 and sharing a flat they decided to tell each other of the men who had asked to marry them. Philippa's 'list' was soon done. As Iris's list went on and on Philippa asked crossly whether it might not save time if Iris listed the men who had *not* yet asked her to marry them. Indeed, they soon competed for Tommy Balogh's attentions, as also for those of Philippa's future husband Michael (M.R.D.) Foot.

'Most friendships exist in a state of frozen and un-developing semi-hostility', remarks Baffin in *The Black Prince*. In order to thaw such a frozen relationship and neutralise him as a potentially hostile witness, Rachel embarks on a serious flirtation with Bradley in that novel: there may be an echo of Iris and Philippa's attempt to break down ancient barriers through embarking on a brief and tentative affair in 1968. It would have been odd had there been no love-hatred, no jealous or dark currents at flow between the two women.

In the novel Rachel's flirtation with Bradley is a not wholly successful manoeuvre: Rachel and Bradley remain locked within a strange paradoxical history of closeness and distance. In an analogous manner the barriers that Iris wanted removed with Philippa did not permanently come down either. Iris's scattered journal references during the next month suggest that the affair only partly resolved the awkwardness they felt with one another. Soon Iris is apologising in her letters to Philippa at having been swallowed up once again by public demands on her time and energy. She and John invented the phrase 'getting owled' for predatory attacks at parties by admirers: new social demands could not always be evaded. And a 1985 journal entry after lunch together runs, typically: 'I was disappointed, as I always am, by seeing Philippa. My fault.'

Meanwhile Iris's fame constantly grew. The disparity between their reputations must on occasion have struck Philippa forcibly. She was far too 'morally tough' and high-minded to have given in to envy, but would have been inhuman never to have experienced that emotion. There was a deep incongruence. All her adult life Philippa had to suffer the mild humiliation of discovering that third parties had cultivated her acquaintance in hopes thereby of gaining an introduction to Iris. The latter's popularity was notable long before she published and is hard to exaggerate after her novelistic success. The long lists of close (often distinguished) friends catalogued in her journals can dizzy the reader.

The attention Iris received as a thinker may on occasion have perplexed or rankled. Iris's philosophic reputation remains higher in the USA than in Oxford and Philippa would account for this by saying 'Iris had a spiritual life' which made little sense to Philippa, who had, instead, a 'moral' life. 'Iris left us, in the end', she would add. Iris's most influential philosophic exemplum is the tale of D and M in *The Sovereignty of Good,* where M (mother-in-law) works hard to re-imagine D (daughter-in-law) in order to perceive her with greater accuracy. This is a fable intended to show the central importance of the hidden inner life: it also proposes that this inner world is more consequential than the outer, public realm celebrated by contemporary philosophers. Philippa sometimes spoke of admirers of this trope as if they must be feeble-minded. I agreed with Martha Nussbaum that the ideas that Murdoch shares with her more conventional contemporaries require for their full exploration her own different and riskier type of writing, which only she, with her complex erotic gifts, attempted to deliver; and I found Iris's philosophy more satisfying because more venturesome. This split was painfully illustrated around 1993 when a Festschrift for Philippa was being put together. Philippa was deputed to invite a contributory essay from Iris, who proffered the script of a lecture on the Ontological Proof in relation to Good, not God. It then fell to Philippa – or so she decided – to turn this down. She used the high-handed excuse that its flavour was 'too theological', while privately fearing that the essay was not yet ready for publication. Perhaps both reasons obtained. If there were remarkable qualities of will-power on display both in enlisting and then in rejecting Iris's contribution, some cruelty was also implicit. Philippa recalled this incident as 'very painful'.

During their so-called 'philosophical' Friday lunches *à deux* that continued into Iris's last illness Philippa would on occasion lock the front door to prevent Iris escaping and walking home or – as she sometimes begged – 'going to Wales'. Determination that John should enjoy respite from care was the reason Philippa gave for this, but John, while enjoying this furlough, also intuited an old asperity between the women, with its roots deep in the past. Philippa was not invited back to Iris and John's and – after Iris's death and his own re-marriage – John allowed his friendship with her to lapse. That was a source of sadness, albeit a workable one.

Philippa and Iris, Wales, 1998

***

She had helped me so generously that on 16 December 2000 I delivered a complete transcript of the biography to her. Nervous about her possible response, I was greatly relieved when she rang twice and enthusiastically. My journal suggests that she reported gratifyingly that it was 'comical, sad, gripping ... you don't know what you've done – don't understand how good it is – it's *marvellous*'. But she had objections and concerns. Some of these appear within a long letter to me. She helped me respect the feelings – and the privacy – of some players in Iris's story. She was hurt when I referred to Oxford philosophy as 'dried up'. Other suggestions she refused to commit to writing and would discuss only face-to face.

I asked her when we met what needed expanding; she mentioned John Bayley's growing and in the end vital importance, and Iris's goodness. It upset her that Donald MacKinnon, who had been obsessionally in love with Iris, had reportedly described her at a dinner-party as 'an evil woman'. Even if he had used these precise words – and Philippa argued that this was reported speech, therefore second-hand and unreliable – he could not have meant it. Deferring to her better judgement I adopted the wording that she thought – knowing Donald so well for half a century – represented the view he might have wished recorded: 'There was real evil there'.

A year before this I had been in touch with Donald's widow Lois, and visited her in Aberdeen. Philippa was hugely relieved, after decades of misunderstanding, that Lois now sent the biography 'all her best wishes', that she avowed that there was never at any time physical expression to Donald's and Iris's affection, that she 'attached no blame' and devoutly wished '"*Requiescant in Pace*" including herself in that prayer'. It seemed probable that Lois may at most have discovered her husband and Iris holding hands, which helps throw light on the scandal in *The Bell* that breaks merely because Michael and Nick are disturbed doing the same. As the narrator of *The Black Prince* observes, 'Only take someone's hand in a certain way and the world is changed for ever'.

Philippa had other anxieties. One was Canetti's contention that Iris had in 1952 laid out Franz Steiner's body, with the scandalous implication that love-making with her had killed him. My partner Jim O'Neill persuaded her that it was important to show Iris as something more and other than a mere bluestocking: that sentence stayed.

But her greatest anxiety concerned Iris's Communist connections. In the summer of 1983 Iris's ex-colleague at St Anne's Jenifer Hart had been hounded by police and journalists after being named in print as a Soviet spy: her husband Professor Herbert Hart suffered a nervous collapse and was for a while institutionalised. Iris, too, had spied during the war for the CP, copying Treasury papers, then leaving these copies in a tree that was a dead-letter drop in Kensington Gardens. Philippa was very alarmed at the possibility of a repeat scandal.

To compound Philippa's fears, her sister Marion, who took over the Seaforth flat Philippa had shared with Iris during the war (and stayed in for nearly sixty years), told me that, when she moved in in August 1945, graffiti on the walls strongly suggested that the flat had been in continuous use as a place for CP cell meetings: since these scribblings were low on the wall, the comrades evidently sat on the floor. Marion believed Iris to have absented herself during these meetings.

I did not remove all mention of her spying but – feeling misgivings – omitted both dead-letter drops and graffiti. In a similar spirit of accommodation I left out all mention of affairs her sister Marion had had, even though these (to my mind) helped show how bohemian and – as it were – Murdochian was the milieu all three shared. At the time that Philippa became Tommy Balogh's lover, Marion entered a liaison with Balogh's childhood friend and fellow-economist Nickie Kaldor, and both Hungarians together with their lovers Philippa, Iris and Marion made use when in London of a small flat in Chelsea Cloisters. 'What tales that flat could have told', Philippa laughed.

Then, in October 2001 the Oxford academic and writer John Jones, the *TLS*'s reviewer of the biography, took me to task for downplaying the theme of espionage. I had written that Iris doubtless copied only 'information of little moment about colleagues and Treasury doings', adding that she would probably not have hesitated to pass on information of greater moment too. But I had no entitlement to make such assumptions. Jones recalled, with much circumstantial detail, Iris telling him in a pub in the late 1940s about her wartime spying and copying of Treasury papers, and mentioning a Captain who was her CP 'minder'. Jones appeared possessive about Iris and about his memories of her – not a rare syndrome: he recorded other memories soon afterwards in an *LRB* Diary.

Two things followed. The first was that Philippa broke off a fifty-year friendship with John Jones and his wife the painter Jean Jones, and never communicated with either again. The second was that the review licensed me in the paperback edition to re-insert the dead-letter drops. The graffiti however I omitted and never mentioned. It may in this connection be recalled that Canetti in *Party in the Blitz* alleges that Iris was involved in spying for the CP abroad post-war. In the event, as we now know, what obsessed the media and wholly overshadowed the news that she had once spied for the CP were details of Iris's last illness and love life.

***

The strange three-way relationship between Iris and John and Jean Jones I rendered anonymous. It is one tribute to the oddnesses of the Bayley marriage that friendship between the two couples survived for so long. The Bayleys never in thirty years invited the Joneses to Steeple Aston but Jean would nonetheless arrive uninvited and unannounced by taxi, interrupting Iris at work until a series of open rows dissuaded her. They must count among the large number of people who saw Iris as their private property. Iris would have drinks in Oxford with John Jones at Jean's instigation, and both Bayleys sometimes had supper, as Jean called it, with them.

The disturbance Rain Carter causes to Mor's marriage in *The Sandcastle* may owe something to Iris's friendship with Donald MacKinnon; it may also owe something to the near ménage-á-trois that she and the Joneses had experimented with. John Bayley spoke often of John Jones as a 'mini-Canetti', also comparing him with Dickens's hypocritical Pecksniff, or with Trollope's sententious Bishop, with Jean playing the role of the domineering Mrs Proudie. Jean in John Bayley's view acted pander and would-be controller of this ménage, thus exasperating Iris and seeing to it that Iris and John Jones's affair never got off the ground. John Jones's lack of deep interest in Iris may also have conduced to matters not proceeding far. Both Joneses were conceited, seeing such an affair as 'no less than their due'. The jealousy between John Bayley and John Jones was recorded in the latter's *Telegraph* obituary: 'Jones minded intensely that his books were not more famous, and that he had not been rewarded by promotion in the academy. It was a very dark day in Holywell Cottage when his great rival – and friend – John Bayley became the Warton Professor of English Literature'. For half a century John Bayley kept his own jealousy somewhat disguised.

***

By comparison with Philippa, John Bayley had few editorial suggestions to my biography and only one big veto, designed to protect his beloved middle brother Michael. Michael was a Brigadier and career soldier who fell in love with the wife of his commanding officer in the Grenadier Guards, Miles Fitzalan-Howard, around 1949. He stayed devoted to Anne over sixty years until her death in 2013, at which he was distraught. Michael died in 2016. Though their relationship was thought to be platonic, Anne, in a sometimes stormy but Catholic and so indissoluble marriage, returned Michael's affection. This pattern of a *cavaliere servente* faithfully in love for years with a married woman first figured in *An Unofficial Rose* in 1962, where Felix Meecham is an army officer loyal to Anne Peronett. Mrs Olivia Bayley upset Iris by charging her with borrowing from life. Exactly this *cavaliere servente* motif recurs in *Nuns and Soldiers* (1980), where the Count has long been in love with Gertrude Openshaw. With notable exceptions it is situational logic rather than character that Iris plunders in her fiction.

Olivia was as we have noted 'insanely' ambitious for the marriages of her sons and not least for Michael, her favourite. She nonetheless chaperoned Michael and Anne on successive holidays in Kenya, Cyprus and Barbados. She must have had increasingly mixed feelings when in 1975, after the death of a cousin, Miles became seventeenth Duke of Norfolk and Anne Duchess. It was Anne Norfolk who found Michael's flat in Pont St, which had belonged to a Norfolk child; Michael who found the Norfolks' house in the Chilterns, in Hambleden, Oxfordshire. In March 1970 Iris noted in her journal '….chez Howards Sunday…. When John and I arrived [Michael] was trimming the laurel hedge outside the house. [Olivia] later: "I hate to see him running round like a tame cat. He has given the whole of his life to that woman…" '.

The Duchess served as Help the Hospices' first chairman, and from 1998 its president; Michael, long retired first from the Army and then the Churches Conservation Trust, worked with her. Like both Felix and the Count he was essentially solitary, with few if any friends, and this solitariness fascinated both Iris and, equally, John – who loved Michael best of all his family, though he claimed never to understand him; (Michael often claimed the same to me of John.)

***

I last visited Philippa in August 2010 when she was bed-ridden and had weeks only left to live. She wanted Proust's account of the death of Bergotte read at her Somerville memorial, which I accordingly did. She had always loved visiting us in Wales, where she made one tradition out of getting up for lunch, saying 'I don't *do* mornings', and another of bringing with her a capon, and porcini to stuff it with, from Oxford market. She now asked what tree we planned to plant in Wales in her memory, and when I said 'a cherry tree' she looked owlish and joked 'Only ONE?!' We duly planted an avenue of trees stretching more than a hundred yards from orchard to lake.

She seemed at peace, inquiring repeatedly 'How are you *really*?'. She minded about the well-being of friends and was not to be fobbed off with shallow or polite replies. She also asked – referring to the biography of Frank Thompson I was writing – 'How is Frank *really*?'

She was incredulous that I had just published some of Iris's letters from the 1940s in *A Writer at War*, which included one from 1945 about her ex-husband Michael having had an affair at Winchester that left him fearful that he might be gay. This hurt and angered him and made him consider – as he told me over lunch – taking me to court: happily a sense of humour and proportion supervened. I did not dream that the *Sunday Times* would acquire serial rights and would foreground the most compromising letters on the cover of its magazine. Philippa spoke of her ex-husband as an 'ass', the faults of whose character as revealed in his autobiography *Memories of an SOE Historian* – snobbery and fabrication – she excoriated, characterising conversation with him nowadays as 'like trying to speak Urdu'.

And then she started to speak, again and again, of the extraordinariness of Iris. She changed the topic for one brief moment to Iris's lover and Somerville colleague Margaret Hubbard, who nearly destroyed her marriage: how unfathomable that Iris should have fallen for someone 'so raucous'. But then she moved back to Iris Murdoch herself. Her last words to me were '*What an astonishing person Iris was… astonishing*'. She died at home on her ninetieth birthday.

22. Canetti's Sting

Canetti was centrally important both to Iris's personal and artistic life; and a profusion of new evidence since my biography was published has made me re-consider their relationship – the biographer's fate. On 8 August 2000 Johanna Canetti sent me transcripts of her father's toxic and scandalous reminiscences of Iris. Three pages of transcript had gone missing and the notes were in a state of confusion. A section concerned with a woman who spied for the CP after the war might refer to Murdoch, or someone else. These notes are entitled by Canetti's stenographer 'Notebooks and Diaries', a form of words whose significance I did not then grasp.

Elias Canetti

Canetti, who had won the Nobel prize for Literature in 1981 and was polyglot, had produced an only child neither especially interested in literature nor able to communicate in English. Indeed, Johanna writes to me only in German. He accordingly found her a disappointment, if not a disgrace. He liked complaining about his womenfolk. His pages find fault with Iris, whom he convicts of every possible sin: of dress, of being 'as ambitious as an arch-criminal', of obtuseness, of low social origins and of pursuing him to start an affair he neither wanted nor found congenial. He thinks her philosophy lame and has little good to say about her novels. He tries to destroy the reputation of his lover, then life-long friend-at-a-distance.

Canetti's biographer recently made clear that this portrait was never meant for publication. Canetti made a distinction between his notebooks, which might be published, and his many diaries, closed until 2024. His writings on Dame Iris resemble diary-entries: they begin, after all, with the key signifier: 'Yesterday, the thick philosophical tome by Iris Murdoch arrived'. 'Yesterday' suggests diary notes. In these *Tagebücher* or diaries he lets rip with – and also disguises – obsessions, rages and moods that he could not otherwise control. His biographer calls this a method of instinctual discharge (*Triebabfuhr*): here was the means by which he calmed himself down, by working himself up. It was how this eighty-eight year-old habitually struggled to regain his equanimity.

Unfortunately the distinction between diaries and notebooks is not always clear, and this licensed his daughter and publisher to proceed in concocting a book parts of which – incidentally – Canetti had destroyed by fire around 1992, 'disgusted', as he put this, 'by the past'. He changed his mind and re-dictated it in 1993. Among the burnt pages were some concerning his intense resentment or grudge against his first wife Veza. By the time he re-wrote, he had displaced this resentment onto Iris Murdoch… He boasts that he idealises some friends; others he chooses to 'dunk in pitch'. That suggests god-like power, exercised randomly. Misogyny is one constant and its target arbitrary.

Johanna Canetti did not tell the editors of his memoir about this burning until some time after its publication in 2003. Had they learnt earlier, they might have reconsidered the appropriateness of going ahead. An English translation was published in 2005 as *Party in the Blitz*. This book helped me come to realise that there were dark aspects of Canetti I had deliberately omitted, for fear that Iris's infatuation with him should seem incomprehensible. The time for prettifying Canetti has passed.

Perhaps because his deepest wish was to eschew definition, it is hard to get Canetti's measure. But recent publication of his biography and of key letter-runs has brought him into focus. It was during her affair with Canetti (1952-54) that Iris wrote scorning Sartre's inadequate representation of love as little more than 'the battle of two hypnotists in a closed room'. This failed to flatter her Platonic view of love as potentially self-transcending …but it accords with Canetti's account of their relationship as locked into a Strindbergian power-war or deadly competition. It is also consonant with my earlier speculation that he may have used Iris sexually like a boy (see ch.8). I used to think him the more powerful – but now consider him only the more power-obsessed.

***

He had known Iris since their affair in the early fifties and they continued friends until his death in 1994: he often boasted of having 'discovered' her. His pride in the success of the many younger women artist-cum-mistresses such as Friedl Benedikt and Iris whom he groomed, encouraged and bedded was essential to him. It belonged to his conception of himself as someone addicted to 'instilling confidence' in his disciples and 'teaching them who they are'. He resembles in this a latter-day Svengali, who in George du Maurier's 1895 novel, seduces, dominates and exploits a young English girl called Trilby, turning her into a famous singer. Much in his later treatment of her reads as pure jealousy of a disciple who – over a lifetime – had the impertinence to outshine her Master.

Canetti's major work of theory *Crowds and Power* (1962) dealt with the question of how rulers command crowds through transferring 'Stings'. Murdoch explicated thus: 'Each command when we obey leaves behind in us its "sting". This … remains in us unchanged. We do not forget or forgive any command. This in turn provides us with a major source of our energy: the desire for a reversal, the desire "to get rid of our stings".' Canetti elevates Stings to a level so abstract and metaphysical that they have little air within which to breathe. Yet if Canetti's theory of Stings is considered as an aspect of egoism, it starts to make sense.

Bradley in *The Black Prince* could be explicating Canetti's doctrine of Stings when he says, 'The ego is engaged in filing damage done to its vanity…. The mind, so constantly busy with its own welfare, is always sensitively filing and sorting the ways in which self-respect has been damaged.' The crucial word here is 'vanity'. It is the egotistical mind that collects and nurses grievances or Stings.

***

The same year as *Party in the Blitz* came out in English (2005), Professor Hanuschek's 800 page authorised biography of Elias Canetti attempted a rounded picture of man and writer. In so doing, it necessarily attacked the comical and 'flat' portrait to be found in John Bayley's memoir *Iris*, where Canetti appears as the tyrannical God-Monster from Hampstead; and it also contested some implications of my portrait of Canetti, in *Iris Murdoch: A Life* (2001). Although translated from German into Japanese, Spanish, and Dutch, no English translation of *Elias Canetti* is under way. I offer my own best attempt at a translation of key passages with due diffidence.

Was Canetti a good or a bad man, asks his biographer? 'Above all was he a man capable of transformations or metamorphoses [*Verwandlungen*], a Proteus, it was a matter of containing all human possibilities and of exploring them'. *Verwandlung* is another major theme in *Crowds and Power*, where it purportedly means 'a kind of empathy based on identification'. Canetti himself defined the *Dichter* or Poet-seer – which is how he saw himself – as a Master of Transformations.

Yet *Verwandlung*, which Canetti so charged with contradictory meanings, may also have unofficial resonances that he never intended: his self-perception as a shape-changer or trickster connects with his twin propensities for jealousy and lying. His biographer acknowledges his 'pathological' jealousy, and connects this with power and control, but excuses such frailties as symptoms of weakness.

Canetti recorded a remarkable testimony about his manic lying. '… I have always to remember exactly what I have said to this person and to that, and, as I never give up on anyone, I am forced to continue this game with ingenuity and circumspection. It is as if I live in many novels at the same time, instead of writing them. The incompatibility of these fictions together, the tension between them I need.... The risk of confrontation I love above anything in the world; in little and also in large I cause [such confrontations] myself and know how at the last minute either to impede or guide [the outcome]'. This apologia for lying was written on 1 May

1954 at the height of Canetti's affair with Iris; exactly two weeks later, on 14 May, she would fall in love with John Bayley and note in her journal Canetti's 'willingness to deceive people for their good'. This self-confessed addiction to manipulating others – a form of capricious power-play – is dressed up in highfaluting terms (*Verwandlung*). If the 'philosophy' is hard to make sense of, the mendacity at least is clear.

His biographer excuses Canetti's habitual untruths either as jokes, pastiche Viennese cabaret turns, or mere teasing. On April Fool's Day 1952 Canetti rang the dying Franz Steiner to pretend that his beloved poems had – as he so devoutly longed – been published. When Steiner understood that this was a hoax, Michael Hamburger watched him change colour while carrying off this humiliation. The tale bears the unique Canetti stamp of cruelty-dressed-up-as-levity that Iris caught so beautifully in two Canetti-inspired characters. Mischa Fox taunts and teases Rainborough while the latter sweats over having hidden Anna in his cupboard in *The Flight from the Enchanter*. Mischa's name connects him to mischief. And Julius King in *A Fairly Honourable Defeat* playfully yet deliberately delays Axel and Simon's birthday dinner so that it burns, while carefully insulting them with the gift of a large pink teddy-bear; Julius's malice helps unsettle, then destroy his friend Rupert's life.

Hanuschek exonerates Canetti as a weak man, an advocacy endorsed by an important letter-run discovered in 2003 in a Paris basement, from Canetti and his first wife Veza over a period of nearly forty years to Canetti's gay brother Georges. Veza believed that her husband was a great man who got matters spot-on in art, but fumbled life. She took on the role of navigator of the real world for Canetti, whom she regarded as essentially both genius and child. These letters show how fragile Canetti's psychological economy was, given to bouts of paranoia, drink, adultery, depression, doubt, breakdown and suicidal impulses.

***

The damaging stories about Canetti that I toned down or omitted generally pertained to his love of power-play. Given his central importance within Iris's imaginative universe and his ghostly presence within her fiction, the most recent debates about these now need documenting. In 1947 Canetti ordered his sometime mistress the writer Friedl Benedikt to abort her child-to-be by another writer, Willy Goldmann. Although Friedl was happily pregnant, she obeyed Canetti's cruel injunction.

Hanuschek acknowledges that Canetti told Friedl that if she had this child he would never see her again. But just before this Hanuschek carefully places Veza Canetti's judgement that her husband was 'hopelessly romantic, selfless, naïve, he actually came across as someone weak and above all vulnerable'. Eyebrows need not rise at 'selfless': he was capable of real generosity. Hanuschek then quotes Canetti's claim that he was at this time 'living in the service of three witches' or hag-ridden, each throwing her weight around. His wife Veza threatened divorce, Friedl was playing complicated games, while the third was his official mistress Marie-Louise von Motesiczky. This paints Canetti as the victim of his womenfolk, which is indeed how he saw himself. But that bullies are essentially weak should surprise nobody.

His propensity for mischief was widely reported, and consequential. The writer Bernice Rubens in 2005 published her memoir *When I Grow Up* with its intemperate reminiscence: 'One day, I was driving up Haverstock Hill and Mr Canetti, deep in filthy thought, crossed the road in front of me. It was not a pedestrian crossing, and I could, quite legally, have killed him on the spot'. She continues: 'he had but one single talent. That of self-promotion. He created mystery about himself. I thought it all rather pathetic. My father met him once and declared him evil. And as it turned out, he was right, though evil might have been an overstatement. He did not have the imagination to be evil. He was wicked rather, depraved, vicious and spiteful. His own life was dull and uneventful, and to compensate he would create intrigue in the lives of other people.' Bernice Rubens told me that Canetti pretended to envy Rubens for bearing children, while Veza confided he had put her through many abortions.

Canetti had interfered comprehensively in Rubens's marriage, choreographing first of all her husband Rudi's affair with Christine Porter (who bore Rudi's child) and simultaneously Bernice's affair with Allan Forbes. I withheld the fact that, when Canetti introduced Bernice and her future lover to one another at the Cosmo Restaurant in Swiss Cottage, he had advertised successfully in the *New Statesman* for a bed-sit on behalf of the American Forbes, (without informing him) specifying that this accommodation be close to the street where Bernice lived. In this manner he was able to present them to one another, *fait accompli*, as neighbours.

Just as Canetti had earlier helped oversee Forbes's affair with his former mistress Friedl, who had recently died, so Canetti first willed and then choreographed Rubens's and Forbes's subsequent affair. This was a habit Iris borrowed to create Julius King's machinations in *A Fairly Honourable Defeat*: Julius conspires by lying to create an affair between Rupert and his sister-in-law Morgan. And one explanation of Iris's curious apparent silence in real life about the darkness of Canetti's character is surely because she displaces into her fiction an understanding that she herself stays innocent of.

Diana Athill in her prize-winning memoir *Somewhere Towards the End* (2008) records Canetti's propensity for intrigue. Athill befriended the funny, warm, charming and indiscreet Vienna-born painter Marie-Louise von Motesiczky. When Marie-Louise discovered that Athill had published Canetti, she became excited and started talking: Motesiczky had become Canetti's 'official' mistress around 1941 and remained so for thirty years. She led a quiet life, circumscribed by painting and care for her aged mother. When Canetti's first wife Veza died in 1963, Marie-Louise out of respect for Veza's memory did not press her own case but continued to wait patiently in the wings as an 'extra' in the play.

Then in July 1973 two journalists staying in her house in Compayne Gardens stunned Marie-Louise with the news that Canetti had been living for ten years with a much younger woman called Hera Buschor, who worked at the Zürich Kunsthaus: they were married and shared a flat and a two-year old daughter. Athill comments: 'Her seclusion seemed to have spared her the knowledge of Canetti's many other women: … [so] that the revelation of his being married had brought their affair to a sudden and agonizing end'. When Marie-Louise first cut Canetti dead in the street, he visibly trembled.

***

Canetti's relationship with England and Englishness is a major topic in his *Party in the Blitz* and helps throw further light on his treatment of Iris. Although Viennese by adoption and temperament, his connection with Britain was a long one. He fled to London as a refugee in January 1939 and kept a flat in Thurlow Road until 1988: around fifty years of residency. He learnt English as a child in Manchester in 1911 before he knew German and he held a UK passport and stayed a British citizen to the end of his life. He also called himself an Englishman by attachment, loving it twice over on account of the affection for it of his wife. Yet he remained an exotic here.

The *New Statesman*'s deputy literary editor Janet Adam Smith told me she invited Canetti to review a book on Hieronymus Bosch around 1949. Canetti's grand-standing – 'Exactly who would be appearing in the same issue?' – i.e were they worthy of his company? – and his condition that there be no sub-editing, caused her to withdraw her offer. Adam Smith referred to Canetti as an intellectual 'Merdle': the social and financial outsider and fraudster in Dickens's *Little Dorrit* who takes everybody in, before his exposure.

Canetti's growing resentment of England was surely prompted by lack of recognition. The reception in Britain in 1962 of *Crowds and Power*, which had eaten up decades of his life, hurt further. While the *New Left Review* and *Sunday Times* reviewed it favourably, the *TLS* was hostile and the anthropologist Geoffrey Gorer gave it a *stinging* reception in the *Observer*, starting with the quip that 'there is less to this book than meets the eye', deploring its incomprehensible neglect of Freud and its outdated anthropology. Canetti's friend Mary Douglas confided that she agreed.

Although George Steiner in *Encounter* defended Canetti's debt to the tradition of *Kulturphilosophie*, this foreignness of Canetti's approach may account in part for an undercurrent which he clearly resented. Diana Athill, who edited the English translation of Canetti's *Aphorisms*, found his ideas pompous, self-important, and vain. This groundswell of antipathy may help explain Canetti's curious rhetoric about English 'arrogance'. Although he sometimes seems to mean a combination of modesty and self-possession, he doubtless encountered superciliousness or hostility.

Canetti's greatest ally was Dame Iris. When his German publisher reissued *Crowds and Power* in 1973, Canetti, despite hesitating over whether her name was sufficiently well-known in Germany, used her praise on his book jacket. In 1981 his much-acclaimed memoirs helped win him the Nobel Prize for Literature; he refused permission for them to be translated into English or published in the UK. In 1982 the *Sunday Times* printed Dame Iris's short letter, under the title 'No resentment': 'Your article… suggests that Elias Canetti is not allowing publication of his autobiography in Britain because he resents neglect of his work in this country. This is not his motive; he wishes simply to avoid hurting the feelings of certain people who live here.' There are few references to anyone in these islands in these first three autobiographies. But Murdoch defends him loyally and inaccurately: concern for the feelings of others is scarcely his trade-mark. Penguin's 1977 decision to delete *Auto da Fe* from its backlist surely exacerbated his resentment. Neglect of his work in England stung Canetti; and he was doubly stung by the acclaim accorded his pupil Iris. He later decided to 'to get rid of his stings' by stinging back.

***

Hanushchek reports that references to Iris within Canetti's *Nachlass* or literary estate – in theory closed until 2024 – are few and off-hand. When Veza's death in 1963 disturbed him intensely he wrote about dismissing a mind-boggling total of forty surviving women friends and/or mistresses, among whom he specifies 'Iris'. Soon Canetti and Iris went together to a restaurant he and Veza had frequented. While he recounted his life without Veza, she 'scarcely concealed her unease…. But then she has evaded death. She experiences death differently than me'. He earlier criticised her for being busy with emotion, commenting: 'She is so shallow, as Veza was so deep'. In 1992 Dame Iris flew to Zürich, where Canetti recorded her as a broadly-built woman bearing a huge tin of old inedible sweets painted with English tin-soldiers for Canetti's daughter (then aged over twenty). Johanna recalled her as chaotic. Such references suggest Canetti's indifference to Iris.

This indifference is compounded in *Party in the Blitz*, where he chronicled their affair inaccurately, insinuating that Iris had not been slow to instigate it. He was not confused: he lists, correctly, the professions of those Iris loved (ancient historian, economist, theologian &tc), and adds insightfully that these represented her 'alter egos' (*Verwandlungen*), whom she absorbed during 'endless' conversations. Thus her male characters were conceived. He noted critically her aptitude for intent listening and patient cross-questioning – capacities, after all, he shared. She collected hungrily, he tells us, usable confidences, 'like a house-wife doing her shopping'.

None the less, there is a strange mismatch between his jaundiced account of their affair forty years later, and her journal contemporary with it. Canetti convicts Dame Iris of initiating a one-sided affair to which he was indifferent. Many of his accusations reduce to matters of taste; this last claim is debatable as a matter of record.

Four entries from Murdoch's journal:

> April 12 1953: C. made love to me savagely, tearing my clothes off.
> June 24 1953: We made love with great fierceness.... He said: 'you are not defenceless against me, because I love you. I do, although I don't say it often'.
> July 25 1953: C's birthday... He said 'I love you' at Crawford St – and then cursed himself for saying it again. I said he needn't repeat it for two years. He said it yet again as we were walking along to Carol's, & kissed me in the street.
> Jan 10 1954: C. so gentle, he fears that I may too much identify myself with Friedl. 'You are yourself!' he keeps telling me, 'I don't love you just because of that.'

Party in the Blitz expends two contemptuous pages on a diaphanous blouse she wore at a dinner in Hampton Court, with the stupid intention of seducing Aymer Maxwell, who was gay. Iris's journal reference to this same dinner expatiates only on Aymer's touching devotion to – and fear of – Canetti. 'At dinner at Hampton Court [Aymer] gave me an opening to say I thought C. a great writer, & absolutely pushed me into it!' Eleven days later Canetti warned her against Aymer (whom he called a werewolf), saying 'Aymer would do anything he could to drive a wedge between us, even to trying to seduce me. He added, if you do do anything you regret, remember that I am merciful! ... I was exasperated extremely by this – but touched too, in an absurd way'. In *Party in the Blitz* he remembers self-pityingly: 'It seemed not to have crossed her mind to *wonder what it* [her seductiveness] *might do to me.*'

Though he represents their affair as entirely one-sided, Canetti recalled, even in *Party in the Blitz*, her face at moments as as beautiful as that of a Memling Madonna. On 30 June 1954 Canetti, having learnt that Murdoch and Bayley were lovers, commanded that their affair cease. They obeyed his edict for eleven weeks until 17 September, even when visiting Paris and staying in separate hotels. Nothing here endorses Canetti's later claim to indifference: on the contrary, he again and again depicts himself as competing jealously with her.

He was an émigré who had lost his culture, his chosen language and his beloved city (Vienna). Murdoch was at home in these islands and a don in Oxford, where he passionately desired to be recognised, staging his play *The Numbered* at the Oxford Playhouse where it flopped in 1956, and hungering to meet Isaiah Berlin. That never happened, though Dame Iris knew him. Hence his attack on Oxford, which had left a *Stachel* or sting that never healed.

He was eldest of three brothers competing for the affections of a mother whose willpower makes her seem almost demented; Iris had all the deep self-contentment and solipsism of a much-loved only child. He was also, if not a blocked writer, then – despite winning the Nobel – a disappointed one. He intended eight novels, but completed only one; and he finished three volumes of autobiography instead of five. Iris by contrast wrote with alarming facility, and won greater literary and social acclaim than he. 'Vulgar' success he calls it, jealously. 'She has published 24 novels' gets repeated three times.

She also had more lovers and admirers than he and he puts on record his wonderment at her strange loyalty to each: something he had never previously encountered. Loyalty to friends is not conspicuous in *Party in the Blitz*. Iris was, he notes incredulously, the only woman in his life who never sought to capture him. 'This is the only time in my life that I was with a woman who didn't seek to hold me to her'. Her independence frightened him.

Iris's most unforgiveable crime was that she was the only person who listened more than he did: he uses '*greedily*' to document this. There are eight separate passages in *Party in the Blitz* where he boasts about his own famous gift for listening even to those who bored him. 'Everyone tells everything to Canetti', one intimate avowed. Canetti liked and needed to feel that 'my willingness to listen led to a dependency, a craving'. Before meeting a writer for the first time, he carefully read *all* their published work: thus he could, partly by flattery, enter into others and, through an intense power of curiosity, transform himself. As a result, everyone gave away their secrets. Yet he secretly enjoyed talking even better than listening. Iris spotted and elicited his Mr Toad-like boastfulness. And there can be such a thing as 'listener's rape', where the person confiding comes to feel his privacy has been violated, his inner being 'robbed', a sin compounded if they then recreate and disseminate fictional versions of you.

Iris's ultimate crime in his view was to listen, steal and cannibalise her friends' lives with more inwardness than Canetti. 'I told her everything', he bitterly laments. 'She got to hear about all the people I knew, and also a good many of those I had known … she took it all in. She wanted to hear everything I had to say.... But I never ... understood in what spirit she listened to me talking about my present friends ... she had a buried robber's nature, and her aim was to rob each one of her lovers not of his heart, but more of his mind; she was generally, greedily silent: she made a lot of booty out of me [i.e in the novels] but mixed with so much other prey that I'd feel ashamed'. He surely recognised himself in Mischa Fox and Julius King, while the portrait of the power-obsessed Charles Arrowby in *The Sea, The Sea* would have been impossible without intimate knowledge of him. Plucking out the heart of the mystery of others was Canetti's expertise; and perhaps Iris – in her cool reflections of Canetti in the novels – did this even more effectively.

All his life Canetti claimed that his job was to overcome death, an obsession that seems further evidence of egomania. If loss and death are, as one Buddhist teacher argues, the ultimate insult to ego – the ultimate *Sting* – by contrast how moving and attractive is Murdoch's belief that what connects us to truthful vision is love and humility.

23. Hedda Gabler and other matters

Doris Lessing, Iris's contemporary and a very different novelist, was sceptical about discipleship. She recalled Tolstoi mocked and bullied by his second-rate disciple Chertkov; Maxim Gorkiy's disciple Kryuchkov paid by the KGB and implicated in Gorki's murder and Benny Lévy accused of brainwashing Sartre and faking the latter's last writings. I preferred not to resemble these equivocal figures; and my discipleship was simplified by the fact I felt no rivalry with Iris. She was publishing the novels I should have liked to write and was happy to read.

Discipleship is a principal Iris Murdoch subject. *Under the Net* concerns a group of Londoners whose lives and concerns are influenced by the good and innocent Hugo Belfounder: white discipleship. In *The Flight from the Enchanter* the cast are so-called 'creatures' of the morally equivocal Mischa Fox: black discipleship. But each of her novels makes use of courts, covens or cults and late novel titles such as *The Philosopher's Pupil* and *The Good Apprentice* suggest that her obsession with fathers endured.

She was herself a professional disciple. Canetti, who listed her surrogate fathers in his memoir *Party in the Blitz* by their professions – Balogh, Franz Steiner, Momigliano, Fraenkel, MacKinnon, himself – portrayed Iris's discipleships as parasitical: vampirish, cannibal, piratical, sucking out the essence of those she listened to with passionate stilled attention and then displaying her booty in her novels with impure intent.

Canetti's black view of discipleship distantly echoes Harold Bloom's in *The Anxiety of Influence* (1973). Bloom memorably pictures the literary master-disciple relation mainly as an oedipal – and cannibalistic – drama: the jealous acolyte's secret wish, beneath public admiration, is for a diminution of the reputation of the older artist so that his 'Mana', prestige or power can be appropriated. The older artist can then be turned into a John-the-Baptist heralding the significant arrival of the younger. This may shed light on how the moralist who gave 'attention' a central place in the moral life appears to have mis-judged a number of her closest friendships.

When she died, the *TLS* listed some novelists purportedly influenced by Iris: A.S. Byatt, Candia McWilliam, Alan Hollinghurst, Marina Warner, A.N. Wilson. This is an incomplete and a partial list and there are other writers for whom she remains important. Be that as it may, a minority who during her life broadcast their friendship with Murdoch changed their tune thereafter. Her utility had now passed. One well-known disciple was reported as boasting of having now 'turned into Murdoch' and having supplanted the original. Philippa Foot – who at no point ever publicised her closeness to Murdoch – remarked in 1998, 'Iris had the knack of making each of her friends feel unique and *as if each was the only one*. But only the very egocentric believed this.' When Iris's life started to become public property it was hard to sustain the fiction that she belonged to any one friend: some changed tack.

Philip Hensher, who admired her in his youth, now charged her with being 'insanely readable', a bizarrely self-admiring phrase. In an ungenerous introduction to *A Fairly Honourable Defeat* he charges her with idly transmuting a Sikh family into a Pakistani one. It is perfectly true that she could be careless. But this particular sloppiness is Hensher's: chapter eleven of that novel makes clear the Sikh lives downstairs, the Pakistani family upstairs. Such attacks might have pleased Harold Bloom and Canetti alike.

The Iris Murdoch conference happens every two years at Kingston University and elsewhere, attracting around a hundred participants gathered from most continents. Many are literary critics or philosophers; a few are theologians. One thing we all share is that the novelist and philosopher whose work we assemble to celebrate and explore is often referred to as 'Iris', *tout court*. This makes for a disturbing simplicity: it also suggests the easy familiarity said to breed contempt. Surely Woolf scholars don't refer to her as Virginia and nor are there conferences where the first names Muriel or Doris are bandied about? Do their respective scholars refer to Morgan (Forster), Henry (James) or Charles (Dickens)?

At conference I primly emphasise her proper style, 'Dame Iris', while reflecting on my complicity in thus helping enter her into the national consciousness. In October 1997 John Bayley announced that he was writing his first memoir. I offered to step down and stop writing; this was declined. We were in Wales, chatting in the kitchen. He was fretting about possible titles. And after trying out various options, I suggested 'Why not simply *Iris*?'. YES, John instantly asseverated, and 'Iris' she became, in his memoir in the UK (in the US *Elegy for Iris*) as also in the film made from his first two memoirs, with all its implications of hokey and inauthentic familiarity. The film has undoubtedly helped keep her name 'current', albeit for lamentable reasons.

I published Dame Iris's authorised biography in 2001; it is surely one point of life-writing to aspire to make its subject walk-and-talk, providing a vicarious sense of intimacy without excluding complexities or mysteries that might – ideally – lead readers back to the work. There are writers whose life-stories nonetheless generate a national charismatic cult, often because their works, as Auden put this, are in better taste than their lives. Writers such as 'Rabbie Burns' or Byron are celebrated for their amorous propensities: the reader's gaze is inevitably distracted and disturbed by the legend. It is disquieting if Iris is joining their ranks, and she has penetrated the public consciousness in this unexpected way. In any case she now belongs, for better and for worse, to the nation.

***

Tony Quinton asked me over the telephone around 2001, 'Do you still like Iris?' and, when I paused, gave an instance or two of a biographer who, through closer acquaintance, had fallen out of love with his subject. Quinton's question gave me pause. The average time dedicated by the contemporary biographer to his task is – I learn – five years: my voluntary enslavement has continued for much longer.

When she died in 1999 Alan Bennett in his annual *LRB* Christmas diary recorded: 'Dame Iris Murdoch dies and gets excellent reviews, all saying how (morally) good she was, though hers was not goodness that seemed to require much effort, just a grace she had been given; so she was plump and she was also good, both attributes she had been born with and didn't trouble herself over…'. That Iris had trodden the same political path as Amis and Larkin, from radical beginnings towards a reactionary old age cast further doubt for Bennett on the 'kindliness and general benevolence' behind which she was 'masked'. On what basis had it become a received idea to write of Iris's 'goodness', for which Bennett saw little evidence?

A.N. Wilson gave a memorable riposte. Iris took almost no practical interest in day-to-day politics. Moreover, did Bennett seriously consider Iris's late support for John Major more culpable than the support the young radical Iris and Amis had given Joe Stalin? Wilson went on to point out that she was joyous; generous; a contemplative rather than an active sister, as befitted a writer. There was also the palpable fact, not to be analysed, that she was deeply lovable. She said a universal Yes to life, which was perhaps one reason why so many people felt joy in her company. You felt in her presence, Wilson recalled, that life was a serious business, and that she was engaged in a struggle that was not necessarily easy or complete…

A dark reading of this struggle might be found within her work. Her novels offer many examples of a woman figure who, by compelling attention, somehow feeds off the life-force of her admirers. In *The Unicorn* the mixture of *princesse lointaine*, madonna and whore represented by Hannah fascinates and claims a high final casualty rate among her acolytes, among whom she is at last cast as a 'pale vampire … a death-dealing enchantress'. Hannah's talent for collecting admirers echoes Iris's; and the word 'vamp' – John Bayley early pointed out to me in connection with the young Iris – derives from 'vampire'. Did Iris also compel an attention as a writer and thinker that she had not earned?

I brood over this 'enchantment' as if it offered an analogy to my own case-history. She has occupied my mind for much of my adult life. I first published my study of her fiction *The Saint and Artist* in 1986 (a second and third edition followed); this was followed in 1997 by what started as a seventieth birthday tribute, *Existentialists and Mystics*, a collection for scholars of her writings on philosophy and literature. Then came the authorised biography in 2001, her wartime letters and a diary in 2010, and finally in 2012 in a biography of Frank Thompson, who had loved her during the war. Although I've also published monographs on others (Dostoevsky, Fowles, Angus Wilson) and studies of Buddhism and the Welsh Marches, I've returned again and again to Iris.

***

The Bayleys' lives and destinies have been so mixed with ours over the last twenty years that objectivity is difficult. Until after John died on 12 January 2015 my partner and I knew nothing of John's request to have his ashes scattered in our garden, so that when we now look out of the window of our house in Wales in summer we see a dark red Charles de Mills Gallica rose fertilised by his remains.

His reasons for this choice of venue are not obscure. He and Iris spent many months with us in Wales in 1996-98. Then, the year following Iris's death, John married quietly his old friend Audi Villers, also from our house and in its neighbouring church. So John's choice of our garden to

John and Audi Bayley's wedding, 2000

accommodate his ashes was a neat piece of equivocation, honouring both marriages. When Audi enquired, on his honeymoon night in a Reykavik hotel in 2000, whether he was happy, he replied, with typical John-like ingenuousness, 'Yes, but I do wish Iris could be here with us too'. Audi took excellent care of him for fifteen years, and he was loved, fed and washed.

In his final years, Audi employed Polish-Buddhist friends of ours – Edytka, Malgosiata, Martyna – to help tend him in his wheelchair in Oxford and Lanzarote and look after his needs. I lived in Krakow, teaching at the Jagiellonian University, in 1990-92; and since Iris had earlier influenced my and my partner's decisions to become Buddhist, the contribution of these Poles was accompanied by some sense of 'what goes around comes around', and of Iris's continuing blessing. When, on the tenth anniversary of their marriage, Audi asked him over breakfast whether he could remember why today was special, John replied 'Let me think', and then after some minutes announced triumphantly: 'The murder of Richard III on Bosworth Field'.

I was Iris's executor, but not literary executor, so that my duties ended when Probate was declared: John's failure to nominate any scholars to help oversee her estate was in the view of some another example of fecklessness. Though I thought I'd given all my Iris correspondence to Kingston University, I still find caches of letters and cards from her – thirty most recently. John charged me with helping dispose of the contents of her Cornwall Gardens flat and the sale of the flat and even now I come across the odd relic.

When I venture into central London it is with Iris's *A to Z*, superscale, and very useful albeit it covers only central London. There are caches of the stones everywhere that she collected and treasured. Smiling protectively from its kitchen shelf is a Gandhara Buddha that she bequeathed me. John gave us his glass Army flask for whisky or brandy from Normandy 1944, whose removable steel cover functions as a cup. He also gave us Iris's 'world-wide stamp album', started around 1930 when she was eleven, running from Abyssinia to Zanzibar and Zululand. In an envelope marked 'Valuable Stamps' are twelve stamps bearing Edward VIII's head. Probably such gifts arrived as a 'thank you' for our help as carers.

The making of Richard Eyre's film *Iris* created for all who knew her a new sense of unreality and a new level of confusion. It felt like having entered an uncanny Hall of Mirrors. In January 2001 I sat in a Hammersmith school watching Dame Judi Dench in a series of repeat 'takes', dying as Iris in a mocked-up hospital room. 'Best boys' kept kindly proffering polystyrene cups of tea and the hope that this scene did not upset me… I protested that I should far prefer to witness Dame Judi pretending to die many times than return to the actual and singular event less than two years earlier. On the day of her death Iris had – thank God – been unconscious, yet in a visible distress that was upsetting to witness.

I met Dame Judi earlier that day in St Pauls Girls school, wearing a fright wig and giving the strange and touching lecture that comes near the end of the film, but which contains (like the whole film) no words that Iris in life either wrote or spoke. She soon invited me to Fortnums, where we drank – what else? – banana milk-shakes. 'Am I like?' she asked. 'Not fat enough', she laughed to hear. She shared with Iris being a Dublin-born Protestant, but representing Dame Iris thus in her decline disturbed her considerably. She had another shoot starting soon in *The Shipping News,* for which she was practicing a Newfoundland accent to play Agnis Hamm, a role happily too remote to trouble her.

We were interrupted in Fortnums by a fan who came over to our table apologetically to thank Dame Judi for her portrayal many years before of Hedda Gabler, a performance which, he explained, had changed the subsequent course of his life and for which he was duly grateful. Judi Dench listened politely and, after many minutes, scribbled on a paper napkin and passed this under the table. Her message read: 'I have never in my life played Hedda Gabler. But if you tell them, it takes an extra hour…'. The next time we met was at the Apollo Theatre, Shaftesbury Avenue in London on 26 June 2002, where Josephine Hart and I concocted a fund-raising Celebration of Dame Iris's life. At the dinner that ensued she added, 'Nor have I ever read the damn thing'.

This tale might serve as a parable about the fallibility of memory. I feared the making of the film and agreed to act as consultant if only to warn of palpable absurdities or untruths. One early draft script had Valentine Cunningham witnessing the Bayley wedding in 1956, when he would have been eleven years old. Another had Iris and Canetti holding hands at a London party: unimaginable and in neither's style. Sir Richard Eyre reminded me in 2002, when he, John and I went onstage together at the Cheltenham Literature Festival, that it was I who suggested that John Bayley's assertion that Iris 'never went to bed with another woman' was not to be taken literally; and who pointed him towards her confusing early love-life. I asked instead of a fee for a small donation to go towards my eighty-four year-old mother's care. John, though attacked for profiteering, in fact made no money from the film: he had (typically) signed away all his rights on a UK publisher's contract he never bothered to read.

My agent and I declined film producer Scott Rudin's invitation to join forces publicising film and biography together in the USA. However lucrative such an alliance might have been, the Iris of the film was not the one we wanted the world to remember. I felt that a bursary scheme at St Anne's College, Oxford might provide a more appropriate living memorial at the university where she studied and taught for many years. Iris herself was after all just such a girl from an impoverished background for whom the experience of studying at Oxford was life-changing. It is good that this small bursary survives to help students from poorer backgrounds pay for their studies. John contributed to the scheme the large sum that the sale of Iris's library raised.

24. The Fear of an Ending

By selecting stages in my life journey, I see that I have written a fairly eccentric sort of autobiography, a form given to reminding us that a final stage must sooner or later arrive. Recent experience has brought this sharply into focus.

An Iris character, feeling sick after watching a trout having a finger put into its mouth to enable its back neatly to be snapped, thinks to himself: 'Such a rapid passage, such an appalling mystery'. Since the novelist earlier in the same story compares leaping salmon to human souls struggling to reach God, she is reminding us here how mysteriously short our life-span is too. The passage echoes *Ecclesiastes*: 'As the fishes that are taken in an evil net … so are the sons of men snared in an evil time'.

Iris made much of death. She may have been brooding on Franz Steiner and Frank Thompson when in her Gifford lectures she repeatedly spoke of the dead as being 'at peace'. I thought this description a soft focus version of the truth, since the dead have ceased to be anything much at all. She also thought we tend to confuse death with suffering, although the two were secret opposites. Death was the great memento of our nothingness, hence a vital spur to the moral quest. She thought we tended to hope we might cheat mortality by suffering instead, and that Christianity colluded with this delusion. She invited us instead to contemplate dying, as the great saints in all traditions have always done, seeing in it an escape from the pains of individuality.

In so far as I understand this, I think her absolutism romantic in a pejorative sense, and unrealistic. It was not merely that she had, I would judge, both a strong and very healthy ego herself combined with a positive life-force. But my own view of endings changed after witnessing four deaths in as many years.

***

In September 2008 all four of her children assembled from different parts of the country around my mother's bed in her Northwood flat. She was ninety and suffering double pneumonia which we had all agreed should not this time be treated with antibiotics. Her breathing pattern had changed, alternating between rasping and quiet, with an intake followed for several seconds by no apparent breath at all, then a further intake: so-called Cheyne-Stokes breathing. She ceased… only to start again. We were very touched by her GP Dr Goodwin's arrival at an appropriate moment; he reassured us about what was happening, promised that she was unconscious, and explained accurately how the moment of her dying would gently arrive. She finally underwent a small rictus or spasm as if some critical message were passing between brain and heart, before an exhalation resembling a surrender or last letting-go. This GP, we later learnt, had a few days before just witnessed his own wife's unexpected death.

My brave sister Prue, with her nurse's training, invited me to help lay our mother out. I hesitated. I reflected on how deeply our mother, with her innate fastidiousness and old-fashioned sense of appropriate gender roles, would have hated my viewing or handling her so stripped of dignity. I duly excused myself.

Six months later, in March 2009, my youngest brother was diagnosed on his fifty-second birthday with stage four colon cancer that had migrated to his liver. He had endured much suffering over the previous year: the collapse of his marriage, the loss of his job, and a prosecution that resulted from his having liaised with (while never meeting) a woman who had lied on an internet chat-room about her age, turning out to be a minor. Now a stent inserted into his colon to ease digestion punctured it and the surgery that followed opened a big abdominal wound that was never either to close or heal. The changing of the elaborate pressure-dressing protecting this open wound was now a recurrent trauma. He faced his own death within weeks: this happened in the Isabel hospice attached to Welwyn Garden hospital, where staff were magnificent.

Our beloved and beautiful collie Sky, white-coated, brown-eyed, independent-spirited as a princess and wilful to the point of recklessness, continued her life-long habit of finding plastic to chew and around this time fatally perforated her gut. A week of unsuccessful surgery followed before the vet helped her on her way. We buried her in our orchard. She was just five.

Since I was now in my late sixties, this saga of mortality should scarcely have surprised me. Prue's diagnosis with oesophogeal cancer that had metastasised into her lungs and elsewhere happened on her sixty-fourth birthday in 2012. She at once – after some minutes of hearty cursing – started thinking about who might like her house and belongings. There was one unexpected blessing or bonus. Although we communicated at different speeds – I made others think faster; Prue slowed us all down so that we noticed more – we had eight months to rediscover how much we meant to one another. I promised her that I would write this memoir and dedicate it to her memory. She specified the excellent and exceptional close friends plus me that she wanted at her death-bed and on New Year's Day 2013 I duly sped from Wales to Norwich, where we all camped out while she died in the small hours of the morning.

Prue

Not long before her death my sister still insisted on a substantial ongoing supply of thyroid pills. She had given up installation of a stairlift, recognising that she was too frail to be likely ever to use it, that this would be money down the drain, but she hedged her bets nonetheless. I admired her too for stubbornly allowing herself wiggle-room and a hope of survival. She had long been anxious about her end, about probate and executors: she and I would discuss how far our last months and the manner of our dying should condition how we are remembered.

My partner jokes that I'm fine in a crisis while ordinary day-to-day vicissitudes overwhelm me.... Anticipating a death can be a revelation of pure suffering. Such vigils entail the hardest waiting, as if time itself had slowed down or changed itself into something strange, becoming a new substance. Survivors can be caught between the fear of the patient dying on our watch, and the equal anguish of their continuing to suffer instead. Grief approaches anger, equal products of powerlessness.

What became clear is that we cannot all the time be staring into the abyss, or into some unimaginable black hole. And Iris's comments on death and suffering belong on an unhelpful plane of abstraction. Moreover if multiple griefs can undermine your hold on life, then the ego – with all its bold reflex denials of mortality – has a certain pragmatic intelligence.

***

There is much more of course to be said about the place of grief in human life, and in 1962 my father's first cousin Cyrus Sulzberger published *My Brother Death*, his own meditation on death and dying through the ages. His book is mercifully short, it has a learned bibliography, and there are chapters on suicide, death in battle, religious death, and so on. The tone is world-weary, sententious, *fin-de-siecle*. It borrows explicitly from Robert Burton's *Anatomy of Melancholy* but recalls Ernest Dowson's 'They are not long, the days of wine and roses' and I still remember the solemn prose-poetry of its ending: 'There to the east, the terrific sun is again rising between a cypress and a cypress.... Now come, my brother Death; now old, old, old, with hair like thistledown, I sink with fatigue, into the soft Aegean waters that bear me northward and backward in time'.

Who is old and tired here? Cyrus, writing from his house on the Greek island of Spetsai, is affecting to be as ancient and jaded as the world itself, trying to find and conjure wisdom – like the Preacher in *Ecclesiastes* – out of the endless, senseless cycles of life and death.

My Grandmother Florence – Cy's aunt – ascribed Cyrus's bleak attitu-

MY
BROTHER
Death
Cyrus Sulzberger

To face death, since all men are alike condemned to die, is the beginning of mastery over life's terrors; to view death and to spurn it or accept it, either with equanimity, that is the justification. How easy is death for those who know how to meet it, striding across its silent iciness with pure, clean courage. We all have our Antarctic to traverse. Take heart from these splendid men and women, our colleagues and companions, who knew how to make the journey."

dinising to indigestion. She remarked drily, 'It must have been something he ate that didn't agree with him'. There was common sense here. She spotted that he was cranking up emotions for effect, and that this was not entirely 'natural'.

I was a schoolboy in 1962 and had not yet read William Empson's witty and penetrating poem 'Ignorance of Death' (1942), which argues that Death is a topic we should on the whole shut up about. '...Because we have neither hereditary nor direct knowledge of death/ It is the trigger of the literary man's biggest gun.... Otherwise I feel very blank upon this topic, / And think that though important, and proper for anyone to bring up, / It is one that most people should be prepared to be blank upon.' Willingness to be blank would imply willingness not to be 'in the know' Empson's sentiment surely sounds exactly the right note.

***

After Iris's death M.R.D. Foot wrote to me that 'Her light was once marvellously bright; and you are lucky to have bathed in so much of it'. I felt that luck. My enslavement brought many rewards, from a new career as free-lance writer to an RSL Fellowship and new acquaintances. Moreover, with all its imperfections I still feel at home in her work and thought; and agree with Martha Nussbaum that 'the complex moral and literary richness of Murdoch's best novels grows more evident all the time'; and with Martin Amis that she was the pre-eminent English novelist of her generation, and that there can be 'no argument about the depth, the complexity, and indeed the beauty of Murdoch's mind: the novels attest to this…'.

'Is your work on Propertius going to be a great work of scholarship?' asks Theo in *The Nice and the Good*. 'Is it necessary?... It's mediocre, it's a time-filler. Why do you do it?' Willy reflects for a moment before replying, 'Love needs to be expressed, it needs to do work.... And if there is an indubitable good within one's reach, one stretches out one's hand'. Celebrating Iris's work and thought still seems an indubitable good within my reach. I miss her championing of the inner life and the power of attention, as also her company in the strange and compelling journey of each new novel; and her presence, warm, comforting, loving, attentive.

If when I die there are any obituaries, I imagine these may record my discipleship. Fine. The relationship between biographer and subject, Alison Lurie has observed, can take the form of a one-sided love affair, often confessed at the end of the acknowledgments in the finished book, when, 'after thanking interviewees and researchers and editors, the biographer apologises to his or her spouse or partner for what sounds rather like an adulterous affair, one that diverted time and attention… from a real-life partner'. My partner Jim has been forgiving, the source both of many insights and of unstinting love and support. John Bayley witnessed our civil partnership in Brixton Town Hall in December 2004. Meeting him forty years ago through a small ad in *Time Out* is the happiest single thing that ever happened to me. He is the best human being I know: the most generous, kindest, most skilful, with a perfect recall for the architecture and the detail alike of others' lives. I have counted my luck ever since.

End Notes

p.17 *7 November 1909* At 6 pm, West End Synagogue, 160 W 82nd St, NYC. Reception St Regis hotel

p.19 *Eli Jacques Kahn* In 1938. Beatrice died in 1962 & Eli married Liselotte Hirschmann Myller in 1964. Eli died 1972. He and Liselotte lived at 1185 Park Avenue. See his *NYT* obit.

p 19 *West End Avenue* Nettie's *Kentucky Cardinal* bears the address 48, 94th St., NYC

p.24 *a welcome addition* Letter from Flo's father to Heinrich/Henry Conradi

p.24 *witnessed* She gave him Elizabeth B Browning's *Sonnets from the Portuguese* inscribed 'To My Emil, My Beloved, Dec 8 1914' and marking its famous sonnet 43 'How do I love thee? Let me count the ways' with a star of David.

p.48 *the second war alone* E.g 'shoe cleaning machines, medicine bottles that poured out a predetermined exact dose, the TEC cable locator for locating faults in portable cable, illuminated bookrests for reading in bed or an armchair, and many, many others, not all of them electrical' Gordon Conradi, *Three Score Years and Ten* (1978), p 21.

p.49 *late eighteenth century* Cousin Felix Levy maintained that the family changed its names from Leon to Levy after a father-son quarrel in the late eighteenth century. Levys and Cohens – as the two priestly tribes – would normally be requested by the Rabbi to 'read' in synagogue, while Felix's branch were never – at Dennington Park Road – so invited. … Possibly it was Asher Leon who became Asher Levy. There is a Yehuda Lieb on the family tree who cousin George Rigal hypothesised was possibly known as Asher Leon Levy. He was probably the father of Aaron Levy born 1800.

p.52 *whom married well* Nan [Anna], Katie, Ben m Bertha, Josie, George (who alone stayed Isaacs) m Hilda, Alec m Betty, Ruby, Cyril m Molly, Manny m Iris.

p.52 *their big house* Ies and Dorothy Vandenberg, Cape Farewell, Loddon Drive, Wargrave

p.55 *throw at you* See *Guardian* 12 Oct 2005

p.56 *arrival in 1958* I wrote him a letter of appreciation after laughing out loud at his autobiography *Life's Rich Pageant* and got an amiable reply.

p.65 *in The Unicorn* See his entry in *ODNB* and also http://enockfamily-history.co.uk/John_Philip_W_Gaskell_-_1926-2001.htm

p.67 *An Unofficial Rose* She explained how the novel title came from Rupert Brooke's poem 'Grantchester' and how it illuminated the 'formless' Anne – referred to within the title – whose lack of definition offended her form-obsessed husband Randall. She proposed that this contrast (form–versus-formless) was one that could be observed in life. Another question came from David Palmer-Jones who asked whether she felt with the passing of the years "more enchanted or more disenchanted?". After dodging she came down on the side of dis- enchantment.

p.79 *sort of light* p.349

p.80 *them, or worse* Martha Nussbaum,'When She Was Good' review of *Iris Murdoch: A Life*, New Republic, December 31, 2001.

p.82 a *male homosexual Living on Paper: Letters from IM 1934-95* eds. A. Rowe and A. Horner p 293; see also p 304

p.82 *the younger man Ibid*, p.260

p.85 *recurrent preoccupations* For example from Lecture One: 'a work of art seems to be a person, a jumble, greater than the sum of its parts.... A moral being must become an artist or mystic – *a fortiori* today when religion has been demythologised...' Plato recurred, identifying fact and value. From Lecture Two, 'we survey the misery of the world more calmly in art and religion...'. She defended consciousness and 'inwardness' throughout.

p.90 *in her demonology* I loaned her Vols 3 and 4 of Heidegger's *Nietzsche*, to help what became *Metaphysics as a Guide to Morals*.

p.90 *Heidegger helped spawn* I had that year (1982) published a monograph on John Fowles's post-modernity

p.91 *work that year* Iris Murdoch, *The Saint and the Artist*

p.92 *where she was* Compare 'I Will Tell You Everything' Rosemary Hill, *LRB* Vol. 32 No. 8 · 22 April 2010 pp 41-42; and Nussbaum, *New Republic, Ibid*.

p.97 *Saxon Minister* Heinrich in 1879 calls him Ambassador. Strictly speaking a legation was run by a Minister, not an Ambassador, but possibly this was a matter either of loose usage or a special arrangement between Saxony and France.

p.97 *philo-semitic* In 1891 Baron von Seebach is recorded as accompanying the Zionist Paul Friedmann, much exercised by the recent Russian pogroms, on board his private steam-yacht *Israel* together with 24 immigrants they had chosen in Krakow on a trip to Palestine, where they were to settle.

p.99 *daughter of a Banker* Lion Abraham Goldschmidt

p.99 *hospitable to refugees* Two days before Fromatte's visit to the legation, Mme Fould died (July 2, 1870 in Trouville-sur-Mer).

p.100 *separate legation in Paris* It closed only on July 19th 1870, on which day Washburne was put in charge of Saxon affairs, archives and the well-being of its citizens. See *A Biography of Elihu Benjamin Washburne* by M Washburne, vol 4 (2007) p 36.

p.101 *protection and assistance* See Michael Hill, *Elihu Washburne* (2012) p 27.

p.101 *Ambassadors or Ministers* USA, Switzerland, Denmark, Holland, Sweden and Belgium.

p.102 *daily more desparate* Washburne, vol 4 pp 76 and 80.

p.105 *he had loved* Leopold's biographer Charlotte Zeepvat makes no mention of this monument. William may – according to Freda – also have helped build St George's Anglican Church in Paris.

p.105 *death by fire* Evidence of death by fire is a family tree sent to Eric Conradi from a Dresden relative c 1950

p.105 *in need of his help* A Dresden relative wrote to Eric c 1949 that Henry and Fromatte visited Dresden in 1892 staying in the Grand Hotel and distributing *bon-bons* to relatives.

p.105 *Royal Collection today* Moritz Conradi was an associate of Antoine Claudet, who operated one of the first daguerreotype studios in London from June 1841. Claudet received many honours, among which were his appointment, in 1853, as 'Photographer-in-ordinary' to Queen Victoria and the award, ten years later, of an honour from Napoleon III.

p 107 *the Russian court* Under Nicholas I (1825-55) Moritz was still studying at the Dresden Academy (1840-43), then at the Berlin Academy (1844-?) and after that freshly out of Art school and so making his name. In the 1861 census he appears as Maurice [sic] Conrady, "Artist, Portrait Painter" aged 35 [mis-transcribed from his real age of 30], b Germany a Lodger at no 3, Alma Terrace, St Pancras, Marylebone, together with a domestic servant and a railway clerk.

p.107 *Marylebone in 1887* Between April and June

p.107 *refugees and artists* Henry writes in his naturalisation papers that he & his family lived at 7 Lower James St (off Golden Square) for four years, then no 8 Lower James St for four and a half years, before moving to 18 Golden Square. The revolutions of 1830 and 1848, the agitation for Italian unification, the Franco-Prussian war, and the Paris Commune, all created their own mini-waves of refugees, many of whom landed among the multi-lingual back streets of Soho.

p.107 *houses and land* By contrast in the UK it was not until 1902 that a Midwives's Act was passed <www.unfpa.org/sowmy/resources/docs/main_report/en_SOWMR_Part1.pdf>

p.108 *a largish windfall* £10,000 thought Jules in 1957. However since that sum in 1880 had a buying power equivalent to £750,000 today, Jules almost certainly mis-remembered: Henry seems to have died without capital. Jules also thought the war-bonds Austrian, but, since he was 87 probably confused the two legations.

p.109 *stilted in English* see also 19 August 1918, from 23 Fawley Rd., Crediton Hill, West Hampstead, NW to Dear Florence, 'Thinking that a sincere friendly and well-meant word is always welcome, and I hope well received by you, I beg to send you my most sincere and heartiest congratulations for your birthday tomorrow, the 20th of this month, as far as I am informed…'

p.110 *£2 per week* See Lieut-Colonel H.P. Picot, C.B.E.: *The British Interned in Switzerland* (1919), *passim*. See also: http://www.swissinfo.ch/eng/first-world-war_1914—how-war-changed-swiss-life/38367288.

p.113 *200 Swiss Francs* A solution, however, was soon happily found. At the request of the Minister, H.M.'s Government desposited £25,000 at the Swiss Bankverein in London, upon which the Swiss National Bank opened an equivalent credit in notes in favour of the Minister at Berne. Mr. Grant Duff was thus enabled to issue cash in exchange for cheques, and so facilitate the return of stranded British visitors.

p.115 *Leon and his father* His mother had died in 1904, his sister Adele in 1910, and his half-brother Armand had emigrated to the USA.

p.118 *at the LSE* 'Training for Social Work' 1938-9 … the Certificate in Social Science and Administration seemed to be a mix of theory / academic work in a range of sociological and economics subjects, along with practical experience. The introduction to the Certificate course states: "The course is meant for both men and women who wish to devote themselves professionally to public administration or social work, and for those who desire to devote the whole or some part of their leisure to voluntary social work." The course was usually run over two years, but in exceptional cases (LSE graduates, or students with prior training in economic and sociological theory plus practical experience) could be taken in one year.

p.118 *sofa or camp-bed* My mother's oft-repeated allegation. Although a war-time airgraph between the brothers refers to 'our room', in any case Gordon had no private room of his own.

p.120 *with great power* http://www.espncricinfo.com/wisdenalmanack/content/story/151866.html

p.121 *Normandy and Belgium* So he attests in his military papers held by the W.O.

p.124 *now Ghana* From 9 Jan 43 in the Field Survey Company of the West African Engineers.

p.126 *to fight in it* *The Trust: The Private and Powerful Family Behind the 'New York Times'* (2000) by S. Tifft and A. Jones, *passim*.

p.127 *Marina's sudden death* *The Trust*, p 529. This was Punch's revenge for Cy snubbing him in the Paris office in the 1950's and for Punch's father making clear he preferred Cy to him: Cy was more erudite, masculine, and better-educated. Marina died July 1976 from an embolism following hysterectomy from cancer.

p.127 *voisinage* Anna Mikhailovna's phrase in *War and Peace* to describe Nikolai and Sonya.

p.129 *partners in the firm and possibly two decades earlier.* Though the firm is frequently said to have been founded in 1834 by George Cohen, he was in fact born only in 1828 and would only have been six years old then; so – assuming the date to be correct – it may possibly be his father Moss Cohen who started the company. Three out of the five sons became partners: Moss (b. 1858), Michael (b. 1861) & Barnett (b. 1865). The two oldest sons from each family became directors.

p.131 *Great Wheel* The Great Wheel was built for the Empire of India Exhibition at Earls Court in 1895 and demolished in 1907.

p.132 *about his health* During his 18 months in Paris there were three deaths at home – uncle Phil, aunt Lizzie, and Lawrie's seven-year old brother Alfred. Hannah advised Lawrie to sit shiva only for the statutory week. There was an outbreak of cholera in Paris too, so Hannah's solicitude about her son's health there is understandable.

p.137 *suit the stock exchange* Cousin Michael Levy, 2016: 'My father was Felix. During the time I was in the 600 Group, there were the following relatives Philip (Pidge) Levy, Lewis Levy, Percy Levy, Brian Levy, Cyril Cohen, Harold Cohen, Michael Cohen, Cedric Rigal and probably more that I have overlooked. No it didn't seem claustrophobic to me. It was big enough, with many branches and subsidiary companies, and the family were pretty much all in Head Office … I did find that the family leant over backwards to try to show that I was treated like any other employee, and in my opinion leant too far! For the record when I started Head Office was at Hammersmith Broadway, but it soon moved to a new building at White City opposite the BBC. In the 50's the scrap side was still very large with numerous branches around the country and some overseas operations. The original George Cohens traded in new and secondhand steel, and process plant. But there were already some engineering subsidiaries, and some were acquired during that time.'

p.144 *John Murray* 'A Beach Escape' – anonymously, in *The New Contemptibles* ed. Douglas Williams (John Murray, 1940).

p.144 *necessarily downplays* See, for an unvarnished account, e.g. Derek Lang: *Return to St Valery* (1989).

p.146 *five 'stuck'* Three charges were withdrawn: purloining petrol and/or paraffin and having repairs carried out on a civilian motor-bike.

p.146 *most trying conditions* 27 Feb 1943

p.147 *provost marshal* See *Black Market Britain 1939-55* (2013) by M. Roodhouse.

p.155 *she then dropped him* Letter to Michael Howard, Kingston University Archive.

p.156 *never to do so* Nonetheless when Tony Quinton told me of IM's name being linked with that of Goronwy Rees's son Daniel I didn't explore this until recently, when Rees's daughter told me the family was 'quite unable to shed any light on it'. He had purportedly put on a play called '*Darling I think I love you*'. Jenny Rees 26/11/2016.

p.157 *intimacies simultaneously* 'The Metaphysical Hostess', *English Literary History* XLVIII (Summer, 1981), pp. 427–53.

p.157 *towards envy* *Existentialists and Mystics* p 398

p.158 *their lives importance* *Persons and Polemics* (1994) pp 2-9.

p.160 *summer of 1954* Heywood was unsure about the exact date of this party, but certain it was before he left Oxford in 1954, when *Under the Net* was published on 30 May to considerable acclaim. Since John's room had been a nun's cell, the party was necessarily small. John kept busy serving tea and cakes and probably wine, while Olivia tactfully let him do all the work. Heywood spoke to Rachel Cecil about Bloomsbury, a world she had known long and, as Desmond McCarthy's daughter, at first hand. He also exchanged a few words with Iris on this, his first formal meeting, which he thus had cause to remember. And Olivia too spoke to Heywood kindly, 'as though we had known each other for a long time,' perhaps about novels, the subject of his research. No other record of this party has come to light.

p.166 *very diffused to me* See *Living on Paper* p 251 (1964), and p 347 (1967).

p.167 *one reviewer* See Frances Wilson, *The Observer* (29 July 2012).

p.167 *IM has been* 'I Will Tell You Everything' Rosemary Hill in *LRB* Vol 32 no 8 22 April 2010 wrote that the prospect of IM as a 'a role model for young women today… seems neither likely nor at all desirable'. Sophie Ratcliffe nonetheless wrote to me 'My mother gave me your biography for Christmas the year it came out and I adored it and was reminded again how brilliant it is. I found that long quotation about Mary Wollstonecraft as pitched at Iris ('she needs nobody's condescension' – that's probably a misquotation, I'm writing from memory) that began one chapter extraordinarily moving – it was a very important book to me at the time, for many reasons, and remains so. Thank you for writing it....' Dec 2015. Lara Feigel expressed similar sentiments in 2013. She wrote: 'For me reading your Murdoch biography was really important in my moment of deciding to be an academic.

At the time, Fay Weldon gave me what still seems to me excellent careers advice: think of someone whose life you'd like to have at 50 and then think how you're going to have it. I looked around – I was doing internships in publishing at the time – and couldn't see anyone whose life I'd like, but then I read your Murdoch biography and thought that she'd had an enviable and inspiring life and that it showed academia needn't be incompatible with writing in many different forms. So I decided to do my PhD.' (22 Oct 2018)

p.168 *for what purpose* LTA Feb 21st 2005. 'there was no 'black leather sofa' … nothing was happening … and the whole meeting was by previous arrangement, as usual when she brought a picnic. No I never had seven women a week, or any sort of affair with Iris'.

p.169 *her own weight* Galen Strawson, rev of A.N. Wilson, *Iris Murdoch as I knew her, Guardian*, 6 Sep 2003.

p.169 *without guile Iris*, p 24

p.169 *things is OK Living on Paper* p 265: 10 June 1964

p.170 *private telephone calls* Around this time (5 April 1965) she wrote to Brigid Brophy as follows: 'Keep in mind that I am very rarely alone when telephoning especially now that the new model 'Cedar Lodge' [work started Feb 1964] is in operation, with all rooms knocked into one… usual difficulty about leaving John. His chief drawback is tendency to mope like dog in kennels when I'm not here…' (pp 292-3),

p.170 *vague and nebulous Ibid*, p 321

p.171 *I also commend seriousness* p 261

p.171 *steady in my attachments* p 268

p.172 *Harcourt Terrace, SW10* p 309

p.173 *experience of an adult* The theme recurs. Otto in *The Italian Girl*: 'To be good is just never to lose [innocence]'; Theo in *The Nice and the Good*, longs to 'regain at least the untempered innocence of a well-guarded child'; Lucius in *Henry and Cato* writes a Haiku elegising lost innocence; Daisy in *Nuns and Soldiers*; ends up seeking innocence, 'a quest suited to human powers'.

p.175 *unconscious prig* June 9 2000

p.179 *happiness with me* Feb 25 1998

p.179 *to be disrespectful* June 2000

p.181 *closeness and distance* Bradley's having observed Rachel and Arnold's murderous marital fight makes Rachel feel compromised. Her flirtation with Bradley is power-play designed to exclude and so pay back Arnold while neutralising Bradley as a potentially hostile witness.

p.183 *decades of misunderstanding* April 6 2000 a propos my visit to Lois McKinnon Philippa Foot wrote 'For the dreadful past one can only think 'The pity of it!' It was all so unnecessary! Why did Donald behave so unwisely? I don't know. It still disturbs me much. But good, good, for what you and Lois managed together.'

p.184 *during those meetings* She was thought to have been required by the CP to leave the party on taking up her war-work at the Treasury in 1942, while staying on as a clandestine member.

p.184 *reviewer of the biography* *TLS* 5 Oct 2001 'She Loved and Sang'

p.184 *make such assumptions* There might – conceivably – still be papers in Moscow that would throw light on when IM's active CP membership ceased…

p.185 *Warton Professor* <http://www.telegraph.co.uk/obituaries/2016/03/19/john-jones-oxford-don—-obituary/

p.186 *few editorial suggestions* I did however at his request omit any reference to either Iris's mother's alcoholism or her probable Alzheimers.

p.186 *returned Michael's affection* Michael and John's old friend Gloria Richardson believed Anne Norfolk was jealous of her and 'deeply in love with Michael'.

p.186 *plunders in her fiction* In *Henry and Cato* the tension between mother and son within a big house may have been inspired by Iris's visits to Whitfield where George Clive (d. 1999) – who is otherwise wholly unlike Henry – lived a bachelor existence with his mother Lady Mary (née Pakenham, d 2010) who conceivably shared with Gertrude in the novel a doubt about any suitor of her son being good enough. Analogously *The Message to the Planet* (1989) appears distantly to reflect a real-life love-triangle involving Patrick and Susan Gardiner and their painter-lodger, with whom Susan, who died in 2006, fell in love. From IM's journal June 19 1975 'Susan G has gone off with a penniless painter to whom they rented a flat cheaply. She now lives in Twyford with this painter. Amazing.'.

p.187 *so raucous* Margaret Hubbard b. 16 June 1924, d. 28 April 2011.

p.189 *only in German* Johanna later read Romance languages and in 2007 translated *Nouvelles classiques* into German [*Klassische französische Erzählungen*].

p.189 *closed until 2024* A third category, irrelevant to our discussion here, was his cryptic *Merkbüchern*, meant only for their author's use, which comprised appointments, dates, deadlines, plus thoughts deemed worthy of being written down. He left a huge literary estate, about 120 boxes of which about 110 are currently accessible. Maybe fifty of these relate to work-in-progress for *Crowds and Power*. Source: Sven Hanuschek.

p.189 *of going ahead* E-mail from Hanuschek, 26 Oct 2014, who consulted with Kristian Wachinger in Sep 2014. Even if fore-knowledge of this burning had caused them to decide against publishing *Party in the Blitz*, however, Canetti's reminiscences including his *Tagebücher* would still presumably have entered the public domain in 2024 when he decreed that his literary estate be opened. They might by then have created a smaller impact.

p.190 *hypnotists in a closed room* See *Sartre, Romantic Rationalist* (1953) *passim*.

p.190 *get rid of our stings* *Existentialists and Mystics*, p 188.

p.191 *800 page authorized biography* It was celebrated, together with other Canetti-related books in Ritchie Robertson 'The Great Hater' *TLS* Sep 2, 2005.

p.191 *and of exploring them* *'… ein Proteus, dem es gerade darum ging, alle menschlichen Möglichkeiten in sich zu haben und sie auch zu erkunden.'*

p.191 *based on identification* See Ritchie Robertson, *Passim*. See also E. Canetti, *The Human Province*, tr. J. Neugroschel, (New York 1978) pp.39-40, an entry for 1943: "*On metamorphosis*. When I stepped out to eat today, a car came driving at my right, the kind used to deliver packages for shops… Through my gaze at her and hers at me, I had changed into the girl at the wheel; and was now driving along in the car."

p.191 *contradictory meanings* Some Canetti scholars suggest that *Verwandlung* is an aspect not just of rebellion against power (through empathic identification), but also of despotism or power itself. This scarcely suggests a simple system of thought, and it will correctly be concluded that no serious study of Canetti's thinking is attempted in these pages. J.P. Arnason and D Roberts in their *Elias Canetti's Counter-Image of Society: Crowds, Power, Transformation*, (Camden Hse, NY, 2004) p 127 argue that EC's Transformation is double : it is the common ground both of despotism and also of subversion…

p.192 *gay brother Georges* From "*Dearest Georg": Love, Literature, and Power in Dark Times: the Letters of Elias, Veza and Georges Canetti, 1933-48*, eds K. Lauer and K. Wachinger. Transl D Dollenmayer. (2009). An excellent precis in English is be found online – with quotations from the letters themselves in German – by Prof W.C. Donahue at Duke U: *In Her Own Words Veza Canetti's Briefe an Georges (Letters to Georges).*

p.192 *Willy Goldmann* Ines Schlenker and Kristian Wachinger, eds of *Elias Canetti und Marie-Louise von Motesiczky: Liebhaber ohne Addresse, Briefwechsel 1942-1992* (2011) p 92 describe Friedl as Canetti's *Schülerin* and finally '*Geliebte*' or mistress until 1951. Canetti's role in this abortion was independently attested around 1998-9 by Friedl's sister Susie in Paris, her lover Allan Forbes in Boston, and her first cousin Margaret Gardiner in Hampstead, in whose house Friedl stayed in World War II.

p.193 *cruel injunction* "*Diese Position der Schwäche wirft ein anderes Licht auf die Frage von Friedl Benedikts Schwangerschaft und Abtreibung*" [p 367]. Hanuschek believes that Canetti's 'position of weakness throws a different light on the question of Friedl Benedikt's pregnancy and abortion'.

p.194 *two-year old daughter* EC and Hera Buschor married December 1971; Joanna Canetti was born 23 June 1972; M-L's letter to Hera making clear she has just learnt is dated 25 July 1973; Hera d April 1988 aged 55.

p.194 *visibly trembled* Friendship somehow survived, and the recently published (untranslated) letters of Marie-Louise and Canetti throw further light on his curious capacity for *Verwandlung* or transformation. See *Liebhaber ohne Addresse L Briefwechsel 1942-1992* (2011) Edited by I. Schlenker and K. Wachinger. While Marie-Louise handled the new situation with simple dignity, Canetti justified himself by saying that he thanked God he had kept her in ignorance for ten years, for by this means he forfeited neither her delightful company, nor her paintings which were 'essential' to him. Moreover 'noone can feel as much bitterness against me as I do myself'. Though Canetti had confided to his diary his boredom with Marie-Louise, he soon invented another ingenious Transformation: he tried to console her by claiming that he hated this second wife because she was a German, and that he summonsed his first wife's ghost from her grave to curse his second. Marie-Louise was unimpressed. She dwells on her jealous hurt – in one letter lamenting heart-breakingly that she has been deprived of the care of Canetti's child, of dressing and feeding it, and monitoring its growth.

p.193 *TLS was hostile* *TLS*, Nov 2 1962 p 839, anon., 'Measurement and Myth'.

p.193 *privately agreed* She thought Canetti's focus on *Trieben* or drives – she used the German word – 'hopelessly out-dated'.

p.193 *Kulturphilosophie* December 1962, pp 85-6

p.193 *Aphorisms* Canetti made British publication of his *Aphorisms* his stated price for the issuing of his memoirs in English

p.193 *or hostility* However those inclined to think Canetti-phobia uniquely English might read the pages on Canetti in *Mein Leben* (1999) translated as *The Author of Myself* (2001) by Marcel Reich-Ranicki, doyenne of post-war German literary critics, who knew Canetti for twenty years, finding him a vain and self-important mythomaniac.

p.196 *loyally and inaccurately* See e.g. Athill: '[Canetti] has taken so violently against the British, I think because they had failed to recognise his genius … that he determined never to be published in this country.'

p.197 *in an absurd way* Entries from July 10 and July 21 1953

p.197 *their affair cease* On June 30th 1953; conveyed by IM to JB July 3

p.198 *meet Isaiah Berlin* Source: Frank Hauser who directed Canetti's *The Numbered* at the Oxford Playhouse in 1956. Carol and Francis Graham-Harrison who were close to Canetti – Carol translated *Crowds and Power* into English – also recalled his frustration at not managing to meet Isaiah Berlin.

p.199 *feel ashamed* Pp 216, 222, 223, 226. It's hard to know what he means here. If IM's portraits had been uniquely of him – rather as he plundered his brother George as the psychiatrist in *Auto-da-Fe*, also called George – would he have felt *less* ashamed ?

p.200 *last writings* Doris Lessing, *Walking in the Shade*, p 275

p.202 *Alan Bennett* Alan Bennett *LRB* Vol. 22 No. 2 20 Jan 2000 pp. 3-8. 'Nobody explains (or seems to think an explanation required) how this unworldly woman managed to be made a dame by Mrs Thatcher and was laden with honorary degrees; sheer inadvertence perhaps.... In a later obituary it's said that she approved of the Falklands War and one begins to see that for all her goodness and mild appeal she may have trod the same path as her contemporaries Amis and Larkin. Masked though she was in kindliness and general benevolence she may have ended up as far from her radical beginnings as they did, Dame Iris's spiritual journey not all that different from Paul Johnson's.'

p.213 *attest to this* 'Age will win', *Guardian*, 21 Dec 2001. Amis also writes of 'the fabulous profusion of her talent' and of her novels constituting 'an extraordinarily vigorous imperium'.

p.213 *real-life partner* Lurie on Edmund Gordon's *The Invention of Angela Carter: A Biography*, *NYRB* March 9 2017

Acknowledgements

Relatives have greatly helped this book. Around 1972 I recorded on to cassettes the memories of my grandmother and several surviving great-aunts. My ingenious brother Richard was able forty years later to rescue these interviews and transfer their contents to CD. He also shared many valuable reminiscences. My maternal cousin George Rigal completed years of hard work on the Cohen/Levy side of the family and my father's cousin Eric Phillips did the same for the Josephis. I'm indebted to my father's book *Three Score Years and Ten* (1978), a history he compiled of his family firm and also to a privately distributed book on the 600 Company in its centennial year (1934). Cousins Mike and Lynn Levy answered many queries. I've benefitted from the kind encouragement of many friends and relatives who looked at chapters in draft: Prof Rosemary Ashton, Aurea Carpenter, Martin Conradi, Margaret Drabble, Simon Edwards, Jenny Hartley, Michael Holroyd, Robert Hutchison, Jane Jantet, Paddy Page and David Schneider. Prof Dick Shannon, Prof Robert Tombs alike helped my researches into Paris in 1870-71. So did Patricia Touton-Victor. Some material in Part Three appeared first in the *Iris Murdoch Review*. Prof Sven Hanuschek assisted many enquiries about Elias Canetti. Daphne Turner – as often in the past – offered both support and detailed practical advice, reading and helping edit the book in draft as in proof. Anne Chisholm generously helped me see how the material might be edited and organised. I could neither have attempted nor completed this book without the constant support and patient feedback of my partner Jim O'Neill. All errors and infelicities are mine alone.

I'm grateful to the Jewish Museum in London who provided the photo of Lawrie Levy and siblings; to Leo Phillips who gave me permission to use the photo of his father Tom Phillips's sketches of Dame Iris Murdoch and to Somerville College who found Norm Schindler's photo of Prof Philippa Foot.

Index